IN THE WHOLE CHRIST

MOST REV. EMILE GUERRY
Archbishop of Cambrai

IN THE WHOLE CHRIST

Prayerful Meditations on the Mystery of the Church

> *. . . for the edifying of the body of Christ;
> until we all meet in the unity of faith and
> of the knowledge of the Son of God, unto
> a perfect man, unto the measure of the
> age of the fullness of Christ . . .*
>
> (Ephes., IV, 12, 13)

*Translated from French
by* M. G. CARROLL

SOCIETY OF ST. PAUL
NEW YORK - CANFIELD - DERBY - DETROIT

Original title

DANS LE CHRIST TOTAL

par Monseigneur Guerry
Archeveque de Cambrai

Published by Desclee, De Brouwer & Cie.
Bruges.

NIHIL OBSTAT:

    E. HARDWICK,
    Censor Deputatus.

Die 3.a Septembris 1957.

IMPRIMATUR:

    CAROLUS GRANT,
    Vic. Gen.

Northantoniae, die 8.a Septembris 1957.

"Our union with Christ in the Body of the Church . . . is so intimate that a
very ancient and constant tradition of the Fathers—in harmony with
the words of St. Paul: *Christ is the Head of the Body,
the Church* (Col., I, 18)—teaches that the divine
Redeemer together with His social Body
constitutes one mystical person,
or, as St. Augustine
expresses it,
the whole Christ."

Pope Pius XII: *Encyclical on the Mystical Body of Christ.*
(English Translation: Canon Smith. C.T.S. p. 42).

Library of Congress Catalog Card Number 59-101-33

CONTENTS

PART ONE

The Mystery of the Personal Christ

CHAPTER ONE

THE CALL OF THE HEAD

His Sovereignty and His life-giving action
—over men's minds:

—over men's hearts:

—over men's wills:

—over men's consciences:

PART THREE

The Mystery of the Catholic Church

Christ's activity in the Catholic Church
animated by His Spirit

CHAPTER ONE

CREDO ECCLESIAM

II. *The Mystery of the hierarchy*

III. *The Mystery of the fundamental marks of the Church*

IV. *Participation in the Mysteries of Christ in the Sacraments*

CHAPTER TWO

THE PRINCIPAL TRAITS OF THE CHRISTIAN'S LIFE IN THE WHOLE CHRIST

Conclusion

INTRODUCTION

AD PATREM, IN CHRISTO, CUM MARIA.
TO THE FATHER, IN CHRIST, WITH MARY.

WHAT a whole program of action is contained in these words!
The phrases they compose, each in itself filled with light and
with life, have been drawn from the Sacred Scripture.

What an excellent motto for a bishop's coat of arms!

What a conception of religion! It is the very opposite of a
purely moralistic or legal conception of the nature of religion;
for these are living words pointing to living relations with living
Persons.

What an orientation of the spiritual life! . . .

In 1936, we published a book entitled *Vers le Père*, wherein
we attempted to write a commentary on the first words of this
device.[1]

---

1. (English translation, 1947: *God the Father:* A.H.C. Downes—Sheed & Ward).
This book attempts to describe our filial life in our relations with the Father, such as
that life has been revealed to us by Christ. This is a field of spiritual doctrine about
which many Christians still know nothing. The Preface contains the words: "We are
sons only through the Son, with the Son, *in the Son.*" The Twenty Seventh Meditation:
In the Church, the Mystical Body of Christ, glances at the collective plan of the Redemption of the sons in the Son: "Men do not receive the life of the Son in a state of isolation from one another. They and the Son are to be members of one same family. They
and He are to constitute a supernatural organism, living and one. Christians are all one
with Christ and *in* Christ" (translation: Downes, p. 55). And the final meditation ends
with these words: "The prayer of the Head in His Glory must become the ardent and
uninterrupted prayer of the Whole Christ, the prayer of all who would have Him reign
in their souls and would enter the Kingdom of the Spirit of Love. For the Holy Ghost,
the Spirit of Jesus, by vivifying and unifying souls interiorly, would realize the unity
of the whole body in the one Church. He comes to recapitulate the whole of dispersed
humanity in Christ, that they may live with the life of the Only Son of the Father.
He comes to lead all men to their consummation in God, in the unity of divine love,
until at last the Whole Christ will grow to perfect stature for the Glory of the Father:
'until we all meet into the unity of faith and of the knowledge of the Son of God, unto
a perfect man, unto the measure of the age of the fullness of Christ.'" (translation:
Downes, p. 182).

The aim of this second book is to propose for the reader's prayerful reflection, the second phrase of the device: *In Christo* —which, for the purpose of our present context, we translate as: *In the Whole Christ.* We owe the phrase: "The Whole Christ," to St. Augustine; and Pope Pius XII has used it in two passages of his magnificent Encyclical: *Mystici Corporis Christi* (1943). We have quoted these passages as an epigraph to this book.

Saint Paul does not use this particular phrase, Saint Augustine being its author some three centuries later. But it is a perfect expression of the whole Pauline doctrine: the unity of all men, both Jews and Gentiles, with God, in Christ. He presented this as a mystery, indeed as *the* mystery, the great mystery which was revealed to him by the Lord. And so, he declared: ". . . there is neither Gentile nor Jew, circumcision nor uncircumcision, Barbarian nor Scythian, bond nor free. But Christ is all in all." (*Col.*, III, 11).

It is this mystery of the unity of Christians with Christ and in Christ that we propose to contemplate in this book. It is this mystery of the Whole Christ which we invite souls to ponder in its many facets as subjects of their prayer, and which we have presented in what we call "prayerful meditations." Now, this expresses perfectly our aim here, to induce our readers to take as the subject of their prayer a mystery which epitomizes our whole religion.[1]

There is no question here of a new or speculative study on the Mystical Body. There are many such, of a profoundly scientific kind, and we are greatly indebted to them here. But these very valuable works often remain inaccessible to the general body of the faithful. Why should we not seek to give the benefit of the riches contained in such works, to the considerable number of souls who are seriously striving to live their Christianity?

When one begins to relish the "sweetness" of the Faith—as the Vatican Council so unerringly expresses it[2] through a deeper penetration of its mysteries in the light and under the inspiration of the Holy Ghost, one cannot agree to allow this sweetness to remain the privilege of a small *élite* of the learned. One regards it as a duty, especially if one is a priest, to communicate its

---

1. Thus, we thought it good and useful to append to each meditation, a prayer centered on its subject. Nothing, most decidedly, can equal in spiritual value the prayer which wells up spontaneously in the soul. Furthermore, as often as the theme permitted, we have simply reproduced the best of all prayers—that which, in the Church's liturgy, coincides in subject with our theme. But, in every case, it is the soul's own meditation which should provoke the prayer.

2. Constitution *de fide Catholica* (Denz. 1791).

benefits to all these souls, today so numerous, who, tired of a merely sentimental piety, are eager to know more intimately and more substantially the message of Christ and His Mystery.

For our part, we have sought to answer this need and, in a modest way, to fulfill this duty. We have limited ourselves to being a simple guide for the personal prayer of our readers. It is they who must, by their prayer, obtain light from Christ, in their interior lives. To aid them, we have confined ourselves to recalling some truths about the dogma of the Mystical Body, and to indicating—without development—some points of doctrine, so as to leave to the personal initiative of each reader, the task of deepening his own appreciation, by meditation and prayer. It is our wish that this book may enable them to linger prayerfully on the truth, the dogma, the doctrine, the theology and the liturgy, here presented. For it is the "lifting up"—the "elevation" —of the soul to, and in, the Mystery, which is of importance here.

We do not, so to speak, step back from the mystery to view it from without, even for the purpose of admiring its beauty.

We do not make a purely intellectual study of a mystery, for thereby we would ignore the fact that, in its essence and by very definition, a mystery is not an abstract truth. We approach it with a respect in which there is both reverent fear and holy trust, as a hidden, living reality, wholly supernatural and divine, in itself a world of light—as something very great whose transcendence dominates and vastly surpasses us, but is at the same time a presence very near to our souls.

We approach it with a humble soul, in hopeful expectation of a gift completely unmerited by us.

We welcome it with a lively faith, fully open and completely ready to receive that gift.

We advance step by step into the heart of the mystery, with a soul which is convinced of its own powerlessness in face of such splendor, but also obediently ready to allow itself to be penetrated with that splendor as profoundly as is pleasing to the Infinite Love of God, Who has revealed and given the mystery to us that we may enter into it.

Finally, with a soul full of adoration, freely offered and surrendered to love, we communicate in the mystery, in its light and in its life.

That is why we have called this book: *In the Whole Christ*, and not *The Whole Christ*, which latter title might indicate a study of the doctrine from *without*. It must be deeply pondered from *within* itself, if we are to live the doctrine and if it is to communicate its light and life to us. It is imperative to stress this phenomenon of interiority and assimilation.

＊　　＊　　＊

What is the life contained in this doctrine? That of Christ —but, we must immediately add, of the Whole Christ. How is this so?

First of all, we must distinguish between the life of the Whole Christ, on the one hand, and the life which Christ lived on earth, and that which He now lives in the glory of His Father, on the other. Certainly, we shall frequently have occasion to turn our thoughts to the earthly life of the Savior; and, in the whole of the first part of our book, we shall contemplate the life of our Head in the glory of His Father.

But there is a third life of Christ, which the Apostle Saint Paul has revealed to us as *the mystery*—for which reason, it is called "Mystical": a real, yet mysterious, life which Christ lives, by His Spirit, in His Body which is the Church.[1]

It is the life of the mystical Christ—that is to say, of that social being in which the personal Christ and His Church are united to the point of forming, "in a sense, one single (mystical) person," as Saint Thomas says (III, q. 49, a. 1). On one occasion, Saint Paul calls this union simply "Christ"; and it is quite clear from the context, that he intends to include in this title both the Christ-Head and His Body.[2] Elsewhere, he says: "For you are all one in Christ Jesus" (*Gal.*, III, 28).

The Whole Christ is Our Lord Jesus Christ, and we, His members. We form but one in the same life which He gives and which we receive from Him, in and through the Church.[3]

---

1. "We pass now, Venerable Brethren . . . to explain why the Body of Christ, which is the Church, must be called *mystical* . . . This word serves to distinguish the social Body of the Church, of which Christ is the Head and ruler, from His physical Body which, born of the Virgin Mother of God, is now seated at the right hand of the Father, and lies hidden beneath the Eucharistic veils. Furthermore . . . we are enabled thereby to differentiate it from any body of the natural order, whether physical or moral." *Mystici Corporis Christi:* (translation: Canon Smith, p. 36-37).

2. (*I Cor.*, XII, 12): "For as the body is one and hath many members; and all the members of the body, whereas they are many, yet are one body; so also is *Christ.*"

3. "What raises the Christian society to a level utterly surpassing any order of nature is the Spirit of the Redeemer, the source of all graces, gifts and miraculous powers, *perennially* and intimately pervading the Church and acting in her." *Mystici Corporis Christi* (Canon Smith translation, p. 38).

It is this unique mystery, the mysterious reality, which souls are invited to contemplate throughout the three parts of our book. These three parts are not, therefore, independent of one another, as though added extrinsically one to the other. But the mystery of the Whole Christ is so rich and so profound that it is impossible for us to deal with it all together, to seize upon it fully in one all-embracing intuition.

We would prefer to regard these three parts, therefore, as though they were three versions of the same picture, painted from three distinct viewpoints.[1] Or, to be more explicit, as the mystery of the Whole Christ, presented as in a sense comprising three mysteries, each containing the others.[2]

*   *   *

PART ONE

The theme of the first part is *the mystery of the Personal Christ,* the mystery of the Head, the mystery of the Person of Christ, considered in His greatness, His personal plenitude, His primacy in all and over all, His universal authority and sovereignty, and in His uniqueness as the only source of life.

This transcendence of Christ is the privilege of the hypostatic union. Because He is the Son of God, Christ, as man, holds the primacy over all things: He is King of the minds, hearts and wills of all men, and holds the sovereignty over the whole creation and the entire universe. It is through this grace of union that Christ possesses the fullness of life; and, because He is thus the only source of life, because all Redemption is in Him, He is the Head Who animates and leads His whole Body, the Head Who builds His Body by the power of His Holy Spirit.

The Christ-Head has a double title, therefore, to our adoration—that of His vivifying action and that of His absolute primacy. By this adoration, we learn to know Him more intimately; to love Him more ardently; to give ourselves more generously to Him; and also to understand in what sense the Church is His "complement" and in what sense, therefore, we can speak of "the Whole Christ."

---

1. Hence it is that the same truth can figure in different passages but under distinct aspects just as, to continue our metaphor, the same objects appear in each of the pictures, but in a different light and from another angle.

2. This explains why, from the outset, in the first part, we are clearly concerned with the mystery of the Church, contemplated in Christ. The second part is equally concerned with the *Church,* but under its social aspect. Again, the third part is meditation on the *visible* Church as containing this mystery.

At the very outset, it is of the utmost importance to dismiss as impossible the idea, in any shape or form, that it was necessary for Christ to be completed in order to reach His personal fullness. The Church can add nothing to this plenitude of life possessed by the personal Christ in Himself. Indeed, the reverse is true: the Church receives all from Him. She is only the manifestation, to all ages, of all the full riches and abundance of grace which lives in the Head of the Mystical Body. In this sense, it is true to say that the Church is the extension and communication of Christ; that she is the life of Christ, propagated and continuing through the members of His Body.

In this sense, too, the metaphor of the body, which Saint Paul uses to convey some idea of the unity of Christians with Christ, has rich overtones. Christ is the Head, the Leader; we are His members in His Body which is the Church. But, immediately, the metaphor demands further interpretation, on pain of falsifying the truth. For, in the human body, the head can do nothing without being one with the body, having no life other than that it shares with the body. Head and body are united to form one physical unity.

On the contrary, Christ possesses in Himself a fullness of life which is absolutely independent of His members. That fullness is in Him as in its source. It is from Him and by Him that it is communicated to His members. Furthermore, in this profound unity, the Personality of Christ is absolutely distinct from the personality of the members. There is union—a union so profound and intimate that Saint Paul, seeking for an image by which to convey it, compared it with the union of "two in one flesh" effected by Holy Matrimony. But there is neither fusion, nor confusion, nor absorption of all or of any one, in Christ.

Christ respects each one's personality to the point of not wishing to impose His sovereignty on him from without. What He desires is the homage of a free, loving will. He makes an offer. He issues a call. He asks for generous collaboration in His mission of Redemption. And so, we thought it well, at the end of the first part and before entering into the mighty undertaking of the world's salvation, that the living member should offer himself to the personal Christ for this work which He desires to confide to him.

✻   ✻   ✻

PART TWO

In Part Two, the Whole Christ begins to act, revealing Himself to the soul. This is a very important stage to be reached in the Spiritual Life. If the soul adheres to it with all its faith inspired by charity, the deepening of the doctrine of the Mystical Body will effect *a real change of outlook* within it. The soul will relinquish its more or less individualist conception of life, of religion, of its own destiny, in favor of a conception of all these which is social and collective. It will gain a live realization that it is a member of a great Body. And thereby the mystery of the Mystical Body becomes a living reality in the depths of that soul.

Up to this stage, the Christian may have lived in spiritual and even pious individualism, without having been aware of this. Such a soul indeed sought to love Christ, and this very sincerely, claiming that Christ was its all in all. It ardently desired the social reign of Our Lord. Equally, it knew that love for one's neighbor is a commandment like unto the first.

In what respect, therefore, is the discovery of the Whole Christ capable of producing so important a change in the soul?

It is possible, as is frequently seen, for a person to love Christ and also to love the other members; but, so to speak, in separate compartments, *side by side*. It is something quite different to love the others *in* Christ, to love in them the Whole Christ with one and the same love.

It is possible, and again quite common, to know that there is a commandment of charity and a virtue of charity, but to regard the commandment and the virtue as simply *taking their place* among the other virtues and the other commandments. It is quite another thing to realize that charity is *the* commandment—that it is "the whole Law"; that the virtue of charity contains all the other virtues and is their very soul, so that it becomes "the bond of perfection," as Saint Paul calls it.

It is possible, and of frequent occurrence, to regard charity as *giving to others,* and to be ready to practice it in the form of gifts to others at every opportunity. It is something quite different to realize the *unity* and the collective life which we form together in Christ, and which we ought to live *with the others,* in Him.

Again, it is possible, and of frequent occurrence, for a person to live in the same religious, family or social community, and yet to lead there an isolated, independent, individualist life, seeking his own pleasure. How many Christians there are who live their own isolated spiritual lives in the very heart of this great community, the Church!

It is quite another matter to understand that Christ asks us to act *with the other members,* to pray with them, to suffer with them, *to develop spiritually together* in Christ, to help the others to give themselves to God—so that we and they may give ourselves *together* to God, in Christ and through Christ.

Finally, it is possible, and quite common, for a person to realize that each has his own personal destiny to work out, side by side with the other members, and to believe that one is alone responsible for one's own personal salvation. This conception is so widespread that, in reaction against it, there are some today who fall into the error of declaring that they give no thought to their own personal salvation.

It is quite a different matter to realize that, while it is true that each person is responsible for his own personal salvation, he is also responsible for the salvation of the others; that he should seek his salvation with the others; and that this salvation can neither be envisaged nor effected apart from the others, without the others, without the whole Body, without "the Communion of Saints."

The second part of our book presents this entire doctrine of the Whole Christ for the prayerful meditation of the Christian soul. It examines from within, the intimate nature of the living community formed in Christ by Christians who participate in the riches of Christ and in the very life of Christ. We see this life spreading along a vertical line—from Christ to His members—in the form of all the gifts of Christ; and thus we perceive the unity of the Mystical Body. We see this life growing to perfection in charity along a horizontal line—from each member to all the others—in all the forms of the ascetical life and of the theological life.

In a word, this second part considers the mystery of the Whole Christ as *the mystery of the interior and profound unity of the living community of the members of His Body.*

❊   ❊   ❊

PART THREE

This living community of Christians in Christ, forming a body animated by the Holy Ghost—this Mystical Body—is the Church itself: the visible, hierarchic, sacramental Church. This is yet another aspect of the mystery of the Whole Christ: *the mystery of the Catholic Church.*

Part Three deals with the mystery of the Whole Christ from this aspect. It would be from the purpose of this book to describe the institutions and the machinery of the Catholic Church, as used to be done in comparatively recent treatises on the Church, written from the standpoint of Canon Law and of Apologetics.

For the past few decades, however, Catholic Theology has very happily rediscovered, and is plumbing the depths of, the mystery of the Church. This new development is opening up perspectives rich in light and in promise, for the life of the Church itself and for that of Christians. It is our aim, here, simply to enter into this rediscovered country of large horizons—to invite souls to turn to this Mystery and to open themselves wide to it.

It is the Mystery of the Church in its essence, in its general characteristics, in its transcendence; the mystery of its "marks" and of its properties, considered from within; the mystery of its hierarchy and of the sacramental order by which Christ communicates His life to us and makes us participate in His own mysteries, by renewing them in us; the mystery of the Holy Ghost animating the Church and imprinting on the Christian life in Christ a particular configuration, with certain fundamental traits of which we treat in the final meditations.

In all three parts, we have consistently presented this Christian life in Christ as essentially a *theological* life—a life of faith, hope and charity, linking and uniting us with Jesus Christ, with the Whole Christ; and as being essentially our living incorporation in Christ, our ever more profound union with Him—a union which lifts up our souls, with Him, to a communion in the life of the Blessed Trinity.

Consistently, too, we have considered this life of the Whole Christ in His redemptive and apostolic mission. We also thought it necessary to underline very specially the character of virility, of courage, of self-mastery, which, especially at the present time, participation in the life of the Church demands; for the Church is in the world to save the world—to live in the heart of the distress of a world which ignores her or is actively hostile to her.

This whole book has been designed for the purpose of transmitting to many souls Christ's invitation to work with Him for the extension of His Mystical Body, His call to the apostolate— which is nothing less than cooperation with Him in the building of the Whole Christ.

✠ EMILE GUERRY.

PART ONE

THE MYSTERY
OF THE PERSONAL CHRIST

THE LORDSHIP OF JESUS CHRIST

OUR HEAD

Only Source of Life in His Mystical Body

HIS SPLENDOR
HIS UNIVERSAL SOVEREIGNTY
HIS POWERS
HIS LIFE-GIVING ACTION

"One Lord."
(*Ephes.*, IV, 5)

FOREWORD

The Christian who desires to approach the Mystery of the Whole Christ, must above all contemplate long and earnestly the Person of Our Lord Jesus Christ in the exercise of His role as Head of the Mystical Body. It is necessary that he should ponder the Mystery of the Personal Christ.

The primary purpose of Part One of these meditations, is to induce in the Christian soul, an enlightened and loving knowledge of the Head of the Mystical Body. The soul is led to admire His splendor, His perfections and His powers. It becomes conscious, in a very special way, of His universal sovereignty and His primacy over all humanity. It contemplates Christ as the source of the life of all souls, as possessing in Himself the fullness of the Divinity and the plenitude of human nature. It feels the compelling power of the Mystery of the Whole Christ, and hears the first whisperings of the call of love addressed to it by the Christ-Head, inviting the soul to cooperate with Him in one and the same magnificent work—the salvation of the world.

Part One is equally concerned with orientating the spiritual life of the soul towards an ardent and generous adaptability in relation to the Head of the Mystical Body. The Christian feels that he is being gradually involved, in a personal manner, and as a member of Christ, in an undertaking so vast that it sweeps aside all his own little plans and transforms the whole meaning of his life. He does not know as yet, to what extent it will please the Head of the Mystical Body to "draw" him in His loving-kindness (Jeremias, xxxi, 3).

He understands, however, that he can no longer be taken up with himself, with his egotism and his narrow ideals. He feels that he can no longer refuse to give himself to Jesus Christ in order to cooperate, in Him and with Him, in the Redemption of mankind. In their different forms, it is the same prayer which, at the end of each meditation, will well up constantly in his soul: a prayer for grace, a desire for light to understand each truth more clearly, a thirst for the dispositions which are necessary if he is to answer the call of his Master. He becomes conscious of his vocation of membership in a great Body. Already in this early part of the book, he senses that this Body is a living community, profoundly united under the sovereignty of the Head, the Source of Life.

CHAPTER ONE

The Call of the Head

*And he hath subjected all things under his
feet and hath made him head over all the
church, which is his body and the fullness
of him who is filled all in all.*

(Ephes., 1, 23, 23)

THE EMINENT SOVEREIGNTY OF
THE DIVINE HEAD OVER THE MINDS OF MEN,
AND HIS LIFE-GIVING ACTION

1. THE MASTER

> *Neither be ye called masters; for one is your master, Christ.*
>
> (Matt., XXIII, 10)

Novelists have depicted Christ as a sentimental dreamer, sweetly insipid and meek. The Gospel, on the contrary, presents Him to us as "the Master." Has this title a special relevance for our spiritual life, and can it help us to know Christ more intimately?

1. *The multitude*

The multitude who listened to Jesus were filled with "admiration" after hearing the Sermon on the Mount (*Matt.*, VII, 28). Why was this? The Gospel gives us the answer.

In the first place, it was admiration for His *teaching:* "the people were in admiration at His doctrine." For this teaching was of a new and arresting kind: the announcing of the Beatitudes; the qualities of the New Law which demanded from the soul sincerity, simplicity and trust in God; the revelation of the heavenly Father; and a whole program concerning relations with one's neighbor, and even with one's enemy. It seemed filled with wisdom. Its immediate effect was to awaken souls to a new hope and a new realization, however discouraged those souls might be.

Admiration also for his *approach,* for the *authority* with which Jesus spoke. This was the quality of His preaching which had already amazed the Doctors most learned in the Law, when, at the age of twelve, Jesus spoke with them in the Temple. (*Luke,* II, 46). The same impression was left by His Sermon on the

Mount: "for He was teaching them as one having power" (*Matt.*, VII, 29). Was He not boldly opposing His New Doctrine to the Old Law—that venerable Law in which no one would have had the blasphemous impertinence to alter a single word? Jesus had dared to say: "You have heard that it was said to them of old . . . But I say unto you . . ."

Finally, what gripped His hearers was the eminent *originality* of the preaching of Jesus, by comparison with that to which they were accustomed. The Gospel underlines this also: "and not as their Scribes and Pharisees." Moreover, the Pharisees were not to miss this difference. No doubt with an ironical inflection, they would say to the Apostles: "Your Master," when they demanded why Jesus did not behave like others (*Matt.*, IX, 11; XVII, 24).

2. *The friends of Jesus: the Apostles and Disciples*

On the lips of the friends of Jesus, this beautiful name *Master* assumed a deeper and more intimate meaning.

Deeper, because through that name they accepted and proclaimed their entire submission to the sovereign authority, no longer of His teaching only, but of His adorable Person. They too had been conquered by His teaching, which had found its way into the very recesses of their souls. They could recall how the power and the compelling strength of His preaching had drawn them away from their little everyday world, from their family, from their work. They were mastered by the extraordinary influence He exercised on them. Every day, they were given ever increasing glimpses of the extent of His power over persons and things. It is this name they use, when, the angry waves whipping the lake and their boat being in peril, they call on Him: "Master . . . we perish" (*Mark*, IV, 38). They appeal to His power over the elements.

Again, is not their use of this name intended by the Apostles and Disciples as the expression of their entire loving dependence on Jesus? They have given to Him the gift of themselves and of their life. He is the Master into Whose hands they have abandoned themselves for the carrying out of something they do not understand. They no longer have any plans for themselves: they belong entirely to Him. With what tenderness and veneration, therefore, they use this name when they converse together about Him.

Lazarus is dead. Jesus comes to weep over the body of His friend. Announcing His arrival to Mary, Martha says: "The Master is come and calleth for thee" (*John*, XI, 28). The Gospel tells us that she spoke these words "secretly," with a suppressed emotion tremulous with her consolation, her happiness, her love, her amazement at such an honor, her gratitude for this touching gesture in which was revealed the infinite tenderness of the Master.

3. The attitude of Jesus

Jesus Himself assumed the title, *Master*. "You call me Master and Lord. And you say well; for so I am" (*John*, XIII, 13). He reserves this title to Himself: "One is your Master, Christ."

Jesus claims to be a new and unique legislator. He does not discuss; He does not put forward reasoned arguments to prove His doctrine. When He performs miracles as the signs which He Himself chooses, it is in order to reveal His Person, His Divinity, His mission. He is no orator prepared to argue; nor is He a Rabbi who repeats a lesson taught by other doctors. He is a Prophet who announces the designs of God. The multitude often confer this title on Him (*Matt.*, XXI, 11 and 46). As a Master, He teaches truth simply and openly, without prolixity or evasions, neither minimizing nor softening it: "Let your speech be: Yea, Yea; No, No." (*Matt.*, V, 37). He is a Leader Who demands that He should be followed, and that those who do so should attach themselves to His Person, should leave all things, and should abandon themselves to His guidance.

O Jesus, our Master, strip us of all vain self-sufficiency, which would prevent us from sitting at Your feet and humbly listening to Your words. Before the sublime Mysteries which You reveal to us, we are but poor and ignorant. Teach us the truth, Your truth; inspire us with the ardent desire to receive that truth, in order that we may spread it to all our brethren in Your Name.

2. THE MASTER AND THE TRUTH

Lord, to whom shall we go? Thou hast the words of eternal life.

(John, VI, 69)

The Gospel shows us how, in dispensing the treasures of truth, Our Lord acts as a Sovereign Master. He thus manifests one of the aspects of the regal freedom with which, now as in former times, Jesus Christ, Head of the Mystical Body, dispenses truth to the members of His Body, when He wishes, as He wishes, and according to the measure of each one's capacity to receive.

1. *When He wishes*

In the communication of divine truth to men, Jesus has chosen to be guided by an economy full of prudence and of wisdom. He did not announce His message of Redemption in its full amplitude all at once. It was necessary that the minds of men should be made ready to accept it, and their souls and hearts made ready to receive it.

Jesus did not reveal Himself immediately as the Son of God, but did so gradually. First, there were the miracles, to astonish men and to set them wondering about Him. Then came implicit declarations, becoming less and less veiled. Finally, He spoke explicitly and clearly, especially in the company of the Disciples.

The Master Himself admitted His Apostles into the secret of this discreet and gradual method of enlightenment: "I have yet many things to say to you; but you cannot bear them now" (*John,* XVI, 12). How often they were astonished at His words! They did not understand, and Jesus reproached them for this (*Mark,* VII, 18; VIII, 18). It was His wish that they should gradually discover for themselves, under the action of the heavenly Father (*John,* XVI, 13) and through their intimate contact with Himself, the mystery of His Person. For an understanding of all He would say to them, a new and final illumination was necessary to them; and this He promised through the Holy Spirit Whom He would send to them (*John,* XVI, 13).

The public Revelation ended with the last of the Apostles. But each member of the Mystical Body must now achieve his own personal union with the mystery of Christ, his Head. He can do so only with the help of the Spirit of Jesus Who, now as always, forms each soul according to a progressive method adapted to the disposition of each.

2. *As He wishes*

Being a Master in the art of teaching, Jesus uses, with full freedom and as He sees most fitting, very diverse methods of instruction. Brief statements, deliberately obscure in order to provoke thought; sentences calculated to shock the mind into vivid attention; comparisons which flood a truth with sudden light; parables which instruct, but which demand proper dispositions of soul to be understood (*Mark,* IV, 12); and finally, direct teaching.

Jesus teaches His Apostles to seek wisdom from three great books. First, *the book of the Holy Scriptures,* on which His own mind is nourished. With profound respect for the Word of God, but always as a Master, He makes use of the sacred texts for His own purpose. He recalls them; He fulfills them; He meets His adversaries text for text; He applies to Himself their prophecies or their symbols; He opposes to them His own Law, not in order to render null the Law or the Prophets, but to perfect them (*Matt.*, V, 17). The second book is *the book of nature.* The lakes and the mountains, the vines and the harvests, the birds of the sky and the flocks of the pasture—all are for Him an occasion for inspiring and instructing the minds of men.

Finally, there is *the book of human life,* composed of the humdrum realities of everyday existence, the joys and the trials of life, the various occupations and labors that are men's daily pattern of living. He saw it all, observed it all, and made use of it all as a means of forming the minds of His Apostles, as a method of correcting their errors: "But apart, He explained all things to His disciples" (*Mark,* IV, 34). He found lessons in all the life around Him: in the laborers and shepherds; the merchants and the tax-gatherers; the fishermen and the vine-tenders; the hired worker and the hunted debtor; the women putting leaven in the dough, or carrying their pitchers to the fountain; the marriage feast, and the burying of the dead.

These three great books are still open before our eyes today. And Jesus, our Head, teaches us at all times, through His Spirit and through the teaching of His Church, to read them, to ponder them, to understand their lessons.

3. *According to the measure of each one's capacity to receive*

Today, as always, Jesus Christ gives His light only to souls who are upright, of good will, humble and simple. The seed of the Word of God must fall on a well-prepared soil, of good rich clay, free from stones and from thorns (*Mark,* IV).

Above all else, Jesus wants souls who desire Him and who seek Him. Nicodemus was such a soul (*John,* III). He was "a ruler of the Jews" who "came to Jesus by night"—which perhaps may appear not very courageous on his part. But what a thirst for enlightenment this action revealed! Moreover, Jesus took very special pains to enlighten him, and to teach him that a man must "be born again" if he is to "see the kingdom of God." When Nicodemus failed to understand this, Jesus patiently explained to him that He was speaking of being "born again of water and the Holy Ghost."

Consider, too, the Samaritan woman. Jesus decided to make

this woman one of the first witnesses to His Divinity. He began by kindling in her a desire for purer things: "If thou didst know the gift of God" (*John,* IV, 10).

The Pharisees were completely lacking in good will and in honest seeking for God, because they proudly believed that they already possessed all truth. Therefore Jesus repulsed them, heaped scorn on them, and refused to answer their insidious questions.

O Jesus, Our Lord, each one of us can trace in the years·that have passed, those moments of enlightenment that have marked our ascent to You. You know, O Lord, whither you would conduct our souls in accordance with the designs You have for each one of us. Teach us to advance daily in the loving knowledge and the practical application of Your truth, through the light of faith, of supernatural prudence and of the gifts of Your Divine Spirit.

3. THE WITNESS TO THE TRUTH

> *For this was I born, and for this came I into the world, that I should give testimony to the truth.*
>
> (John, XVIII, 37)

Our Lord has Himself clearly stated that one of the purposes of the mission of the Incarnate Word was to "give testimony to the truth," and the whole Gospel is the story of that testimony. Did this mission of Christ end with His death? How does He fulfill it today, now that He is in the Glory of the Father?

1. *During His earthly life*

We can define a witness as a person who has seen and who bears testimony to what he has seen. Jesus eminently fulfills these two conditions, as He Himself directly claims: "Amen, amen, I say to thee that we speak what we know and we *testify* what we *have seen*" (*John,* III, 11).

Jesus has seen. His knowledge pierces the heavens and the earth. He sees the Father, the Holy Trinity, the supernatural and divine realities which are beyond the vision of men—mysteries of whose nature, of whose very existence, the human mind can of itself know nothing.

Yet He expresses in the language of men, those invisible realities on which His soul feeds. He *testifies* to them; He reveals them; He vouches for them. He reserves to Himself alone this privilege and this role: "And no man hath ascended into heaven, but He that descended from heaven" (*John*, III, 13). He was in Heaven, reigning in equal glory with the Father. But, by His Incarnation, He descended to live among men, that He might speak "heavenly things" to them (*John*, III, 12), and prepare them to share with Him the glory of Heaven.

At the heart of these Divine Mysteries, is the Mystery of His own Person. He is the Son of God. His whole earthly life was spent in bearing witness to this truth. He insisted on it before His judges, and He died as a martyr to that truth.

2. Today, as Head of the Mystical Body

Now hidden in the glory of His Father, Christ bears witness through His Mystical Body—through His Church, His hierarchy, and each member of His faithful. He relies on every Christian to bear that witness in the world, and in the sight of all those who do not acknowledge it. "Eritis *mihi* testes" (*Acts*, 1, 8). There is precious food for thought in that command given by Christ to His Apostles, at the moment when he was about to be "raised up" so that "a cloud received Him out of their sight."

In the first place, the *subject* of that testimony is no longer an abstract truth: it is a person, it is Christ Himself. "And you shall be witnesses unto *Me*"—witnesses of My life, and especially of My Resurrection. The witnesses were to be those who had seen His life, and it was in this sense that the Apostles understood the Master's command (*Acts*, II, 32; III, 15; V, 32; X, 39).

Again, Christ asked His Apostles to act as witnesses in His stead, since He Himself could no longer be a visible witness. His own mission on earth was to bear witness to the truth, and He now appointed His Apostles to fulfill that mission *in His place and in His Name*. They were, therefore, to be His instruments in that necessary duty of public witness. "You shall be witnesses unto me."

Finally, the members of His Mystical Body, whom Christ calls to share in His mission, should fulfill the two conditions required in a witness. First, they must have *eyes of faith*—contemplative minds which, being filled with the light of the Holy Spirit, have learned to see God's action in the sweep of human history, in the events of their own lives, in nature and in the hearts of men. But they must also *testify:* by word, when necessary; always and above all, by the example of their own lives. They must testify to the Divine Presence—to the peace and strength they derive from the conviction that a beloved Person is really present to them, and that they are intimately united with

Him. They must testify to the power of a mighty Love possessing them and urging them to ceaseless self-sacrifice for others.

O Jesus, Our Head, Who calls us to continue Your witness on earth through our service of the truth, give us a passionate love for that truth. Help us to seek it unfalteringly always and everywhere; to accept it courageously, with all that it demands of us; to defend it with constancy; to confess it without compromise; to serve it with holy intentions; to bear witness to it before others, by our immense charity towards them; and to love it to the point of entire sacrifice of self for Your love.

4. THE MEDIATOR OF TRUTH

> *For there is one God; and one mediator of God and men, the man Christ Jesus.*
>
> (1 Tim., II, 5)

The role of the mediator is to reconcile and unite two extremes with infinity between them: God and men, Light and darkness. This "one mediator" is "the man Christ Jesus," because it is as "man" and as "Christ" that He fulfills this mission. The mediator of truth is primarily a witness: the Revealer. But He is more than just that.

1. *The Person of the Mediator*

In mediation, the person of the mediator is directly and essentially involved, since the mediator himself is the center, the point of encounter, the focus of union. The mediator is not just an intermediary, nor is He simply one factor of union. It is in Him, in His Person, that the reconciliation is effected and the union made. As He is the mediator of truth, it is in Him that men find truth.

It is in Christ that truth must be sought, for it is in Him that the Light dwells. He is "the light of the world" (*John*, VIII, 12).

It is in Him that men can become united with the very Life of God, for He is God made man. It is in Him that they can meet the Father, for the Father is in Him and He is in the Father (*John*, XIV, 10). It is in Him that they can share the Life of the Holy Trinity, for He is One of the Three Divine Persons.

Christ, the Head of the Mystical Body, gazes upon the Holy Trinity face to face. He is in the glory of the Father. His glorified humanity is radiant with triumphant Light. He worships for us who are toiling painfully towards the summits through the darkness of our souls. Yet we know that He sees and knows the Father, and that He will tell us the secrets of the Father. We must open our souls in faith to His secrets, which are communicated to us by the Church and which the Spirit of Truth teaches us to understand in the silence of our souls; still more, must we submit our whole being, in faith, to Christ our Head. By so doing, we hold ourselves in readiness to receive all the inspirations it will please Him to give us, in order that we may fulfill our personal mission in the Mystical Body.

2. *The action of the Mediator*

The person of the mediator of truth is not merely the place where truth is found, in the sense of the "treasure hidden in a field" of which the Gospel speaks (*Matt.*, XIII, 44). A personal action goes out from the Person of Christ, and reaches to every soul in the entire Mystical Body. Though the mediation of Christ has some points of resemblance to earthly mediation, it nevertheless differs radically from such mediation. In human mediation, the result is obtained through reciprocal concessions: the parties are united only through consenting to certain renunciations on both sides. But in the mediation of truth, there is no room for compromise; for what compromise can there be between light and darkness? Light must penetrate the darkness; and the darkness must yield to the light by itself becoming "lightsome."

In the Mystical Body of Christ, there radiates from the Head an illuminating and transforming power—which through faith, through the virtues, and through the gifts of the Holy Ghost—should bring about an assimilation to the Person of the Mediator, a sharing in His riches, an identification with Him Who is the Light. "I am come, a light into the world, that whosoever believeth in me may not remain in darkness . . . And he that walketh in darkness knoweth not whither he goeth. Whilst you have the light, believe in the light, that you may be the children of light" (*John* XII, 46, 35, 36).

O Lord Jesus, when Your Light comes into our souls, it seeks out the most hidden recesses of our being. As the light of the sun, suddenly filling a room, shows up the dust that lay hidden there, so does Your light uncover the depths of our misery. Then, indeed,

the scales fall from the eyes of our soul, and we see ourselves as
we really are. No longer can we play the saint and gaze com-
placently at our supposed virtues. Your light comes to startle our
souls into a realization of the truth.

5. THE TRUTH IN PERSON

I am . . . the Truth.

(John, XV, 6)

By becoming man, the Word has plunged that human nature
which He assumed, into the abyss of Light and of Life which is
Himself, as Son of the Father. His humanity is therefore completely suffused with this Divine Light. "He will reign over men's
minds, because He is the Truth" (Pope Pius XI: Encyclical on
Christ the King).

1. *The doctrine*

"Ego sum veritas." No one, except the Word made Flesh, has
ever made this astounding claim. The mightiest of human thinkers
have found all their glory in being the humble servants of truth.
How many of them, indeed, have groped towards glimpses of the
truth, through long years marked with the anguish of their doubts
and the torment of their famished souls!

Christ Himself has said that He is the Truth: He claims that
Truth and He are One. To seek Him is to seek Truth; to love Him
is to love Truth. For Jesus is the Divine Word, the Son of the
Father, the Wisdom of the Father, "the brightness of his glory
and the figure of his substance" (*Heb.*, 1, 3), "the Light born of
His Light" (Council of Nicaea). Jesus is the Word, in Whom
the Father speaks within the abyss of His own Being; the Word
through Whom, in knowing Himself, God also knows all His
creatures.

The Son is the expression of the Father, consubstantial with
and equal to the Father; and He is at the same time the ideal
expression of all creatures, while being also their Creator (St.
Thomas, 1, q. 34, a. 3). They exist only because, from all eternity,
they have existed in the Word as in their Exemplary Cause . . .
It is in Him that they have life. "In him was life, and the life was

the light of men." (*John*, 1, 4). Things realize their true nature, therefore, only in the measure to which they conform to the idea which their Divine Archetype, the eternal Son of the Father, has had of them. Their truth is to be measured by the fidelity with which they represent this idea and reproduce it.

2. *The applications of the doctrine*

The words of Jesus, declaring that He is the Truth, define as though with letters of light the doctrine that He has come to teach, and our relations with Him.

Christianity, therefore, is not primarily a body of truths: it is an *attachment* to a *living Being* Who incarnates the Truth in His own Divine Person. Nor is it primarily a written code of ethics: it presents a *Model* to be imitated, in the example of the most powerful Personality of history. Neither, however, is Christianity primarily the earthly life of its Divine Founder, sublime indeed as was that life: it is *union with a Person* Who now lives, and will live through all future ages and in eternity.

For a soul which seeks to love God, the problem is more than a study and imitation of His teaching and His example. Such a soul must live in the interior silence of prayer, wherein the voice of the Divine Word Himself can be heard. Ceaseless meditation, deepened by prayer, on the teachings of the Church is necessary to such a soul; for it must thus strive more and more to learn how to listen, in its own silent depths, to the words of light which the Divine Word speaks to it personally at this very moment.

To become in this way the ready pupil of the Divine Word, a soul must first free itself from all human desires and from all attachment to created things, so as to be able to embrace the truth, however demanding it may be. The soul must also realize its utter dependence on God, and must submit humbly to everything which the Master of Truth decides. Only by doing so, can the soul put itself into His Hands, to be formed to holiness by Him.

Finally, an ardent faith in the omnipotence of the Divine Word is required in such a soul. According to the intensity of this faith, will be the strength of the soul's conviction that He Who is the Light will give the light which it seeks, in accordance with the Master's own good pleasure and as a reward for its faith and its hunger for eternal truth.

O Jesus, it is not in learned books and by purely intellectual studies that man can discover the Supreme Truth. For You are

Yourself the living Truth in Person. It is You Who reveal Yourself
to a soul which is detached from earthly things, which seeks You
in all sincerity and with a lively faith, hungry for You, ready to
throw itself wide to Your engulfing light, and to submit itself
always to be formed to holiness by You.

6. THE OMNISCIENCE OF THE HEAD

In whom are hid all the treasures of wis-
dom and of knowledge.

(Colos., II, 3)

"In the manger, on the Cross, in the eternal glory of the
Father, Christ sees and embraces all the members of His Church,
and He sees them far more clearly, embraces them far more lovingly, than does a mother the child of her bosom, far better than
a man knows and loves himself."

(Pope Pius XII: *Mystici Corporis Christi.* English translation,
Canon Smith, C.T.S.).

How does Jesus Christ, the Head, actually know each of the
members of His Mystical Body? In two ways: by His infused
knowledge; and by His beatific vision.

By His Infused Knowledge

1. *The object of this knowledge*

From His place in Heaven, Jesus has within the scope of His
human intelligence, all the occurrences of this earth, through His
infused knowledge. This knowledge is universal, reaching out to
all things, present, past and to come.

The Gospel shows that Jesus, as man, was made aware of
natural occurrences, of the events of history, of the things to
come. He was the Mighty Seer, the Great Prophet. Already, in
Nazareth as in Gethsemani and during His entire earthly existence, He knew our whole life in all its details. He knew in
advance all that would happen to us.

It is equally by this infused knowledge that Jesus knew all
the secrets of men's hearts, for He could read the most hidden
thoughts of those who spoke with Him, uncover the evil designs
of His adversaries, and probe the intimate feelings of the multi-

tude. From his own experience of the searching glances of his Master, Peter could say to Christ with entire conviction: "Lord, thou knowest all things; thou knowest that I love thee." (*John*, XXI, 17).

Finally, it is by this infused knowledge that Jesus knew the supernatural realities in the life of souls, and the wonderful transformations which sanctifying grace effects in them. He contemplated His own human soul, in which was the plenitude of the graces and the gifts of the Holy Spirit; and He had thus experimental knowledge of the Divine Life in His soul.

Now, at this very moment, Jesus possesses that penetrating knowledge in His glorified Humanity. How deeply consoling it is for us to know that, at all times, we live thus within the light of the human intelligence of our glorified Savior!

As God-Man, He knows each one of us individually, with each one's temperament and character, tendencies both good and bad, deficiencies as well as resources. He looks into the heart of each one of us. There He reads our sincere feelings and our generous impulses, our cowardice and failures. He reads our souls with a clearness of gaze far superior to our own, for we tend to see ourselves through the veil of our illusions about what we are. Not even the most secret thought escapes that penetrating gaze.

He sees all the events of our life, their connections and their consequences; He sees our trials and our joys, our successes and our failures . . . He knows the exact moment and the circumstances of our death.

2. *The mode of this knowledge*

Jesus knew and knows today all human occurrences in their *human* aspect, through the ideas and images which were communicated to Him during His earthly life, and which are now communicated to Him, in His glorified Humanity, directly by God, as the Angel receives them in its pure spirit . . . as the prophets received them for unknown events and for events of the future. While, however, the prophets' knowledge was confined to some limited and transient aspects of the future, Christ's prophetic knowledge extended and extends to every detail in the full sweep of the future, for the whole world and for each one of us individually.

It is in this manner that the Eucharistic Christ knows us. Many imagine that Jesus, really present in His Sacrament of Love, sees us with bodily eyes; but this is not so. Imagination has no place in this "mystery of Faith," for it tends to injure this sublime Mystery by deforming and lessening it to the size of our own poor invention. Faith is the secret by which we attain directly to Christ, for it is faith which sweeps away the immense distance separating us from Him. By faith, we enter into what Christ is even now thinking about us, into the fullness of His designs for us, at the moment when we receive Him in Holy Communion or visit Him in His tabernacle.

O Jesus, Our Lord, we shall no longer busy ourselves with imagining what You would do or think were You in our place. The reality is what You are thinking of us and desiring from us here and now. Our whole concern, then, is to enter by faith into Your thoughts and lovingly to fulfill Your wishes through our discharge of the duty of our state now awaiting our attention.

7. HIS KNOWLEDGE THROUGH THE BEATIFIC VISION

No man hath seen God at any time; the only begotten Son who is in the bosom of the Father, he hath declared him.

(John, I, 18)

Christ's beatific vision is not His Divine Knowledge—the knowledge which He possesses as God. It is by this Divine Knowledge alone that He embraces the Divine Essence and knows the full extent of the Divine Power, both what It is and all that It can create. From the first instant of His incarnation, Jesus had possessed the knowledge enjoyed by the Blessed in Heaven— the beatific vision: a knowledge lower than the Divine Knowledge, and superior to infused knowledge. Now in the glory of His Father, He possesses that knowledge in His glorified Humanity

1. *The object of this vision*

In the first place, the human mind of Jesus knew all created things, and knows them now, through the beatific vision, in the light of the Word . . . "everything that is being, has been, or shall be thought, said or done, by any person whomsoever at any time" (Saint Thomas). Jesus has seen and sees all these things in God, in their First Cause, in their Perfect Exemplar, the Divine Word Who He is Himself.

Now as during His earthly life, Jesus sees the Divinity as it is in Itself. He contemplates all Its infinite perfections and their harmonious union in the Divine Essence . . .

Christ's human mind, enlightened by the beatific vision, contemplates with admiration the Three Divine Persons. It sees the Father Who, in knowing Himself, eternally begets the Son—that Son Who is Jesus Himself . . . It sees the Father and the Son Who, in mutual love One for the Other, are one and the same Principle of the Holy Spirit . . .

It contemplates their subsistent relations which constitute the Life of the Blessed Trinity . . . It discovers, in the light of the Word, the whole redemptive plan of Infinite Love; and It adores the Goodness, Wisdom and Mercy of God, Who willed to save mankind at any cost.

2. *The effects of this vision in the soul of Christ*

During His whole earthly life, the Soul of Jesus was inundated, through this beatific vision, with an inexpressible joy— the joy of seeing His Father directly and face to face, of contemplating the happiness of the Holy Trinity, and of being very intimately associated with that happiness; the joy of admiring and adoring the Divine Perfections as They are in Themselves.

On the other hand, however, this beatific vision was a cause of unfathomable suffering for His Soul. The more this Soul became immersed in the immediate vision of the Divine Perfections and the Holiness of God, the greater became Its power to measure the full horror of sin and the frightful misery of sinful humanity. The more It penetrated into the abyss of Infinite Love, and embraced, in one resplendent glance, the whole plan of Divine Goodness and Divine Mercy for each and every person and for all mankind, so much the greater became its suffering at the sight of the sinful ingratitude of men towards the Father, and of the immense unhappiness of men when they stray from God or rebel against Him. The more the Soul of Christ bowed Itself to the rights of God and His justice, the more vivid also became Its realization of all the immolation and sacrifice which would be necessary for the Redemption of the world.

Since His Resurrection and Ascension, and unto eternity, the glorified Soul of Christ can no longer experience any suffering in Itself. But, as Head of His Mystical Body, Christ asks of all His members who seek to love Him and to model their lives on His, that they should accept some part of the sacrifices and immolations which are necessary for the salvation of the world today;

because, by doing so, they will follow Him along the way that
He went in order to win the glory of His own Body and that of
His Mystical Body. Christ knew all these sufferings, and He carried these crosses in bearing His own. But He asks us in our
turn to bear them generously, fully accepting our day-to-day
sufferings as from the Father's Hand, that we may cooperate
with Him in the Redemption of our brethren.

*O Jesus, Who, in the glory of the Father, sees all things in
the fullness of celestial light, give us as intense a realization as
possible of the evil of sin, and a keen sorrow at the thought of all
the disorder and unhappiness into which those are plunged who
have forgotten that they have a Savior and that they are called to
enjoy with You eternally a life of happiness in the vision of glory.*

THE EMINENT SOVEREIGNTY OF

THE DIVINE HEAD OVER THE MINDS OF MEN,

AND HIS LIFE-GIVING ACTION

8.   THE IMMENSITY OF HIS LOVE

> *Yea, I have loved thee with an everlasting
> love: therefore have I drawn thee, taking
> pity on thee.*
>
> (Jeremias, XXXI, 3)

"He was the King of men's hearts because of His incomprehensible Love, Which surpasses all human understanding" (Pope
Pius XI, *Encyclical on Christ the King*).

The Mysteries of the Godhead were not revealed to men by
God in order to keep men at a distance from Him by imposing on
their minds truths which make Him inaccessible to them. On the
contrary, indeed, these Mysteries are the touching manifestations
of that Infinite Love by which God has willed, from all eternity,
to love mankind in His Son and to "draw" mankind to Him. For
these Mysteries are addressed to the understanding as enlightened
by faith and animated by love.

All the Mysteries of Christ are Mysteries of Love

The Mystery of the Incarnation is essentially a mystery of love. "Already before the world began, the only-begotten Son of God strained us to Himself with His eternal and infinite knowledge and with His everlasting love. And to show this love in a visible and most wonderful way, He united our nature hypostatically with Himself." (*Mystici Corporis Christi*. English translation: Canon Smith). What the philosophers cannot fathom is that the abyss between the infinite and the finite should be bridged, that the Divine Word should be made flesh, and that He should submit to the conditions of man's birth, growth and life. This they proclaim as impossible and inconceivable. All things are possible with God; but what the wisdom of the wise cannot understand here is the inscrutibility of the Infinite Love Which inspires and rules this whole Mystery. Saint Paul gives us the key to Its understanding: *Propter nimiam caritatem—*"for his exceeding charity" (*Ephes.*, II, 4). He has loved us beyond our powers to measure the love "wherewith he loved us" (*ibid.*).

The Mystery of the Redemption is essentially a mystery of love. What scandalizes, and sometimes arrests on the very threshold of faith, men of good will who seek to understand the religion of Christ, is that One Who is sinless should have willed to expiate and repair the sin of mankind; that, in order to realize in Himself the full conditions of human kind, He should have accepted the consequences of their sin—suffering and death; that He, the Judge of the living and of the dead, should have consented to appear as a criminal before a human court, and to be nailed to a cross between two malefactors, exposed to the blasphemies of a misguided mob. It is Christ Himself Who has given the answer to all this: "Greater love than this no man hath, that a man lay down his life for his friends." (*John*, XV, 13). He has loved us beyond measure, "unto death, even to the death of the cross" (*Phil.*, II, 8).

The Mystery of the Eucharist is essentially a mystery of love. Because He loved us, Jesus willed to live in our midst by His Real Presence, to offer Himself with us and to feed us with His Sacred Body and His Precious Blood. But here again, the human mind could never of itself imagine or understand such an extraordinary state of affairs: the God-Man, the Lord of all creation, hidden under the appearance of a tiny Host! And again, it is the Gospel which gives us the solution to the problem: "having loved

his own who were in the world, he loved them unto the end"
(*John*, XIII, 1).

The Mystery of the Church is essentially a mystery of love.
Because He loved men, Jesus willed to protect their minds against
the anguish of doubt and the evil of error. Because He loved
them, He directed the Barque of Peter into the heart of the
tempests and through all the vicissitudes of history, in order that
mankind might be guided to port by a Society led by His Holy
Spirit, and that their souls might be vivified by the sacramental
life.

*The Mystery of the Blessed Trinity is essentially a mystery of
love*—the Infinite Love of the Father for the Son and of the
Son for the Father, eternally expressing Itself in the unity of
Their Holy Spirit. Here is a whole world of truths which surpass
the powers of the human understanding. Although It has been
revealed to us by Christ, philosophers were overwhelmed by this
Mystery wherein they admired the infinite fecundity of a Love
which gives Itself from Person to Person in the intimate Life of
the Holy Trinity. But what is really astounding is that Our Lord
Jesus Christ was not content to reveal this Mystery of the Blessed
Trinity as if it were merely an abstract truth with no significance
for us beyond itself. Christ's purpose in taking our nature was
to introduce us into family relationship with the Three Divine
Persons, and to make us share henceforward in the Life of Their
Infinite Love.

Finally, where therefore can this Infinite Love blaze forth
with greater power than in *the Mystery of the Whole Christ*—the
Mystery of His Mystical Body? Jesus Christ has willed to raise
every man to the sublime dignity of son of God, and to let him
share in His infinite riches as the Son of the Eternal Father. He
has willed to gather all men into the unity of His Mystical Body,
vivified by His Charity and animated by His Spirit of Love. Christ
will be "Whole" only when He can present to His Father all His
human brethren who have been conquered by Love, "that God
may be all in all."

*O Jesus, Our Savior, increase our faith in Your Love, so that
we too may be able to say with the beloved Apostle, in the depths
of our souls: "We have known and have believed the charity
which God hath to us" (I John, IV, 16). Do this, we beseech
You, in all the events of our life, and especially in those moments
when we find that all goes wrong with us and our human plans
are in fragments about our feet.*

9. THE DEPTHS AND THE VARIED ASPECTS
OF THE LOVE OF JESUS

I have loved you.

(John, XV, 12)

In Christ, the Head of the Mystical Body, there is such a fullness of love that it is impossible for our poor limited and narrow hearts to open at once and with full understanding, to what Saint Paul calls "the inestimable riches" of His Sacred Heart. And because our views are but partial and stunted, we think that we find contrasts there, or even contradictions. Let us contemplate, with an ardent faith, the harmonious synthesis of Infinite Love in this adorable Heart, the Heart of God.

Christ's love for us is a *personal* love, reaching out to each of us individually as if ours were the only soul in the world. Yet, it is as members of His Mystical Body that He loves us. Although Christ embraces all of us with the same love, inasmuch as we are all united in the unity of His Mystical Body, the intensity of that love is nevertheless in proportion to the mission and the influence which each member exercises in the service of the whole Body.

The love of Christ for us is a *plenitude* which utterly satisfies all the aspirations of our heart, and seems to absorb all our capacity for loving according as it takes possession of all that is within us. And yet, this love awakens in our hearts an *insatiable desire* to meet it with a love which increases more and more, while it also causes us to suffer because we never love with sufficient warmth.

The love of Christ for us is a *disinterested* love, because Jesus does not love us for Himself, but for the sake of His Father and for our own sake, for our good and for our happiness. Yet, it is a terribly *jealous* love, which demands that itself should reign without a rival in the heart, and which draws all to itself.

The love of Christ for us is an infinite tenderness, which brings an ineffable joy to the heart and a sweetness full of peace. Yet, this love makes formidable demands on our natural sloth and calls us imperiously to *self-sacrifice*.

The love of Christ for us is an *infinitely merciful* love, which takes away the sins of the world, which cleanses all the defilements of our souls. Yet, in the very act of penetrating our souls, this love reveals to us, with a more and more blinding clarity, *the abyss of our own misery*.

The love of Christ for us is an *infinitely patient* love, which is never discouraged by our slothful delays, our weak irresolution and our ungenerous refusals. Yet, it is a love which urges us to act, which ceaselessly pursues us, and seeks from us an immediate and practical answer.

The love of Christ gives to our souls a *peace* "which surpasses all understanding"—the peace which Jesus alone can give. Yet, this love creates dissatisfaction and obsessive preoccupation with the Redemption of the world; and constant dissatisfaction at not being sufficiently zealous in our mission as co-operators in the work of Redemption.

The love of Christ awakens in the heart which eagerly longs to meet the Master face to face, a *desire* to be delivered "from the body of this death," in order to possess Him for eternity. Yet, this love increases the ardour of our attachment to life in order that we may be able to heap up greater merit, and work for the extension of the Reign of Christ in the world, during such span of years as it shall please our Heavenly Father to give us.

The love of Christ *purifies* and *detaches* the heart from all that is not the work of Christ. It makes all our human efforts seem weak and unavailing. Yet, this love gives to our smallest actions an inestimable value, inasmuch as they are a means of proving our love and of contributing to the Redemption of souls.

The love of Christ for us is an *infinitely powerful* love by which our hearts are brought under the sweet yoke of His sovereign dominion, in captivity to Him. Yet, it is a love which delivers us, which releases our hearts from the enslaving chains of human passions, and which sets us free from clogging attachment to all created things.

O Jesus, to recognize Your sovereignty over our hearts is to proclaim it our duty to submit to Your Love because You have every right to our submission and to our love. But when once we have begun to feel the sweetness and the strength of Your Love, this duty answers to an imperious need of our poor human hearts. We find our joy in allowing ourselves to be vanquished by You and to be conquered by Your Love.

10. BY HIS MEEKNESS

Ego sum mitis.

(Matt., XI, 29)

The meekness of Jesus has an incomparable power of attraction, and it is the quality He specially chooses to predicate of Himself: "learn of me, because I am meek and humble of heart." (*Matt.*, XI, 29).

1. *This meekness itself*

Let us study, in particular, *His meekness and sweetness with His Apostles;* for it will show us the quality of His sweetness towards each one of us here and now, His sweetness as the Head of that Mystical Body of which each one of us is a member.

For three years, Jesus lived with His Apostles a life shared completely with them. He knew them intimately and read the depths of their souls. He discerned all their human weaknesses, both those which they would have wished to keep hidden from Him and those of which they themselves were unaware. Nay more, He saw their whole future: Peter's denial, the treason of Judas, His abandonment by all those whom He had loved so much. And yet, He never ceased to lavish upon them abundant evidence of an infinitely delicate, untiringly patient affection. With exquisite meekness, He formed and encouraged, sustained and corrected them, and enlightened their dimly groping minds, slow to understand.

Today, we no longer hear the sound of Christ's voice, it is true. We have no longer His gestures and the gentle warmth of His whole attitude, to show the nature of Christ's sweetness towards us. But we know by faith and by doctrine that His attitude remains unchanged, "yesterday, today and the same forever." Jesus is not impatient or irritated with us; nor does He repulse us. On the contrary, today as yesterday, He welcomes us, draws us, and desires to conquer our souls by revealing to them the inexhaustible riches of His Sacred Heart. Indeed, if He complains, it is of not being sufficiently loved; and—as formerly in the Psalms and in His confidences to His Saints—He begs that men should not reject Him, but should answer His advances of love towards them. When faith is pure and lively in a soul, it enables that soul to discern, through all the events of life, the extremely touching manifestations of the love of Christ our Head for the members of His Mystical Body. There are those prevenient graces by which He prepares and disposes the soul for a painful or joyful event; and there are those graces of light, strength and peace by which He illumines, sustains and consoles us in every circumstance. The awareness of Christ's loving glance resting upon our souls, is with us in all the circumstances of our lives.

2. The elements of this sweetness of Christ

a) This sweetness was, in the first place, *the expression of the wonderful equilibrium* which reigned in His whole body.

With us, meekness can be acquired only laboriously as a result of the patient and progressive conquest of the chaos created by our fallen nature and the tyrannical demands of our self-love. In Jesus, meekness is the sign of an extraordinary self-mastery and of perfect order—the perfection of a human will, fully master of the passions, and completely submissive to the Divine Will. Thus, His meekness is power, and it exercises an ascendency over us who know that we are always at the mercy of our passions.

When we seek to understand the soul of Christ, what first strikes us is precisely His supreme mastery. Conqueror of death and of the malice of men; now triumphant in the glory of His Father, from Whom He has received all power over all mankind and over the whole world; freed from the material limitations of the body and of space—Christ dwells in all His fullness, disposing at will of the Divine Treasures and giving them to each soul according as He Himself pleases. But this limitless authority in no way grinds us down. We rapturously contemplate it, and, enthralled by the splendor of Christ's sovereign equilibrium, we endeavor to imitate Him in His meekness. We beg Him to let us share the power of His soul, in order that we may be able, to conquer everything which would deprive us of interior peace and of our painfully preserved spiritual equilibrium.

b) Christ's sweetness was also *the fruit of His penetrating knowledge of men,* of their limitations and their grandeur; while being also the fruit of His intense love for them.

Freed from all limitations of time, this essential element of Christ's meekness continues the same, today, in His glorified humanity as Head of the Mystical Body.

Christ's knowledge reaches intimately to us all. Hence it is that His charity shows itself as merciful understanding, loving pity, and patient meekness. While He condemns with such emphasis and severity evil and sin, He knows how to be patient and to bear with our weaknesses. "The bruised reed he shall not break, and smoking flax he shall not quench." (*Isaias,* XLII, 3). His meekness reflects the eternal patience of God.

But, while He knows the measure of the fundamental poverty of human nature, Christ also clearly sees, in each one of us, the vessel of divine grace, the person loved by God with an infinite love, the child of His Heavenly Father. With all the urgency of His love, He seeks to win this person for His Father. He has for the human soul a respect of the utmost delicacy—that astonishing respect which God shows for the dignity of His creature and for his liberty.

O Jesus, rule our hearts by the power and the sweetness of Your love, that we may learn to open our hearts to all that is divine in the persons around us, and to welcome with meekness the Will of the Father in the smallest details of our daily lives.

11. BY HIS GOODNESS

*"Or despisest thou the riches of his good-
ness and patience and long suffering?"*

(Rom., II, 4)

Goodness is that interior disposition which inclines a person to spread happiness around him. A *good* soul is one that thinks, wishes and does only what is good. In complete forgetfulness of self, such a soul aims only at securing good, happiness and joy for others; and thinks only of giving, never of receiving. Such was Jesus Christ; such He is today as Head of His Mystical Body.

1. *During His earthly life*

Jesus did good: as the Scripture says—"who went about doing good" (*Acts,* X, 38). The Gospels are the evidence of this.

a.) Jesus showed a *merciful and compassionate* goodness towards all suffering—physical, moral and spiritual. "And Jesus went about all the cities and towns . . . healing every disease and every infirmity" (*Matt.,* IX, 35). As Jesus walked the roads of Palestine or entered into the towns, He was surrounded by the afflicted multitude of the sick, the infirm, the paralytics, the possessed, the blind, the deaf and dumb. They had put all their hope in Jesus, because they felt His sympathy going out to them. He did not repulse them with indifference, contempt or distrust, as so many others did. He loved them and pitied them. He wished to cure them. "And, seeing the multitudes, he had compassion on them; because they were distressed and lying like sheep that have no shepherd" (*Matt.*, IX, 36).

What is indeed striking in the attitude of Jesus when faced with a human sorrow or misfortune, is His response of generous understanding and of sincere compassion. Jesus suffers personally at the misfortune of others, and makes their sorrows His own. He puts Himself in their place, His Heart vibrant with human and divine tenderness. Christ's tears at the tomb of Lazarus; His tears over the fate of Jerusalem, and because of the mothers who had lost their children—all show more eloquently than any words, how truly He was a *man*, sharing all the sorrows of His brethren. "I have compassion on the multitude" (*Mark*, VIII, 2); "Come to me, all you that labor and are burdened; and I will refresh you" (*Matt.*, XI, 28). These words, which it pleased God should one day fall from the human lips of His Son made Man, will reverberate their soft compassion to the end of time and even to the uttermost parts of the earth.

The goodness of Jesus is *warm* and *effulgent*. We are not surprised, therefore, to read in the Gospels how close Jesus is to His people, and what an extraordinary attraction He exercised on all those who came to Him. He is besieged by the multitude, who want to see Him, to touch Him, to be near Him, and who never tire of listening to His instructions. They put all their trust and all their hope in Him. It is admirable how easily He can be approached by all; by the humblest, the poorest, the most wretched outcasts of nature and of society. These are the first of the saintly multitudes who, throughout the centuries to come, were to attach themselves to Christ and give themselves to Him because He had first loved them and they had felt the warmth of His love.

2. *Today as Head of the Mystical Body*

Jesus *desires the good* of each member of His Body. Today as yesterday, He brings to all souls His message of Redemption, of freedom and of happiness. He calls them to happiness: "Blessed are those . . ." Of course, the happiness which He promises them is not the mirage given by the frivolous and transient pleasures of this world. It consists in the complete satisfaction of the most noble and most profound aspirations of human nature; in the fulfillment of man's higher faculties through the possession of their object; in the peace of a soul which has attained its place of rest. But this happiness does not stifle and exclude the legitimate joys of this world: it purifies them, increases them, and makes them meritorious of eternal life.

b) Jesus, as Head of His Mystical Body, is the *inexhaustible source of all the supernatural and divine benefits* which He confers on His members at every moment. One of the elements of our joy in Heaven will be to contemplate, in the Light of the Eternal Word, the innumerable graces which have been lavished on the soul of each one of God's elect—on that of the Blessed Virgin Mary and on those of all the great Saints throughout the centuries. All these graces have sprung from the Heart of Christ; and it is with rapture that the soul contemplates, with eyes of splendid faith, this Infinite Goodness which, now and at every moment, is ceaselessly communicated to all the members of the Mystical Body by Christ our Head.

c) However marvellous this generosity of our Head in His gifts, the greatest wonder of all is that—now as formerly, though under another form—*He gives Himself to us.* Jesus can no longer experience sensible pity or the sufferings of immolation, in His Glorified Body; but He still gives us His Life. In the Holy Eucharist, He gives us His Divine Life and the Celestial Life of His Humanity; by sanctifying grace, He gives us participation in His Divine Life. In His Mystical Body, He forms a constant community of life with us, in order that we may enjoy with Him an ineffable share in the Life of the Three Divine Persons.

O Jesus, living image of the infinite Goodness of the Father Who is in Heaven, increase in all the members of Your Mystical Body, an unshakable faith in the Goodness of Your Sacred Heart. Grant them, especially in times of sorrow and trial, a firm conviction that You are guiding them, and that it is impossible for You to will anything which is not for their real good and their true happiness.

THE EMINENT SOVEREIGNTY OF
THE DIVINE HEAD OVER THE WILL OF MEN
AND HIS LIFE-GIVING ACTION

12.   THE CHRISTIAN VOCATION

Follow me.

(John, I, 43; Matt., IX, 9)

The Christian vocation consists in the call to participate in the Mystery of Christ. The Mystery of Christ is the Mystery of the Son of God becoming man in order to save the world by the sacrifice of His life and by the institution of His Mystical Body. There are four essential elements, therefore, in the Christian vocation.

1.   *Participation in the LIFE of the Son*

The Son of God became man in order that, like Him and through Him, all men should be made the sons of God. The Christian vocation is primarily, therefore, *a vocation to sonship.* The Christian is he who, by Baptism, becomes a son of God through participation in the Divine Sonship of Jesus. This is not, of course, a participation in the hypostatic union, which is the unique and absolutely incommunicable privilege of the Son as God. It is, however, a participation in the Divine Life as possessed by Jesus Christ through the sanctifying grace in His human soul. It is a participation in the sanctifying grace of the Head, which grace He possesses in its plenitude in order to communicate it to the members of His Body.

2.   *Participation in the MISSION of the Son*

Jesus Christ does not call souls to enjoy the benefits of His Life as Son of God, in order that they may rest in the consolations and sweetness of intimacy with Him. He attracts them to Himself and gives them His Life in abundance, in order to associate them with His Redemptive Mission. The Son was made flesh to save the world: His Mission as Savior is therefore inseparable from His very Being.

Jesus offered His invitation to the Twelve with the words: "Come after me"—but He immediately added: "and I will make you to become fishers of men" (*Mark*, 1, 19). The fact that the Twelve Apostles were called to serve the Mystical Body, is undoubtedly one of the spiritual events which demonstrates, in the clearest manner, the entire mastery of Christ the Head over the members of His Body.

In a sense, it is the same call from the same Head which is given to every Christian. It is the same vocation—the same participation in the Redemptive Mission of Christ. For the Christian vocation is essentially *apostolic and redemptive*.

3. *Participation in the SACRIFICE of the Son*

How has Christ saved the world? By each of His prayers and by each of His actions; but all His actions were directed towards His Sacrifice, which is the crown of His whole Life and the Key to its meaning.

To aim at following Christ to the foot of Calvary, but with no desire to participate in His sacrifice, is to mutilate the Christian vocation and deprive it of all significance.

How many of those, however, who have decided to follow the Master to the utmost of His call, realize that the Christian vocation is a vocation to sacrifice and to self-oblation? Many indeed declare their readiness to be adopted sons of God, because it is heartening for a man to know that he is the object of the Heavenly Father's love. But the vocation of sonship leads inexorably to Golgotha: "But that the world may know that I love the Father . . . arise, let us go hence" (*John*, 14, 31), said Jesus, setting off for the place of His Sacrifice.

Numerous, also, are the souls who wish to cooperate in the Redemption of the world. But they do not understand that the apostolate is not just the simple blossoming of a generous nature or the satisfaction of devoted service. Those who were "Apostles" in the full sense of the word, have followed their Master to the total giving of their lives for the salvation of their brethren.

4. *Participation in the FORMATION of the WHOLE CHRIST*

Finally, the Christian vocation is a call to the soul to live, deeply and fully, its life as a *member* of the Mystical Body of

Christ. It is therefore a vocation of membership, which can be fully realized only in the unity of the Mystical Body and in the life of that Body. This does not imply a lessening of the soul's dignity, as though it were being regarded as merely a little cell in an immense organism. On the contrary, indeed, this unity in the Mystical Body throws into greater prominence the astonishing fecundity of the soul. Alone, what could any soul do for the Redemption of the world, however generous and apostolic it might be? Through this unity, however, it becomes rich and powerful with all the richness and power of the Mystical Body of Christ.

For such a soul, life takes on its full, luminous meaning, as personal cooperation in the formation of the Whole Christ. This mighty work is free from the limitations of time: the soul will continue eternally to fulfill it, for the glory of Christ Who has deigned to call that soul to the most perfect possible assimilation with Him. The realization of this truth makes the Christian understand that his personality, even to the most intimate depths of his faculties and his gifts, is meaningless except as related to this mission reserved for it in the Mystical Body of Christ.

O Jesus, Our Lord, give to Your disciples a realization of the immense responsibility which lies in the choice implied by their Christian vocation. Do not permit them to minimize that sublime vocation.

13. THE PRIESTLY VOCATION

You have not chosen me; but I have chosen you.

(John, XV, 16)

The vocation to the priesthood is an absolutely free gift of the Infinite Love of God. "Neither doth any man take the honor to himself, but he that is called by God, as Aaron was" (*Heb.*, V, 4). The answer to this call is a free, personal act. But it is also the act which most clearly manifests Christ's conquest of the wills of His members, and His concern for the social needs of His Mystical Body.

1. The call of Christ in the Bishop's Call

Since it is the service of the Mystical Body which is all important, the priestly vocation consists essentially in the call of the Church. Aware of the needs of all the faithful of his diocese, the Bishop calls to the different Sacred Orders a candidate for the priesthood. This, however, is not a choice which he makes arbitrarily; for the Church has laid down the conditions governing it. These conditions are the interior and exterior signs which reveal that God has given such a vocation to the candidate.

The interior signs are a right intention and the required physical, moral and intellectual qualities which, being the gifts of the Creator, can point to the existence of a call from God. The exterior signs are the various circumstances of the candidate's life, which can show whither Providence is leading him.

There is admirable wisdom in this doctrine, for it avoids two possible extremes. On the one hand, it guards against the individualism of a personal "inspiration" which would lead some men to imagine that they have a vocation and to claim the right to be ordained; on the other hand, it guards against whim and undue interference on the part of the Bishop.

In this matter, the Bishop, who is responsible to God and to the Sovereign Pontiff for the proper conduct of his diocese, acts as Head. But he does so in the name of God, and as the representative of the One Head, Jesus Christ.

2. The call of Christ in the personal graces of the chosen

The right intention shows itself in various ways. It is the desire to give to life a noble ideal and a higher fruitfulness; it is the attraction of sacrifice and self-oblation for others; it is a very ardent love for Christ, expressed by a compelling desire to imitate Him and to participate in His Redemptive Mission; it is the conviction that there cannot be a more useful, more urgent, more necessary mission to men than that of the priest, since it answers the most noble, most profound, most essentially human of all needs—those of the mind, of the soul, of social life; it is the very lively consciousness of the frightful distress of mankind deprived of God.

Whatever the direction taken by these desires, it is Christ Who calls these souls by means of them; for it is His grace which kindles such desires. Again, it is He Who makes use of a particular occasion through which the challenge of a true vocation is issued to a young soul. It may be the example of a saintly priest, the atmosphere of a good Catholic family, a disillusionment which lays bare the transience of earthly things, a few words in a sermon which strike vividly home as the Voice of God, the splendor of a liturgical ceremony, and so forth. When a young man reaches a considered and firm decision to seek the priesthood, with a full realization that he is entering on the hard way of self-oblation and sacrifice and is not just acting on an impulse of pious imagination or passing fervor, this is the surest sign that the grace of God is stronger in him than the repugnances of human nature, and that Christ our Head has chosen him to be an Apostle.

3. *The call of Christ in the needs of souls and of the Church*

Certain souls fail to solve the problem of their priestly vocation, because they consider it solely on the personal plane—that of inclination, of taste, of security. But the problem of vocation is a social one: the problem of serving the Mystical Body and the needs of the Church. There is one question, therefore, which should exercise the minds of those who are seeking to reach a decision of this kind, and which should be kept before them by their spiritual directors: "What are the most pressing needs of the Church today? To what parts of the apostolic field does the Master of the harvest now prefer to call His laborers? Which ministries does the development of the Mystical Body most urgently demand?" In this way, the sad cries of the sheep who are without a shepherd, and the appeals of famished souls who have found no one to give them the Bread of Life, will find an answering sympathy in generous hearts. The profound tragedy of deserted churches and empty tabernacles will become to them a living sorrow; and, in the depths of their souls, Christ will awaken the echo of the Good Shepherd's burning appeal: "There are so many sheep who are not yet of my fold; who, then, will help me to gather them in?"

O Jesus, let many young souls hear the call of Your Love. Make them realize that, for a soul eager to shape its life to the height of a great ideal, there is no more exalted and more fruitful exercise of human liberty than the act by which it renounces all things in order to yield to the sweet yoke of Your Will—to You Whom the soul has met and loved, in the full bloom of its youth.

14. THE RELIGIOUS VOCATION

*One thing is wanting unto thee. Go sell
what thou hast and give to the poor; and
thou shalt have treasure in heaven. And
come, follow me.*

(Mark, X, 21)

The story of the social activity of religious congregations
makes inspiring reading. Through their monasteries, rich in
prayer and in penance; through their educational establishments
and their institutions for works of charity and of the apostolate
—the Mystical Body of Christ carries out its life-giving mission
among men. It is Jesus Christ, the Head of His Mystical Body,
Who prays, teaches, acts, heals, and brings consolation to men.
But the religious vocation has another significance in the Mystical Body: namely, the social aspect of its essentially spiritual
nature.

1. *The hierarchy of values*

In a world which flings itself headlong into the fevered pursuit of earthly riches and material things, there is an urgent need
for those who, by the example of their poverty and detachment,
proclaim the hierarchy of values—the primacy of things spiritual,
supernatural and divine. The witness of religious souls devoted
entirely to the One Thing Necessary, is supremely helpful to
Christians themselves, who are indeed aware of this order of
values but are in danger of neglecting it through their anxious
care to provide for the material needs of their families.

But, in order that it may have its full meaning, the religious
vocation must appear in its positive aspect, as something more
than a practical detachment from and sincere renunciation of
earthly possessions—which detachment and renunciation cannot
always be imitated by the laity, or at least only in spirit. This
positive aspect is that of a *veritable holocaust* offered to God
through the dedication of one's whole being, in order to proclaim
that He is the only Supreme Good worthy of the soul's attachment. How splendid is the radiance, in the Mystical Body, of
those who, faithful to their religious vocation, profess the
superiority of spiritual values and reveal to the world "the
unsearchable riches of Christ" (*Ephes.*, III, 8).

2. *The exclusiveness of the Love of Christ*

In the midst of a world which is the slave of the senses and of hunger for the pleasures of the flesh, there is urgent need for those who, by the example of their whole life, prove that chastity is possible, is fruitful, and ensures a greater freedom to serve the needs of men. For Christian married couples who realize the grandeur of human love when it is expressed as a total giving of one to the other; who realize, also, all the strength and support given to their union, even unto eternity, by the Sacrament and the love of Christ—the presence near them of consecrated souls, is a light which purifies and an example which inspires.

When, however, a young soul has understood that he or she could love another person while at the same time loving Christ, but that the heart would be "divided"—*divisus* (1 *Cor.*, VII, 33) —then it is that he or she has discovered the full exclusiveness of the love of Christ. Such a discovery is one of the most certain signs that Christ has chosen that soul by making it understand the rights and the demands of His love.

The religious vocation is not, therefore, a stifling of the powers of the heart; rather is it the full blossoming of those powers, through their being directed towards Him Who wishes to be loved entirely and for Himself. Because such souls consecrate themselves to Christ with their whole heart and their whole being, theirs is a greater intensity of love in the Mystical Body, and Christ can rejoice in them.

3. *Submission to God*

In a world which seeks to emancipate itself from all authority and even from the Divine Law, there is a great need of those who, by the whole tenor of their lives, proclaim the dignity of obedience and the necessity for discipline in all human relationships.

The dignity of obedience stems from the fact that it is not submission to another person, as a person; for, since all souls enjoy an equal personal dignity in the eyes of God, no one has an intrinsic right to rule another. It is to God Himself that we submit when we obey those who exercise authority only in His Name and for the common good. Now, there can be nothing more exalting for man than this aspiring to God and this union of his fickle will with the omnipotent and infinitely wise Will of his Creator and Father.

In order to give this example in every circumstance of the

religious life and despite the reluctance of proud, selfish and rebellious human nature, souls who have entered that Life must live profoundly the consecration they have made of their whole being to God their Father, to the Holy Trinity. On the day of their consecration, they gave back to Him, not only what they had received from His Hands, but also the very essence of their human personality.

Such an immolation of the will is possible only if these souls are sustained in their oblation by the sovereign grace of Christ, their Head. They have delivered into His Hands their whole personal freedom, in order that He may dispose of it, according to His own Will, for the common good of the entire Mystical Body.

O Jesus, we give You thanks for having deigned to choose, for the service of Your Mystical Body, so many souls enamored of perfection and holiness. We rejoice in the pleasure they give You by being the instrument through whom You fulfill that office of Head which is so dear to You in Your relationship with men. For these are souls entirely at Your disposal, and through them You can extend the reign of Your love over the entire human race and prepare the advent of Your Father's Kingdom.

15. THE CHRISTIAN LIFE

Lord, what wilt thou have me to do?
(Acts, IX, 6)

For every member of the Mystical Body, the Christian life is an unceasing warfare: warfare of the upright human spirit against the evil tendencies and the passions of our human nature, in order to establish the Reign of Christ over as many souls as possible and over the relationships of each member with all the others.

1. *The nature of the Christian life*

Jesus reigns supremely over a soul when *that soul is ready to do the Will of Christ, however human nature may shrink from what is required.* What is important here is a *habitual* attitude of submission to this adorable Will of God. Transient weaknesses and faults of human frailty do not affect the sovereign authority of the Head, when the soul is ready to admit its mistakes and deficiencies, humble itself on account of them, and seek the shelter of Christ's Reign of Mercy. But the greatest obstacle to the Reign of Christ our Head, is the will which *rebels* against being led by Our Savior, this being the state of an *evil* will which refuses to submit to the Divine Plan. What Jesus expects from each one of us, is an upright, good and docile will.

Jesus also reigns over souls when, as Head of the Mystical Body, He *exacts abnegation and renunciation of the love of self* which wars against the reign of His charity over the soul. It is especially in these battles against selfishness that the will of the disciple is strengthened, and his sincere love of the Master put to the test. These battles can continue, and there may be a struggle within the soul, a complete revulsion against sacrifice and suffering. But if, in spite of human flinching and of heartbreak in the times of trial, the soul is ready to accept fully the Will of God, it is He Who will finally conquer.

In fine, Jesus reigns over souls when they reach the stage of asking themselves the question of the grace-conquered Paul: "Lord, what wilt thou have me to do?" There can be no words more agreeable to Our Lord, because they express *the generous and unconditional acceptance of all His wishes.* The disciple does not know whither his Master wishes to conduct him; but he submits in advance to all the demands of His love. This shows a generous enthusiasm of the will, identifying itself wholly with the Will of Christ, that it may be led by Him in any direction and at whatever cost.

2. *The mode: How does the grace of God act on our souls?*

"Without me, you can do *nothing*," said Christ. It is only with great difficulty that we convince ourselves of this fundamental inability of our nature to do anything meriting eternal life. We find it hard to realize fully that we are, of ourselves, utterly helpless in all supernatural matters, since we fail to understand the necessity for this intervention of grace at every moment of our lives. Indeed, it is only by the help of divine grace that we shall grasp this truth. For, by His inspirations, Christ must anticipate our actions; His help must accompany them; and it is through Him alone that we can successfully accomplish them.

With a power derived from His divine energy, and not from our consent, the divine grace of Christ "strongly and sweetly" moves us to make our choice fully, and to make our own decisions for good, for virtue and for duty.

It is the grace of Christ which makes us freely reach our personal decisions for what is right and good. This grace not only urges us to do the Divine Will, by inviting us to speak our *fiat* of acceptance; but it is this very grace which causes us to voice our acceptance. In reality, it is Christ Who—actuating His grace within us by the power of His Holy Spirit, and living His Life of Sonship in His members—would again speak in our souls to His Father: "Pater, fiat voluntas tua." Of ourselves, unfortunately, we can always resist and always refuse. But it is "He Who bends and subdues to His wishes, even the most rebellious wills" (*Mystici Corporis Christi*).

We beseech You, O Lord, in Your mercy to grant us the grace of always thinking and doing what is right, so that we, who cannot exist without You, may be able to live according to Your Will. (Collect for the Eighth Sunday after Pentecost).

16. THE CALL TO PERFECTION

Be ye therefore perfect.

(Matt., V, 48)

It is to all souls without exception that Our Lord addresses His call to perfection. Perfection consists in the union of our will with the Divine Will, through charity. In this call, how does Christ, as Head of the Mystical Body, exercise His authority over the wills of men?

1. *The Model*

"He reigns over human wills, because, in *His* human will there is perfect rectitude and perfect submission to the sanctity of the Divine Will." (*Encyclical on Christ the King*).

During His earthly life, the incarnate Son of God possessed two wills, just as He had two natures: His Divine Will and His human will. Since it was a created will, the human will of Christ, like that of every human creature, was dependent on the Divine Will, and could not act spiritually except with divine concurrence. But it was the Divine Word Who was responsible for Christ's desires and wishes, since, as God made man, Christ acted with His human will in accordance with that human nature which He had assumed.

Complete harmony existed between these two wills. As Man,

Christ could not desire anything which was not in full conformity with the Divine Will, because, being the Son of the Father, He could not sin. Christ consented to experience repugnance when faced with the Chalice of His suffering, in order to be like unto His brethren; but His deliberate human will never felt the slightest hesitation in accepting His Father's Will. Jesus could will only what His Father willed and as His Father willed it. He Himself has said: "My meat is to do the will of him that sent me" (*John*, IV, 34).

The things of this world beckon us and pull us in a thousand different directions. The contemplation of this admirable rectitude of Christ's human will in its complete submission to the Divine Will, brings calm and recollection to our souls, while at the same time it invites us to imitate that submission by an entire dependence on the grace of Christ, our Head.

2.   *The Head Who leads and inspires*

In the glory of His Father, whence He exercises His office of Mediator and of Head, Christ is not inert and passive; for He uses His wondrously penetrating and active intelligence and will, in His glorified Humanity. But is it sufficient to say that His Will conforms exactly to the Divine Will? Rather it is plunged in that Will, so that it is now but one with the Divine Will. In Heaven where He can no longer suffer, His sacred Humanity is free from those infirmities of human nature which He deigned to experience while on earth. His will is immersed in the Beatific Love which necessarily accompanies the Vision of Glory in Heaven; whereas, while on earth, Christ had laid aside the beatifying effects of this Love on the sentient part of His Soul, in order that He could suffer among us and for our sake.

Christ wishes that His Mystical Body should grow in holiness, for the law of that Body is that of a continual increase in perfection. He therefore earnestly desires our perfection. It is thus that we must contribute to the formation of the Whole Christ, because it is with our fidelity to His Divine Grace that Christ effects this formation. He desires that each member should unite his will with His own Will, as Head, so that, in Him, we may be in constant union with the Divine Will. This call is ceaselessly renewed in our souls. Because He sees all the needs of His entire Mystical Body, Christ insistently urges souls in their ascent to the ideal of perfection He has assigned to them. He does not allow them to stop on the way, because He knows that for them to rest is to slip back. Ceaselessly, too, He gives the graces of which each soul has need in order to fulfill its mission in the Mystical Body.

3. *The demands made by Christ, our Head, on those who seek perfection*

But those who understand the call of Christ, our Head, must learn the full demands He makes on those members of His Body who have decided to live like Him and under His influence.

Which are the activities of such souls which Christ will accept, bless, fructify and recognize as His own? They are those which proceed from Him and are inspired by Him; those which souls accomplish by reason of the spiritual strength He gives them, and under the impulse of His Holy Spirit; in a word, those which bear His mark, so that He can say of them: "I have accomplished these things in you and with you." On the other hand, those actions which do not find in Him their inspiration and their principle—which proceed rather from our selfish, proud, sensual nature—cannot be referred back to the Head of the Mystical Body; for they are the fruits of a nature abandoned to its passions or not kept under sufficient control.

O Jesus, Our Lord, have pity on our Christian brethren who, through indolence, faint-heartedness or the choking cares of this life, no longer feel the desire for perfection burning in their hearts. Pity yet more, we beseech You, those souls who have settled complacently into their own conception of a religion of ease and self-deception, a surface religion without ideals, a religion involving neither effort nor that divine discontent which urges to greater perfection—a religion, in fine, which deforms the appearance of Your Mystical Body and is treason against the mission given to these souls.

THE EMINENT SOVEREIGNTY OF
THE DIVINE HEAD OVER MEN'S CONSCIENCES
AND HIS LIFE-GIVING ACTION

17. FOR THE PURIFICATION OF CONSCIENCES

Lord God, Lamb of God, Son of the Father,
Who takest away the sins of the world,
have mercy on us.

(From the Gloria in excelsis)

One of the most touching and most beneficent forms of the
sovereign and vivifying authority of Christ, our Head, is certainly
that by which He exercises, now as during His earthly life, His
merciful power of purifying consciences and bringing them His
peace.

1. *Jesus affirms His power of purifying the consciences of men*

When Christ was dining at the house of Simon the Pharisee,
a woman came in, carrying on her shoulder "an alabaster box of
ointment"—that is, of costly perfume. She threw herself at His
feet, and Simon was indignant that Christ should dare to speak
with her who, in the whole town, was known as "the sinner"
(*Luke*, VII, 36 ff.).

But the Divine Master intended to preserve His judgment
free from that of any public opinion, and He affirmed this openly
in order to emphasize His sovereign authority over the consciences of men. For He sees into their depths, and He reads
there the motives of their actions. He knows that a person has
a conscience clean in His sight, purified by remorse, sincerely
penitent and inspired with deep love. He discovers in such a soul
the sensitivity which leads it to redeem its guilty past by making
the instruments of its sins the very material of its loving reparation, according to a fine observation of some of the Fathers. Thus,
the sinful woman in the Gospel brought the repentant tribute of
her tear-filled eyes, her hair, her perfume. And Jesus saw even
more than the sincerity of these actions; for He contrasted each
warm gesture of the sinner with the cold and self-sufficient attitude of him who was daring to criticize and condemn this woman.

Jesus can act with such assurance because He reaches to the
very depths of the human conscience. He knows human souls as

we cannot know them, for we are dependent on more or less exact deductions which result from a psychological analysis or are the fruits of intuition, and which may be misleading. Christ sees human souls exactly as they are. He pierces to the very recesses which are cloaked by an exterior attitude frequently hypocritical and deceptive; He reads behind the overt motives to those of which the conscience is aware but would blush to acknowledge. Probing further still, to the secret motives which unconsciously inspire the soul, Christ reaches to the real depths of the conscience. If the conscience is a sincere one, He purifies the soul from all its past sins: "Go in peace . . . thy sins are forgiven thee." Faced with an authority so sure of itself, "they that sat at meat with him began to say within themselves: Who is this that forgiveth sins also?" (*Luke*, VII, 49).

2. *From the height of Heaven, Christ, the Head of the Mystical Body, now purifies consciences by the ministry of His Church*

On the evening of the Day of Our Lord's glorious Resurrection, the Apostles, with the exception of Thomas, were assembled in "an upper room." Suddenly, Jesus appeared to them and showed them His Hands and His Side. In the midst of their great joy at seeing Him, Christ said to them: "Peace be with you. As the Father hath sent me, I also send you." He announced that He was confiding to them a mission similar to that He had received from the Father—a mission with the same purpose, but in dependence on His. "When He had said this, He breathed on them; and He said to them: Receive ye the Holy Ghost. Whose sins you shall forgive, they are forgiven them; and whose sins you shall retain, they are retained" (*John*, XX, 19-24).

By these words, Christ gave to fallible men the amazing power of pronouncing here on earth, in the tribunal of Penance, decisive sentences which are ratified in Heaven. It is as Sovereign Master, therefore, that He gives this power over the consciences of men. It is from Him that priests receive such power, and by Him and in His name they exercise it, according to the principles of His Gospel, the laws of His Church and the laws of morality. Furthermore, it is to Him that they must one day render an account of this power given to them.

O Jesus, give unto all Your priests an extremely vivid realization of the sublime responsibilities they bear in this sacred ministry of Confession, so that, in administering this wonderful Sacrament, they may submit themselves entirely to the action of

3. *IN THE WHOLE CHRIST*

the Holy Spirit to breathe upon them. Increase in the souls of Christians, faith in this other Sacrament of Your presence and Your love; because You are really present, though with a presence different from that of the Holy Eucharist, in this sacramental power, by the invisible and mysterious presence of Your grace and Your Holy Spirit.

18. FOR THE EDUCATION OF CONSCIENCES

For our glory is this: the testimony of our conscience.

(2 Cor., I, 12)

Our conscience is our sense of duty, of what must be done and what must not be done. Moral conscience is a rational judgment by which we evaluate our personal actions in the light of the moral law. How does Christ, the Head of the Mystical Body, intervene in the education of the consciences of His members?

1. *The law of the Holy Spirit*

The Christian law is not primarily a written law, a code, a treatise on morality: it is first and foremost the law of the Holy Spirit, of the Spirit of Christ, the Soul of the Mystical Body, inspiring, fashioning and guiding the members of His Body. Nor does this law primarily imply exterior obedience to clearly defined precepts. It implies essentially an attitude of fidelity to the Holy Spirit, of docility to grace, a conscience thrown wide to the action of the Head Who, by His Spirit, rules over the members of His Body.

The more intimately the member is united with the Divine Head, and the more generous he is in responding to the inspirations that come to him from Christ and from His Holy Spirit, so much the more readily will Christ fill his soul with an abundance of light by which he will be enabled to know immediately wherein his duty lies. The immense benefit of the interior life is that it gives to souls this clear vision of the path they must follow.

While we thus affirm the primacy of the Holy Spirit in this domain of moral formation, as in all the others; while we affirm the priority of faith in the Divine Action and of confidence in the power of grace as the necessary means in this formation—we do not thereby deny, in the slightest way, the necessity for ascetical practices and for a preliminary purification from sin, if the soul is to be made delicately responsive, more and more, to the influence of the Holy Spirit. Asceticism is necessary in every stage of the spiritual life. It takes various forms. There is an asceticism of the moral virtues which is both a severe mortification and a wonderful liberation; and this is imposed on the soul from the very outset.

Yet, how many errors and failures in the formation of conscience there are which can be explained by the fact that the soul was first presented with a catalogue of moral rules, and invited to battle against its weaknesses and failures. The soul must be placed, first of all, in the presence of Him Who is the source of life, and must be taught that the first rule is an attitude of obedience to Him.

2. *The written laws*

The evangelical law, codified by the Church in a body of precepts, counsels and directions, is the expression of the inspirations and of the working of the Holy Spirit within the soul. The central and first commandment of this law is the commandment of charity—that charity which the Apostle assures us is ceaselessly poured forth in our souls by the Holy Spirit. No contradiction or opposition need be feared between these two laws. The Holy Spirit urges the soul to form its conscience in the light of the written law; and the written law strives to educate the supernatural conscience of the children of God, of the members of Christ, to an ever deepening dependence on the Holy Spirit.

There is another law—the Natural Law—which is written by the Creator, not on paper or in books, but in the depths of every rational being. To imagine that the Holy Spirit would ignore the Natural Law or contradict the natural conscience it engenders, would be to set aside the principles which govern the relationships between nature and grace. Undoubtedly, the voice of conscience is distinct from the Voice of the Spirit: it speaks even within those in whom the Voice of the Spirit has been stifled or has not yet succeeded in making itself heard.

But we must be on our guard against dangerous illusions that spring from confused thinking in this domain. We mean the false idea of the supernatural which is based upon a false human conscience; the illusion of an angelic spirituality which tends to condemn all that is in the least mundane, and to ignore as irrelevant the demands of conscience in the humble daily duties of one's state of life—those of professional conscience, of honesty, of uprightness, of loyalty, and, in a word, of the human virtues.

The Incarnate Word came to serve the whole man, and to exalt the whole man with Himself to the highest communion with the Holy Trinity. Cooperation in the life of the Whole Christ is incompatible with a deliberate violation of the prescriptions of conscience in the relations of man with man, and in the ordinary course of social life. There can be no true sanctity in a person who compromises about his ordinary duties.

O Jesus, Our Lord, when You inspired Your Apostle to write that our glory is the testimony of our conscience, You did not approve a principle of anarchy which would make each one of us the sole judge of his own conduct. Rather was it Your intention to emphasize how highly You, our sole and supreme Judge, esteem that candid, clear and direct glance by which the personal conscience looks inward upon itself in the light of Your Holy Spirit.

19. THE SUPREME JUDGMENT

> *It is he who was appointed by God to be judge of the living and of the dead.*
>
> (Acts, X, 42)

Our Lord Jesus Christ, as God and Man, will be our supreme Judge in His role of Head of the Mystical Body. Because He is the Son of God, the Wisdom born eternally of the Father with Whom He is equal in all things, the power of Judge is eminently fitting for Jesus Christ. But it is also in His glorified Humanity that He will judge us on the Last Day. We may indeed take heart that, as Man, His justice will then be tempered by His mercy. Furthermore, His role of Supreme Judge on the Last Day helps us to a better understanding of His authority, as Head, over our consciences during our life on earth.

1. *The truth of His judgment*

Jesus Christ is not like those earthly judges who are always liable to error, who are victims of an insufficient knowledge of a situation, capable of being influenced by passion or by exterior pressure, and obliged to apply the law and exact obedience to it, without always taking into account that they themselves are fallible men set up in judgment over fellow creatures.

On the contrary, Christ possesses all the qualities which secure just judgment: *wisdom* because He is "full of grace and truth" (*John,* 1, 14); and *zeal for rectitude* which ensures that the sentence will be pronounced only with a loving regard for justice, without hatred or spite. Of course, for this very reason, those, who, during their whole life, have revolted against Christ, have ignored or rejected Him, can await with fear and trembling their appearance before the Supreme Judge, on that day when the power of His Justice is manifested. But those who, despite their failings, and with a consciousness of their poverty and a conviction of their misery, have constantly sought to return to their Divine Master, should await with confidence that moment, in itself so terrible, when the final sentence is pronounced.

Since He is Justice and Truth, Christ will take into consideration, among the very elements of His judgment, His own knowledge and exact appreciation of the limitations and weaknesses of human nature. He will not judge men as He judges the angels. The one thing alone He seeks is that man should acknowledge, in that hour and during his earthly life, that he is a man, that is, a creature, and a sinful creature. This truth will readily be proclaimed by those who, despite their errors, have sought Him humbly during their whole life, and find themselves suddenly face to face with this glorious Humanity of Christ. They will themselves request that the sins which they have humbly confessed on earth, may be revealed; they will themselves acknowledge, in the light of His Holiness, all their sins and all their misery, that the Infinite Goodness of Christ may be made more manifest; they will cast themselves with complete confidence on His Mercy, at the feet of that adorable Master Whom they are at last contemplating in all the spendor of His glory.

2. *The penetration of His Judgment*

Our Lord is not like one of those human judges who can pronounce only on external evidence, and who is compelled to pass sentence in the name of society and to punish actions which are externally and socially evil, whatever may have been the intentions of the culprit.

Christ sees the inner reality: "the searcher of hearts and reins is God" (*Psalm* VII, 10). Nothing escapes the all-seeing eyes of this Judge: "The judge ascends His awful throne. Each secret sin shall then be known" (*Dies Irae*).

Since He is the Head of the Mystical Body, Christ will first judge us on our social behavior towards the other members of that Body. He will judge us on "our innumerable sins, offences and negligences," in their bearing on the common good of the whole Mystical Body. Christ Himself has declared that He will judge us on our acts of charity towards our brethren (*Matt.*, XXV, 31-46). But what will count with Him in that hour, is not the noise which these actions made among men or the attention they attracted: He will look for purity of intention, for generosity of heart, and for that whole world of dispositions and motives which escapes the notice of the world. The modest alms secretly given, the widow's mite, the cup of water given in His Name, and all other charitable actions unseen by men, shall then have their true weight in the balance of the Just Judge.

On that awful day, those searching eyes of the Judge will terrify the hypocrites, the Pharisees, and all those who have hidden their disorderly vices under a mask of virtue. But all those who have multiplied their interior acts of love, who have practiced hidden virtues and offered their sufferings for the redemption of their fellow men, shall hear, in that great hour, their merits openly proclaimed by their Divine Master. Nay more, He will call them to sit by Him that they may join with Him in judging the world (*Matt.*, XIX, 28).

3. *Our bonds of intimacy and of solidarity with our Judge*

Lastly, Jesus Christ is not like those human judges for whom the accused persons are just strangers, unworthy of their interest and even despicable in their eyes.

The Divine Word has taken our human nature. He has lived among us, and knows what it is to suffer as we do. His human Heart has taken pity on our weaknesses, as the Apostle Saint Paul assures us: "For we have not a high priest who cannot have compassion on our infirmities; but one tempted in all things like as we are, without sin. Let us go, therefore, with confidence to the throne of grace; that we may obtain mercy and find grace in seasonable aid" (*Heb.*, IV, 15, 16).

Furthermore, since Christ is the Head of the Mystical Body, He will be judging His own members: those for whom He has given His life; those whom He has incorporated in His Church, to live a life of intimate union with Him; those whom He has led through all dangers, making Himself their constant companion and the ever present witness of their temptations, their indifference, their falls—but also of their good will, their efforts and their victories.

O Jesus, what unshakable confidence it gives us to know that He Who will one day judge us at the supreme tribunal, is the same who will have so often visited us, and Whom we shall have received sacramentally into our souls; the same Lord Who will have consoled, sustained and strengthened us. No other than You, O our incomparable Head, our Redeemer, our elder Brother.

THE EMINENT SOVEREIGNTY OF THE DIVINE HEAD OVER THE MINDS OF MEN, AND HIS LIFE-GIVING ACTION

20. BY THEIR CONSECRATION

> *Know you not that your bodies are the members of Christ? . . . Or know ye not that your members are the temple of the Holy Ghost, who is in you, whom you have from God; and you are not your own?*
>
> (1 Cor., V, 15, 16)

The life-giving action of the Head over His members, is of a spiritual order: it is exercised on the souls of men. Can it, then, be said that Christ is also the Head of our bodies? (*St. Thomas, III, q. 8, a. 2*).

1. *The Gospels*

Jesus performed many miracles on men's bodies. The Evangelists record more than forty such miracles, and are sometimes content with the general formula: "And all that were sick were healed" (*Matt.*, VIII, 16). Why did Jesus perform these miracles?

First of all, in order to prove His Divine Power. He sought to establish His divine and invisible action on the soul, by the clearly visible evidence of His power over the body: "But that you may know that the Son of man hath power on earth to forgive sins (He saith to the sick of the palsy), I say to thee: Arise. Take up thy bed and go into thy house" (*Mark*, II, 10, 11).

Jesus desired, above all else, to kindle in those who witnessed His miracles, an ardent faith in His Divinity. He also desired to manifest His merciful goodness towards those who were suffering, so that He might reach their souls through the healing of their bodies and awaken in them a lively faith in the Omnipotence of His Divine Mercy. Finally, the Divine Master thus sought to prove that, as Son of God, He has sovereign authority over the bodies of men and over their entire being. All the human senses are subject to His power: He gave sight to the blind, hearing to the deaf, speech to the dumb, motion to those who were paralyzed.

Christ does not bring an attitude of angelic spirituality to His relationship with men. He sees men as composed of soul and body, of spirit and matter. He thus shows us the balance we should strike between two contradictory errors: that of materialism, which sees man as matter only, as mere body; and that of angelism, which regards men simply as mere souls. It is impossible to deny the influence of the body on the spiritual life of man through the play of heredity, the influence of personal disposition, and the relationship existing between our human nature and the laws of the universe. But, on the other hand, man's true liberty consists, not in denying these influence to which he is subject, but in a spiritual mastery of them, in a rational acceptance of them, in the subjection of his body to his soul by submitting it to the sovereign dominion of Christ.

2. *It is through the Blessed Eucharist that Christ now exercises His dominion, as Head, over our bodies*

Saint Paul has given the profound explanation of the dignity of our bodies, and has derived from this our duty to respect them: "Your members are the temple of the Holy Ghost" . . . "Glorify and bear God in your bodies."

The first consecration of our body to Christ, the Head of the Mystical Body, was made in our Baptism. As long as the grace of God lives in our souls, our bodies are the temples of the Holy Ghost. Saint Paul adds that they are "the members of Christ." But it is through the Blessed Eucharist that this astounding truth, affirmed by the Apostle, is verified: "Your bodies are the members of Christ."

We must get rid of any crude idea of a kind of *merging* of the Body of Christ with our bodies, in physical unity. Nevertheless, since there is a very intimate, mystical and vital union between the whole being of the communicant and Jesus Christ, the Christian is sanctified, both body and soul, by the Holy Eucharist. There is a sense in which it can be said that Christ regards the body of the communicant as His own Body. He exercises a real influence over it.

Does not the liturgy of the Church frequently celebrate this action of the Blessed Eucharist on our bodies and our souls? She attributes to the Blessed Eucharist numerous effects on the body: the effect on its health;[1] its renovation;[2] the aid[3] and protection[4] it gives; its power of purification,[5] sanctification[6] and salvation.[7]

The Blessed Eucharist exercises a direct purifying action on our bodies in as much as they are the seat of carnal concupiscence This Sacrament calms the impulses of the flesh, stifles its desires, and progressively spiritualizes it by the influence of the sacred Flesh of Christ.[8]

Indirectly, too, the Blessed Eucharist brings special graces to the soul which help it to dominate the concupiscence of the body and to rule as mistress. The special effect of the Blessed Eucharist is to increase charity in the soul. Now, the more the love of God increases in a soul, the less scope there is for evil passions. The disorder of our passions was born of man's revolt against God; and charity restores order to them.

Moreover, when a soul has begun really to know, through faith, the spiritual consolations and the richer joys of Christ's Real Presence; when it has really felt, through a sincere and generous love of Christ, the happiness of a life shared with Him— then earthly things and the pleasures of the senses seem so miserable and vain that the soul, through a thirst for purity, knows only an ever increasing desire to abandon itself more and more to Our Lord Jesus Christ.

O Jesus, we firmly believe that your Resurrection is the cause, the exemplar and the pledge of our own resurrection. We also believe, because You have said it, that You will raise us up on the

1. Secret for Wednesday of the fourth week of Lent.
2. Post-Communion of the 8th Sunday after pentecost (*reparatio*).
3. Post-Communion of the 11th Sunday after Pentecost (*subsidium*).
4. Third prayer before Communion.
5. Post-Communion of the 15th Sunday after Pentecost ("So that its effects, and not our own impulses, may ever prevail in us").
6. Secret of the 3rd Sunday of Lent (*sanctificet*).
7. Post-Communion of the Feast of the Blessed Trinity.
8. Post-Communion asking for the grace of continence: "Et refloreat caro nostra et vigore pudicitiae et castimoniae novitate."

Last Day, and that he who eats Your Flesh and drinks Your Blood has already eternal life dwelling with him. In Holy Communion, You place in our souls a principle of our resurrection and a seed of immortality; and You demand of us that, in each of our Communions, we should abandon ourselves more and more to the transforming action of Your adorable Body.

THE EMINENT SOVEREIGNTY OF THE DIVINE HEAD OVER THE MINDS OF MEN, AND HIS LIFE-GIVING ACTION

21. THE MEANING OF THE UNIVERSE

> *"He commandeth both the wind and the sea; and they obey him."*
>
> (Luke, VIII, 25)

The universe is a huge book in which are written the proofs of the Divine Omnipotence and Goodness of God. But it is Jesus Christ Who teaches us to read that book, so that we may know the meaning of all the wonders of the universe and use them to sing the glory of God's Omnipotence in His sovereign authority over all created things.

1. *Christ's sovereignty over created things*

The ship carrying Jesus and His Apostles was moving slowly towards the opposite shore, through the calm waters of the Lake of Genesareth. "And when they were sailing, Jesus slept." Suddenly, "there came down a storm of wind upon the lake," lashing the waters into huge waves which lifted themselves above "the little ship" and crashed down upon it, threatening to engulf and sink it. The Apostles were terrified, and they awakened their Master with a cry for help: "Master, we perish." Jesus arose and, with a strong voice, He "rebuked the wind and the rage of the water." One word of command from Him flung back the wind and levelled the water: "and there was a calm." Then Jesus pointed the lesson of all this. He gently reproached the Apostles with their want of faith and trust: "Where is your faith?" But they, in the grip of their astonishment and fear, said one to another: "Who is this (think you), that he commandeth both the winds and the sea; and they obey him."

Everything in this scene shows the sovereign dominion of Christ over the elements of creation, and throws His mastery into relief. In contrast with the trembling fear of the Apostles, were His serenity and the immediate power of His words, and His actions, full of calm authority. He acted as Master, by His own power and without the aid of any human means. He did not ask His Father for the power to perform this miracle, but found that power within Himself and at the hour He chose to exercise it. The elements of nature were visibly at His service and bowed to His orders. Without the faintest hesitation or the least doubt, Christ acted as one who is sure that He will be obeyed. The winds and the waves know their Lord, and the sudden calm was, as it were, their homage of submission to Him.

On another occasion, Christ walked on the waters of the lake, which seemed to grow firm under His feet to make a path before Him ... Again, there, were the occasions when He multiplied the loaves and fishes, and when he turned water into wine.[1]

The Gospels present Christ to us, therefore, as the King of the whole creation. All nature is submissive to His commands, to aid Him in the fulfilment of His mission and to prove His Divinity.

2. *The doctrine*

The primary purpose of the whole creation is to *reveal God to man*. The liturgy teaches us that we should "acknowledge God in visible things, that we may through Him be drawn to the love of things invisible" (*Preface of the Nativity*). Jesus has invited us to consider the birds of the air and the lilies of the field, that we may see in them the proofs of the love of Our Father Who is in Heaven (Matt., VI, 26-30). In its whole being, its life, its beauty, every created thing reveals the work of God; for it is the gift of His Love, the shadow of His perfection, the sign of His presence and of His creative authority—in a word, it is the image of God. That

---

1. The homage of nature to its God, in this miracle, has been beautifully expressed by Crashaw in one splendid line: "The modest water saw its Lord, and blushed."— *Translator's note.*

is why Christ loved the whole creation: He found a voice in everything that spoke to Him of His Father.

From nature, too, He derived those splendid comparisons which served so well to bring home to men the truth He preached: "I am the light ... I am the Life ... I am the vine ..." The images of water and fire become the symbols of His mission: "But the water, that I will give him shall become in him a fountain of water, springing up into life everlasting" (*John*, IV, 14). " I am come to cast fire on the earth" (*Luke*, XII, 49). The mountain becomes the symbol of what faith can move (*Matt.*, XVII, 19). And when Christ looked at the harvest ripe for the sickle, He saw it as the image of another harvest—the spiritual harvest of souls (*Luke*, X, 2). It is with the eyes of Christ—with a clear and pure look—that we must see the world; for then it will take on its full meaning for us.

✴ ✴ ✴

The creation has another purpose: *it is a challenge to men, calling upon them to complete it and make it serve the higher aims of the human soul.* For, in themselves the things of nature are not completed, but await man's labor to give them their full significance in the pattern of the universe, in submission to the plan of God and of Jesus Christ. The temporal mission of mankind consists in this collaboration with the creative activity of God, and in the realization of the providential plan which, through Jesus Christ, shapes the world.

✴ ✴ ✴

Finally, the creation has a third and still more exalted purpose, since the Church teaches that the world has been "made for the glory of God" (Vatican Council). It is for men to *return the creation to God,* that God may be glorified in it and by it. By their minds and hearts, by the work of their hands and the aspirations of their souls, by their prayer and their self-oblation, men should lift up the whole creation to God in homage, adoration, thanksgiving. Created things, inanimate or living things, should find in mankind the voice by which they sing the glory of their Creator and proclaim their submission to Him Who has made them.

But because the creation, too, had been wounded by original sin, it needed a Redeemer if it was to fulfill its mission. And because the prayer of man rises to God through Jesus Christ alone, the Son of the Eternal Father took His place at the summit of the whole creation, that He might transform it into a magnificent liturgy, and give to creation its most sublime significance.

O Jesus when You came into our world as God made Man, the whole creation took on a new meaning. You have purified it, delivered it from "the servitude of corruption," and sanctified it by extending the divine contact to all earthly things. You have willed that every creature should groan and travail in pain, "waiting for the adoption of the sons of God"—for the dawn of that day when mankind, in You and through You, the Eternal Son, shall be perfectly the sons of God, for the glory of God, in "the liberty of the glory of the children of God" (Rom., VIII, 19-27).

22. THE RESTORATION OF THE CREATION IN CHRIST

> *"For all are yours; and you are Christ's;*
> *and Christ is God's."*
>
> (1 Cor., III, 23)

How can Christ, as Head of the Mystical Body, extend His Reign over nature and over the entire creation?

1. *Sin has upset the divine plan of the creation*

An admirable order must have existed in God's original plan, not only in the relations between men and their Creator, but also in the microcosm man himself between his senses and his reason, and—a wonderful order indeed!—between man and the creation.

God had prepared for mankind a very pleasant world, adorned with plants and peopled with animals whose purpose was to serve the needs of him whom God gave the earth, as "the paradise of pleasure, to dress it, and to keep it" (*Gen.*, II, 15) and to rule over it. Man then worked easily and with joy, lifting up the whole creation in single praise to God.

By severing the links of dependence and of love which united man to God, His Creator and Father, sin disrupted the whole Divine Order. In man himself, this disruption was the revolt of the senses against reason; while the relationship of harmony between man and nature was also weakened and destroyed.

First of all, from being the servant of man, Nature became for him an occasion of sin, of difficult struggles, of laborious and painful effort; or, on the contrary, it became the source of his egoistic, sensual, disordered pleasures. Since it was one of Nature's fruits which occasioned the first human sin, the earth became infested with briars and thorns. Man had to set about conquering it in the sweat of his brow.

Instead of revealing God to man, the creation became as it were an opaque veil hung between him and his Creator. Nature then caused him to forget his God; for he began to ascribe to Nature itself the powers of life which he found there, without referring them back to their Creator. Furthermore, he began to imagine that he could make himself master of this whole creation, by the unaided progress of his own intelligence and his own knowledge. In such thoughts, his pride reached a pitch of self-sufficiency which led him to believe that God's reign on earth was a thing outmoded.

Finally, sin set man against man, whereas God has disposed all things with a view to establishing a necessary cooperation, and a close union among men for the cultivation and organization of the riches of the world, to the bettering of human life. The murder of Abel by his brother, Cain, began the long story of fratricidal strife among men.

In earth and air, in ocean tides and mountain torrents, in the minerals hidden in the bowels of the earth, in the riches of the vault of heaven, God had placed sufficient and necessary resources for the nourishment, clothing and housing of man, for the well-being of his body and soul, for his development towards higher civilization more and more worthy of him. Sin has transformed all these things into causes of war, of envy and of hatred among men.

2. *The restoration in Christ*

The Incarnate Word came to renew mankind and the whole creation in the pattern of the divine plan. He re-established order in all domains, under His own governance as Head, so that all should henceforth bear the stamp of purification, of detachment and of reparation.

First of all, he re-established *the relationships between man and the creation*. He affirmed *the primacy of man* over all created beings. All things, whether the natural riches of the world, or the results of man's discovery, production and organization, should be at the service of man; sciences, material goods, money, work, technique, society itself. Man must no longer be the slave of created things enthralling his passions. He must use them, master them, control them, in order to acquire self-mastery and to achieve greater perfection of his own nature.

"For all are yours."

At the same time, Christ *has re-established order within man's own being*. He has proclaimed *the primacy of the spirit*. To organize the earthly City for the sole purpose of promoting the enslavement of man to his senses and lower passions, is certainly not the way to ensure the true happiness of the whole man, but, on the contrary, is the sure way to endanger that happiness. All things should be made to serve those elements which essentially constitute the human person: freedom, rationality, a soul capable of acquiring self-mastery with a view to submitting itself to a higher ideal and to One Who infinitely surpasses human nature. "And you are Christ's."

Finally, Jesus Christ has re-established *order among men*, through His Gospel of love, His Law of justice and charity, His Grace and His Church. These alone are sufficiently powerful to aid men to conquer their selfish tendencies, to love one another as brothers, and to effect a magnificent unity of all mankind in Him—in his Mystical Body.

But the Mystical Body is not superimposed on human life as something extraneous to that life. The charity whose ceaseless source is the Heart of Christ and His Mystical Body, enters intimately into the relationships existing necessarily among men as associates in the great task of deriving from the universe the things of life. It is God Who, by a law of nature governing the work and even the very life of the human community, has willed to establish bonds of interdependence among men, which they cannot reject without injuring themselves and injuring society.

O Jesus, when each morning we hold in our hands, at the altar of Sacrifice, the Host and the Wine, the fruits both of nature and of human toil, it is the whole creation which is thus caught up and represented by those elements which You are about to make the matter of Your Sacrifice. In this mighty act of the Holy Mass, You affirm Your sovereign mastery over the universe by changing into Your Sacred Body this bread and this wine—the symbols of our own complete self-oblation and of that of Your Mystical Body. It is in the Holy Mass, too, that You take the lead in that vast movement of adoration, of thanksgiving, of offering and of reparation, which rises to Your Heavenly Father through Your Church and through You. Thus it is that You restore to the Father all that appertains to Him by original and eminent right of property.

23. HEAD OF ALL MANKIND

*All things were created by Him and in
Him. And He is before all; and by Him all
things consist. And He is the head of the
body, the church, who is the beginning,
the firstborn from the dead, that in all
things He may hold the primacy.*

(Colos., I, 16, 17, 18)

The thought of the multitude of men who do not know Christ
and have never heard of Him, is a source of intense pain to the
disciple who sincerely loves his Divine Master. And yet, Christ
is the only Head; for He is the Savior and Redeemer also of those
who do not know Him, but whom He wishes to lead to their true
happiness. In view of this ignorance of men and their indifference towards Christ, how necessary it is to grasp fully the doctrine
of the sovereign authority of the Head over all men without exception.

1. *For Him*

All things were created for Him—for "the firstborn," for
Christ as Man—in order that He might "hold the primacy." Why
was this?

a) *The primacy of the principle of life.* Men have been created in order to participate in the supernatural life. In the eternal
plan of creation, it was decreed that Christ should be "the first-
born," in order that He might be the sole source of the supernatural life which makes men like unto God.

However, do we not say, in the *Credo,* that it was "for us and
for our salvation"that Christ came into the world? Yes; but we
must understand what is meant by this.

Christ is not a means; He is a *principle*—the principle of salvation. It is He Who gives life to the members of His Mystical
Body. It is they who have been chosen *for Him,* to become His
members, to submit to His dominion and leadership as Head, thus
enabling Him to manifest, in His Mystical Body, the full splendor
of the plenitude that is His.

But the members achieve their own perfection by living as
His members, *for Him.* In this sense, it is true to say that He came

for them, to fill up what was wanting in them. They add nothing to Him; on the contrary, it is from Him that they receive all things.

God has drawn up this plan in order that Christ should "hold the primacy."

b) *The primacy of excellence.* Christ is God's masterpiece in human nature, the perfection of the whole creation . . . the Man-God . . . with the fullness of the Divinity; with the fullness of humanity . . . the fullness of perfection and of holiness.

"I . . . will draw all things to myself," said Christ (*John,* XII, 32). Throughout the centuries Christ has been the center of attraction for all those who sought an ideal, a model, a living example. He remains so today, and will remain so through all time. Even those who lack the courage to follow Him, admire Him intensely and regard Him as the glory of all mankind.

Souls who allow themselves to be drawn by Christ, will get nearer to their ideal of holiness. Christ is the supreme summit of holiness. If everything has been ultimately chosen for Him, it is in order that He may reign as sovereign Master in the full brilliance of His glory. But it is only at the end of time, when the Whole Christ is formed, that the full measure of this divine plan of Christ's primacy will be manifested and accomplished. "For Him;" for the Whole Christ!

c) *The primacy of conquest.* Christ is Head by right of conquest, since He has won His sovereignty by His sacrifice and the shedding of His Blood. He has offered this sacrifice for all men without exception; He has shed this Blood for the entire human race. His mission as Head extends, therefore, over all mankind.

2. *In Him*

a) *All men are reconciled in Him with God.*

God has willed to effect a reconciliation of all men with Himself, in Jesus Christ. This idea of reconciliation in the New Dispensation, is both fundamental and essential, since in it are realized the promises of the Old Dispensation. In Christ, the unity broken by sin was restored: unity with God, and—as a result— unity of men among themselves, and the unity of interior harmony within each person.

Christ, the sole Mediator, is the Representative of all men before God. In Him, God gives Himself to men, to save them, to pardon them, to communicate His Life to them. This is a new title which Christ has to His primacy over all men, to the sovereign authority which He exercises over them as their Head.

b) *In Him, all men realize their true vocation.*

"And by him all things consist:" the words of the Apostle are fully applicable to men, for it is Christ Who gives his true meaning to every man. It is in Him that men turn back to their true selves and to their vocation—that vocation which they had in God's plan, and from which they have been cut off by sin. The Word, the Creative Thought of the Father, carried them all eternally in Himself. From the time of His Incarnation, the Word made Flesh carried them in His human mind, in His consciousness as the Man-God; He knew them all in their own being, and also in the place each one was destined to occupy in the whole Mystical Body.

The task for mankind is to realize, in Christ and through Christ, the design which God has had from all eternity for each man: the place he is to take in the Mystical Body. It is this idea which constitutes the truth of their being. By accomplishing it in them, Christ restores them to their true selves, and gives back the true meaning and direction to their lives.

In this way, also, and to the extent to which each person fulfils his mission as a member of the Mystical Body, the whole edifice finds in Him its cohesion, its harmony, its interior strength. For these qualities belong to Christ, Who, as Head directs and governs the whole Mystical Body.

3. *By Him*

a) *The creation.*

"All things were made by Him; and without Him was made nothing that was made" (*John*, I, 3). Mankind has been created by Christ: as the Divine Word, of course—the creative work being common to the Three Divine Persons of the Holy Trinity; but also as the Man-God, as "the instrument conjoined to the Word" and made efficient in His Humanity by the Divine Word.

However, the soul which adores this triumphant Humanity in all Its power and which desires Its full glory, feels a need to explore this matter yet further. How does this Humanity Itself intervene in the creation? Here we come up against a Mystery. The doctrine of the Church has no pronouncement on this; and therefore let it suffice that we ask God's light as we meditate on those words of the Apostle: "and one Lord Jesus Christ, by whom are all things, and we by Him" (1 *Cor.*, VIII, 6) Is it not Christ Who guides all the events of the world? And since He is the Final Cause and the Exemplary Cause, how could He fail to intervene in the creative act?

b) *The Redemption.*

It is *by Him* that the Redemption is applied to all men. Christ is, therefore, the Head of all men, in varying degrees.

First, He is the Head of all the living members of His Mystical Body: of those who have entered into Heaven; and of those who are living on earth in grace and in charity.

He is also the Head of all His members who believe but are in sin. The vital sap no longer rises in these withered branches, even though they remain attached to the stem of the vine. These members remain attached to the Body by the ineffaceable link of their Baptism and by their continuing faith; and thus Christ could renew life in them.

Finally, by His right and His power, Christ is the Head of all those who are not yet part of His Mystical Body. He desires to conquer them; for "he is the Savior of all men" (1 *Tim.*, IV, 10). His Church is undoubtedly only at the beginning of her expansion. In essence, she is missionary. She is the great sign (sacramentum) of Christ radiating beyond those seven Sacraments which these people cannot receive. They are "related to the Mystical Body" (Encyclical on the Mystical Body).

O Lord when, with a growing appreciation of Your Mission as Universal Head we remember the innumerable multitudes of those who do not know You, and we are tempted to doubt, give us an ardent faith in Your ability as Head to carry out the full plan of Your love. That You may act effectively, You await the lively faith of Your disciples, fired with zeal to promote Your social reign over all mankind.

CHAPTER TWO

The Doctrinal Foundations of the Mystery of the Christ-Head

Tu Solus Sanctus!

Tu Solus Dominus!

Tu Solus Altissimus!

(Gloria)

24. THE MYSTERY OF THE INCARNATION

> *For in him dwelleth all the fullness of the*
> *Godhead corporeally. And you are filled in*
> *him, who is the head of all principality*
> *and power.*
>
> (Col., II, 9)

Who, then, is this Infant Who is born in a miserable stable in Bethlehem, His parents being two of the unknown poor who have been turned away from the inns of the town? In face of such complete destitution, is it not derisive to meditate on the greatness of this Child and to regard Him as the Head of humanity? How is the Mystery of the Incarnation in itself a foundation of the universal sovereignty of Christ?

1. *He is the Son of God, the Incarnate Word*

What first claims attention in the Incarnation is the mystery of abasement, of humility and of annihilation which it contains. "(He) emptied Himself, taking the form of a servant, being made in the likeness of men" (*Philip.*, II, 7).

But, from another viewpoint, the Incarnation is the mystery of the magnificence of Christ—the magnificence that is His in *the hypostatic union.*

As God, Christ is the Son of the Father, the Divine Word equal to the Father, possessing the same Divine Nature Which the Father communicates to Him entirely from all eternity. Christ has the same infinite perfection as the Father, the same power, and therefore the same Creator's authority over all creatures.

Furthermore, as Man, Christ is the true Son of God, the Only Son of the Father, in His human nature; since filiation is predicated of the person and not of the nature. While He is truly Man, Christ is no other than the very Person of the Word subsisting in human nature; and He is the Son of God, through the hypostatic union. Herein is His true glory, coming to Him from His Divine Generation in the bosom of the Father.

Jesus, therefore, while truly Man, has the right to receive all that is due to Him as Son of God and that is not incompatible with

His human nature. Consequently, Jesus, as Man—but because He is the Person of the Son—has the right to be adored with that adoration which is reserved to God alone. He has also the right to possess sovereign authority over all creatures.

This is, however, in no way incompatible with human nature, but, on the contrary, is in perfect harmony with it. For the Sacred Humanity of Christ has been raised to the unique splendor of being the Humanity of the Son and of being assumed by no less a Person than the Son of the Father. This Sacred Humanity possesses, therefore, a fullness of grace, of holiness, of beauty, and of many other titles to our admiration and our loving obedience; and therefore this Sacred Humanity has the right to possess a total sovereignty over all creatures.

2. *Christ sums up all humanity in Himself*

Is the Incarnation merely the coming among men of one who is another man, but who is a Man-God, destined to live a very short life in an obscure part of the world? This man, since He is the Son of God, will undoubtedly live an exemplary life; He will be the model of His brethren. Then, by His actions, His sufferings and His sacrifice, He will be the Savior. But all this comes within the pattern of Redemption.

Apart from all the meritorious efficacy of His human actions, the Word, in taking flesh, Himself assumed the essence of human nature in its depths and in its universality.

Christ is indeed a man, similar to other men, truly and fully man. He has assumed human nature: a body which is truly His, a soul which is truly His; a consciousness, intelligence and will, that are truly His.

And yet, this man is not as all the others. Since, as Man-God, He contains and sums up all humanity in Himself, He cannot be bracketed with other men. The unity of the whole human race is henceforth realized in Him, on a transcendent plane.

Adam, not Christ, founded the natural unity of the human race, since this unity derives from the first man. It is precisely because men already formed one whole by the unity of nature, that Christ could incorporate them in a Body which He would animate with His Holy Spirit; a Body of which He would be the Head. Christ is the second Adam, who contains the new, regenerated humanity.

But how is this so?

People live side by side, and communicate among themselves through knowledge and love. Each, however, has his own personality, which sets him apart from the others even while incorporating him with them. Each person has his own particular traits and limitations. Human nature is individualized by the human personality in each of us—*this* "I," *this* "ego," which distinguishes each one of-us from all the others.

In Christ, these limits, these particular traits, these oppositions, do not exist; because in Him human nature is not individualized by a human person. With Him, human nature has not its own co-natural personality; but, from the first instant of conception, it has the Personality of the Word. When Jesus says: "I"— that "I" refers to the Divine Word Himself, since Jesus has a Divine Personality. And that is why this Personality of Christ is so powerful, exercising sovereignty over all men, exceeding them all, able to throw itself wide open to all men, to embrace them all, to communicate itself to all by participation.

3. *Christ is the source of life for mankind*

The Divine Person of the Word, Who is Life, and in Whom and by Whom all things have been created, could not become man without also becoming for the whole human race, the source of Life, by and in this Man-God Whom the Son of God became.

By His dignity as Son of God, Jesus Christ raises human nature to an extraordinary and sublime dignity. The Divine Word, in assuming human nature, places in all human nature the beginning of an elevation to a divine state. The Fathers of the Church declare that God became man in order that man should become a god—a son of God, participating in the Divine Nature. Saint John says: "But as many as received Him, He gave them *power to* be made the sons of God" (*John*, 1, 12). They did not automatically become so by the fact of Christ's Incarnation, because an obstacle—original sin—opposed their entry into the Divine Family. This obstacle remained to be recoved by the Redemption.

But,\with the Incarnation, there was already a radical change in the relationship between God and man. God saw all mankind in His Son Jesus, cradled in the poor manger. He saw them linked with Him, incorporated in Him. It is in the Incarnation that the Mystical Body was fundamentally constituted in germ. For the Incarnation is the union of the divine and the human, it is in this union that our human vocation to divine sonship finds its source.

O Jesus, our Savior, the more we seek to understand, in the silence of prayer, the splendor of Your adorable Person as Son of God, the more are we seized by a kind of dizziness before such an abyss of holiness, of power and love. Yet, it is to the most intimate union with You that You invite us; it is a real participation in Your Life as Son of God that You give us; it is an indissoluble and complete attachment to Your Person that you desire from us. Could You have shown us in a more striking way, our true splendor as Christians?

25. THE REDEMPTIVE SACRIFICE OF THE CROSS

And I, if I be lifted up from the earth, will draw all things to myself.

(John, XII, 32)

In these amazing words, Jesus Christ announced the conquering power of His redemptive Sacrifice and His right to become the Head of His Mystical Body. "By the victory of the Cross, Jesus has merited power and sovereign dominion over all mankind" (*St. Thomas*, III, q. 42). What an astounding paradox this is!

1. *The seeming defeat of the crucified Christ*

Humanly speaking, there was every indication on the eve of the first Good Friday, that Christ's mission on earth had ended in lamentable failure.

Condemned to the most ignominious death by a tribunal composed of enemies exultant in their resounding victory over Him, Christ died on the Cross, utterly destitute, abandoned even by His own.

At the sight of this mangled Body, gripped in agonizing pain; and even while Christ was crying aloud to His Father to pity and pardon His executioners—the crowd was spitefully flinging its jeering taunts at Him that His promises had been void and His mission a lie: "Vah, thou that destroyest the temple of God and in three days buildest it up again; save thyself, coming down from the cross" (*Mark*, XV, 29, 30). And the chief priests, with the Scribes and the Ancients, mocked at Him and at His alleged mission of Savior and of Son of God: "He saved others; himself He cannot save. If he be the king of Israel, let him now come down from the Cross; and we will believe him. He trusted in God: let him now deliver him if he will have him. For he said: I am the Son of God" (*Matt.*, XXVII, 40-43).

Thus, therefore, far from finding in this tragedy a lesson which would make them reflect on their mistakes, these men invoked each claim of Jesus to His titles of Savior, King of Israel, Son of God, in order to emphasize how empty they were and how they furnished decisive proof that He was an impostor.

2. *The real victories of the crucified Christ*

a) *Victory over sin and the effects of sin.* Sin was conquered because Christ destroyed sin as an obstacle to sanctifying grace. The original fall was blotted out, and total reparation was made. The rights of God were vindicated: His Justice, satisfied, The supreme gift of the Son rendered the greatest possible glory to the Father. Infinite Love, Which had taken the initiative by willing the Redemption, by sending the well-beloved Son into the world, could now give Itself with full freedom.

The effects of sin—suffering and death—were also conquered. For Christ willed to make Himself master of these also, by accepting with all His soul the wishes of the Father. God willed that Jesus should enter freely into that pattern of human events which would lead to His death as a consequence of His affirmations of His Divinity. He did not shrink from His sacrifice, but made it the instrument of His triumph. By His heroic acceptance of the Divine Will, He merited for Himself the glorification of His Sacred Humanity; and, for all other men, He won liberation from the bondage of sin.

b) *The transformation of the relationships between men and God.* The Old Law was abolished: Christ brought a new life to redeemed mankind. By His death, He merited for them all the spiritual and divine gifts, the supernatural benefits, and all the graces which were to constitute this renewed life. In essence, He merited for them a new *state;* for, in place of the state of servitude which was mankind's under the Old Law in their relationship with God, the Son of God substituted that state of sonship which He had won for them by His Sacrifice and which was given to them through the Divine Mercy. And all those who, in the long unfolding of the centuries, were to be transformed and divinized by their incorporation in Christ, could receive this life of sonship only through the saving virtue of Christ's liberating Death.

c) *The birth of the Church, The Mystical Body.* The Church was born at the foot of the Cross: born from the Heart of Christ, burning with love, crushed with sorrow, pierced by a lance. His Blood opened the source of divine gifts, which were to give life to the Church, ensure the fruitfulness of her powers of teaching, governing and sanctifying, and also make her the associate of Christ—His "complement" in His redemptive mission.

O my Savior, prevent me from ever being one of those who ignore or blaspheme or disparage Your Holy Cross; or one of those who are scandalized by it and dare not speak of it, because they accuse it of casting its shadow on their human pleasures and greeds. Give me the grace to understand more and more the profound meaning of the Mystery of the Cross. Let me love that Cross whence life is given to me; let me attach myself to it, all the days of my life; let me learn to contemplate in it Your victory over the world, over death and over sin.

26. THE MYSTERY OF THE REDEMPTION

> *As he chose us in him before the foundation of the world . . . In whom we have redemption through his blood, the remission of sins, according to the riches of his grace . . .*
>
> (Ephes., I, 4-7)

How does the mystery of the Redemption constitute a new foundation for the splendor of our Head? The Incarnation and the Redemption are in fact, intimately connected. The Incarnation is already redemptive: in the manger, Christ offers Himself to the sacrifice of the Cross. But, because our minds are not able to grasp at once the depth and sublimity of the whole Mystery of Christ, we must approach that Mystery gradually and by successive stages. As our understanding is deepened, so will our faith be strengthened; for each mystery, more profoundly contemplated, gives to our souls its own special light.

1. *It is God Himself Who, in His redemptive design of Love and of Justice, has chosen and sent Jesus Christ to be, by the Redemption, the Head of redeemed mankind*

—His redemptive design of *love:* "By this hath the charity of God appeared towards us, because God hath sent His only begotten Son into the world, that we may live by him. In this is charity; not as though we had loved God, but because he hath first loved us, and sent his Son to be a propitiation for our sins ... " "God first hath loved us" (1 *John,* IV, 9-10; and 19).

Let us not imagine God, therefore, as waiting, in all the fulness of His wrath, until man had decided to make reparation for his fall, before the divine pardon should be offered to him. It is God Who takes the initiative in the Redemption, by sending His Son into the world to save the world. At any cost, even at the price of the Blood of His Son, God wills to save all men.

Love dominated the whole Mystery of the Redemption: the Love of the Father in His prevenient Mercy and in the gift of His Son; the Love of Jesus, manifested in the entire giving of His life to accomplish this redemptive design.

Since it is God Himself Who has chosen the Savior, His only begotten Son, we are already certain of being saved *in Him* and *by Him.* He is the Holy Victim, chosen and willed by God to be the Redeemer.

—His redemptive design of *justice.* An absolutely pure and sinless victim was demanded to make reparation for the sin of man.

We must not imagine that God simply cancelled sin by an external and arbitrary decision of His Mercy. Sin is a frightful evil—it is *the* evil; and it had blighted everything. Order had to be restored, firstly, within man himself, by a total reformation of his perverse will, by purification and by an entirely new life. Justice demanded this. The rights of God had to be reestablished.

Did this involve a conflict between Love and Justice? By no means, because this Justice is not vindicative justice. It is the justice of Love the Justice which demands and expresses Love. Indeed, in this order of Justice, the Infinite Love of God is manifested all through the more clearly by the fact that He loves sinners, that He sought out sinful humanity in its misery and its servitude, in order to free, recall and save mankind; and even more, by the fact that He willed to give men a share in their own redemption *in Christ and through Christ, their Head.*

2. *The very nature of the Redemption willed by God, demanded that Christ should be Head*

a) Because the Redemption is a *mystery of solidarity*. Jesus Christ is Head because He is the Representative of humanity before God. He is not like an advocate who pleads on behalf of his clients, but regards those clients and their concerns as quite neutral and impersonal to himself. Nor is He as a hostage undergoing a sentence in the place of condemned persons. Being God, He contains all mankind mystically in His Sacred Humanity; being truly Man, He is the Head of the human community. When He offers His life and His death to save us, we are united with Him and in Him.

The Mystery of the Redemption is essentially the supernatural inclusion of mankind in Christ the Head, Who by the free gift of His life as a homage of love, makes reparation for the sin of humanity. In Him, mankind is redeemed and saved.

b) Because the Redemption is, in itself, *a mystery of death and of life*. A mystery of death, because Christ's death for sin was our mystical death to sin. It remains for each one of us to renew this death to sin and to his own selfishness. The mystery of the Redemption is applied to each of us by Baptism, which makes us participate sacramentally in the death of Christ, and by faith, animating a charity which detaches and frees. Now, we can do nothing towards applying to our souls this mystery of death, except with the aid of Christ. It is He Who, by His grace and His Sacrament, works in us, with our free collaboration the mystery of death to our own sinfulness.

It is He also Who, by His grace and His Sacraments, especially Baptism and the Holy Eucharist, works in us the mystery of His Resurrection and His life.

For all this redemptive work continually occurring within us, we are therefore unceasingly dependent on Christ and on His action. This is another title to His Headship over us.

c) Because the Redemption is *a mystery of collective* life. It is as a body, in Christ that we are saved; as united in the Church, His Body; as united in and by the Communion of Saints; as united by the exercise of active charity, after the example of Him Who has given us the supreme proof of love, that He might draw us together in love for one another. After having celebrated the Love of God as shown by the gift of His Son even to the death of the

Cross, Saint John points to its lesson: "My dearest, if God hath so loved us, we also ought to love one another" (1 *John*, IV, 11).

Now, there is One alone Whom God has appointed from all eternity to direct and vivify this whole collective enterprise of mankind's salvation. God has decreed that Christ is the only source of life; and hence, the Head Who leads mankind incorporated in His Church, the Mystical Body, by His Holy Spirit, towards the parousia for the consummation of the Redemption, already accomplished in principle for all mankind on Calvary.

O Jesus, Our Head, among so many titles You have to our love, we love You as the Redeemer of mankind, as our Redeemer, as the One to Whom the human race owes its salvation, its reconciliation with God, its peace, its happiness, its share in the very life of God. Awaken in the souls of all Your disciples a generous and ardent enthusiasm for Your Person as Redeemer, and for Your redemptive mission in which we are all invited to share.

27. THE RESURRECTION AND THE ASCENSION

> He humbled himself, becoming obedient unto death, even to the death of the cross. For which cause, God also hath exalted him and hath given him a name which is above all names . . .
>
> (Philip., II, 8, 9)

The Resurrection marks Christ's triumph—His victory over death and over His enemies. At the time fixed by Him, He emerged from the sepulchre, alive. This proof of His Divinity, a proof which Jesus had Himself foretold, dominates Christian Apologetics. But it is under another, more dogmatic and more interior, aspect that we must consider this important fact, if we wish to gain a better understanding of the mystery of Christ.

1. *The Resurrection; the Ascension; the Redemption of mankind*

The Resurrection and the Ascension are at once a *crowning* and a *commencement*.

They are the *crowning* of the work accomplished by the Son during His mission on earth. "It is consummated," Christ said

when dying on the Cross. On the eve of His Passion, He had said:
"Father . . . I have finished the work which thou gavest me to do.
And now glorify thou me, O Father, with the glory which I had,
before the world was, with thee" (*John*, XVII, 4-5).

The Resurrection and the Ascension are the immediate and
complete answer to this supreme request which Jesus addressed
to His Father. The Father welcomed His Beloved Son into His
Glory. He accepted His sacrifice. Following the Master, Saint
Paul stresses the close link which exists between the obedience
"even to the death of the cross," and the sovereign exaltation of
Jesus Christ in the Resurrection and the Ascension. The Gospel
also underlines the connection between these two facts: "Ought
not Christ to have suffered these things and so to enter into his
glory" (*Luke*, XXIV, 26). And again Saint Paul: "by his own
blood, entered once into the Holies, having obtained eternal
redemption" (*Heb.*, IX, 12).

In recompense for His sacrifice, the Father confers on His
Son, the sovereignty over all men. The Psalmist (1) had already
described this triumphant transmission of the Divine Powers, and
the universal reign of Christ: "Sit thou at my right hand: until
I make thy enemies thy footstool . . . " "Thou art my son; this day
have I begotten thee" (*Psalms* 109 and 2).

While they are the crowning of the earthly mission of Jesus
Christ, the Resurrection and the Ascension are the *commencement* of that work which, from His place of Glory, Christ was
henceforth to carry out among men and in His Mystical Body.
It is as risen from the dead and entered into Glory, that Christ,
as Head of His Body, gives supernatural life to His members. The
Paschal *Preface* celebrates this: "for dying He hath destroyed our
death, and rising again He hath restored our life." By the Resur-
section and the Ascension, Christ has become the "life-giving
Spirit," as Saint Paul calls Him; and, since His glorified Humanity
is freed from those limitations of space and time which are imposed by our bodies, Jesus Christ, as Head, can communicate His
life to the whole Mystical Body, and, by the power of His Holy
Spirit, can enable His members to share in His own Divine Sonship.

Furthermore, the Resurrection and the Ascension do not
stand apart from a Redemption already completed. The Redemption is the synthesis of three mysteries of Jesus Christ, which are

---

1. Saint Paul, in his discourse to the Jews in Antioch of Pisidia, says that it was
by "raising up Jesus" that the Father pronounced this decree (Acts, XIII, 33).

intimately linked with one another, as the liturgy of the Mass affirms on two occasions (in the *Sancta Trinitas* prayers of the Offertory, and in the prayer which immediately follows the Consecration): *"Passionis, Resurrectionis et Ascensionis."* These three facts are inseparable, and constitute the full mystery of Christ the Redeemer.

2. *The triumph of Christ, our Head, in the Resurrection and the Ascension of His members*

In the first place, the Resurrection and the Ascension of the Head of the Mystical Body are the undoubted *pledge* of the resurrection and the ascension of His members. Saint Paul teaches us that this is the unshakable foundation of our Christian Faith: we are certain that we shall one day rise from the dead, because Christ our Head is really risen. "And, if Christ be not risen again, then is our preaching vain; and your faith is also vain... But now Christ is risen from the dead, the first-fruits of them that sleep" (1 *Cor.*, XV).

Furthermore, the Resurrection and the Ascension of Our Head are the exemplary *cause* of our resurrection and ascension. It is the mystery of His Resurrection which is here and now the direct cause of the resurrection of our souls from the depths of sin, and, in power and in hope, of the future resurrection of our bodies. The mystery of His Ascension will one day be the cause of our ascension, of our entry into eternal glory; while here and now, it is this mystery which secures those continual ascensions by which our souls strive daily to reach greater heights of sanctity. It is the glory of the Head to lead to their final reward all His members, whom He has accompanied and sustained during the whole course of their earthly lives, and to whom He has given life (*Heb.*, II, 10).

Christ was not contented merely to go before us to Heaven: He has gone to the Father in order to win our place for us, and there He addresses to His Father those words which He spoke to the Father on the eve of His Passion: "Father, I will that where I am, they also whom thou hast given me may be with me; that they may see my glory which thou hast given me" (*John*, XVII, 24).

Finally, Saint Paul goes still further: "And hath raised us up together and hath made us sit together in the heavenly places, through Christ Jesus; that he might show in the ages to come the abundant riches of his grace, in his bounty towards us in Christ Jesus" (*Ephes.*, II, 6).

The certitude of our faith and our hope is so strong because we are already raised to life in the mind of God; because, since as members we are inseparable from the Head, we have already, in the Person of our Triumphant Head, the right to possess one day those eternal benefits which Christ has won for His members. Everything, therefore, now depends on us—on the fidelity with which, grace assisting us, we allow this divine plan to be realized in our lives. But, in the Mind of God Who sees us in His Son, and in the formal Will of Christ Our Head, we are already raised up and victorious.

O Divine Savior, grant that, instead of being discouraged by the depressing sight of our personal failures, we may experience an increase of faith and of hope, in the loving contemplation of Your heavenly trumphs, so that we may pursue with renewed courage the great works of charity which will prepare here and now the triumph of Your Love in souls.

28. THE CHURCH, THE COMPLEMENT AND FULLNESS OF CHRIST

> . . . the church, which is his body and the
> fullness of him who is fulfilled all in all.
> (Ephes., I, 22-23)

There will always be those who regard the Church as simply an unnecessary intermediary, and who claim to go directly to Christ without any such hindrance. This is the very negation of the Savior's plan. The Church is a living Body, of Which He is the Head. He and the Church are but one. Without the Church, the Whole Christ does not exist; for the Church is His "complement," His fullness. In what sense is this so?

1. *In the Church and through the Church, Christ accomplishes His Redemptive Mission*

The Church is not a new intermediary between Christ and men, since the mediation of the Church is not something added to that of Christ. He is "the One Mediator." But it is He Who associates Himself with the mission of the Church, in order to fulfill His own Mission; because, without the Church, He has not willed to produce the fruits of salvation. Undoubtedly, He could have communicated directly to each soul the supernatural life He had merited for all mankind by His death on the Cross.

But He chose another plan, and it is in the Church and through the Church that He carries out this plan. He wills that the Church should "complete" Him, by using the Church as an instrument for the distribution of all the treasury of spiritual riches contained in Him, and for the communication of His whole life to souls.

2. In the Church and through the Church, Christ has willed to unify all men

The plan of Redemption willed by Jesus Christ, is a collective and social plan. It was not a single person, but a whole people, whom God chose to prepare the world for the Redemption. The Chosen People of Israel were the real figure of the Church; for the Church is the People of God. But with the Church, the message is no longer limited to one nation, but extends to all mankind. The mission of the Church is to unite all men in the unity of a single Body, animated by the Spirit of Christ.

The reasons why Christ has founded and why He directs His Church are to glorify the Heavenly Father by the union of His sons in Him, His Son; to provide an answer for the profound longings of the human race; to conquer sin which divides, by love which unifies.

There is another aspect under which the Church is the "complement" of Christ. With the Church, Christ manifests Himself as the Whole Christ. By "the Whole Christ," we mean Jesus Christ in His glorified Humanity as Head, together with souls He has conquered, incorporated in the Church, and gathered together into the unity of His Mystical Body. The Head and the Body constitute an indivisible whole.

3. In the Church and through the Church, Christ manifests the fullness of His human sanctity

The plenitude of perfection in the Sacred Humanity of Christ, can be expressed only through a multitude of different people. The myriad of Saints through all the ages of the Church, has for its mission to imitate, reproduce and incarnate this or that aspect of the sanctity of Christ, or some one or other of His virtues. Even when all the generations of mankind have passed into eternity, there will not have been, in the world, a greater amount of sanctity than was contained in the adorable Humanity of the Savior. All the holiness of the world will have come from the plenitude of Christ as from its source. In contemplating the

Church here and now, and eternally in Heaven, it is Christ Himself that we discover and learn to know more intimately.

O Church of my Savior, I can no longer separate in my heart my love for you and my love for Christ. For it is in you that I find Christ. It is you who give me His life, and communicate all the graces which He has merited for me by His death on the Cross. But I remember all my human brethren who have not yet entered into the Church. For this whole and universal Redemption of mankind, make me to cooperate in your Mission, which is my Mission also.

29. THE ETERNAL PRIESTHOOD OF THE HEAD

> *Having, therefore, a great high priest that hath passed into the heavens, Jesus the Son of God.*
>
> (Heb., IV, 14)

The priest is the mediator between God and men. His mission is to give men to God and to give God to men. This role of mediator has a twofold aspect: the one, *liturgical;* the other, *pastoral.* As the Head of the Mystical Body, Jesus Christ fulfills in an eminent manner, as He had done on earth, this mission of mediator in its twofold form.

1. *The liturgical function of the mediator*

The priest is a man chosen from among men and set apart from them for a double purpose. On the one hand, he offers to God, on behalf of men, their prayers, sacrifices, pleadings for pardon; and on the other, he is the channel by which divine blessings, divine pardon and divine graces come from God to men.

During His whole earthly life, Our Lord offered, in a liturgy which gave the greatest possible glory to God, His prayers, His supplications, the holiness of each one of His actions, and all the sacrifices which were to culminate, on Calvary, in the supreme and unique oblation of the sacrifice of His life for the salvation of men. Moreover, Christ called down on mankind the mercy and the gifts of His Father. By His sacrifice, He has reconciled God and men.

The priesthood of Christ was so efficacious because, being the Son of God, His whole being was impregnated, to its profoundest depths, with a priestly dignity, quality and power. The priests, who are only men, must receive, by the anointing with Holy Oil and the imposition of hands, a consecration that gives to their liturgical actions a value which makes them agreeable to God, and which makes of the priests themselves the ministers and the instruments of Christ. Christ had no need to receive such anointing. His substantial Consecration is that of the hypostatic union by which, from the first instant of His conception, the Divine Word took possession of His human nature and, superseding the finite personality of that nature, united, in the unity of His Divine Person as Son of God, the two natures, human and divine, which the Man-God must possess. His human nature has been entirely penetrated, sanctified and consecrated by the Divinity. The priesthood of Christ derives essentially, therefore, from His Divine Sonship communicated to the Humanity of Christ—to that Humanity which was to make reparation for mankind, through the sacrifice of Christ. Hence, Saint Paul could write: "So Christ also did not glorify himself, that he might be made a high priest; but he that said unto him: Thou art my Son; this day have I begotten thee. As he saith also in another place: Thou art a priest forever, according to the order of Melchisedech" (*Heb.*, V, 5, 6).

Thus, the liturgical function of this eminent and unique priest finds its consummation in the offering of the sacrifice which He made of His Body and Blood for the remission of sins and the redemption of the world. It sufficed that this sacrifice should be offered once to God the Father by His Beloved Son. Saint Paul tells us this: "we are sanctified by the oblation of the body of Jesus Christ once."

But the Sovereign Priest has willed to continue, under the sacramental rite of a liturgical Sacrifice which His priests would repeat, the redemptive Sacrifice of the Cross, in order to spread abroad its efficacious power and to apply its merits to souls and to His Church. Furthermore, the priesthood of these men and all the Masses which they celebrate, have no value in the eyes of God except through their participation in the present and eternal priesthood of the Sovereign Priest, Who offers unceasingly to His Father, in Glory, the whole liturgy of His Mystical Body.

2. The pastoral function

Because he is a mediator, the priest must be the good shepherd who goes in search of the lost sheep to bring them back to the fold. Christ fulfilled perfectly the mission of Good Shepherd. By His ministry of evangelization, whether in His public preaching or in His friendly visits and personal contacts, Christ conquered souls.

Christ, the Good Shepherd, exercized a constant care for the sheep of His flock. He knew them all by their names; He led them; He gave His life for them. But His very special solicitude was for souls who did not as yet form part of His fold: "And other sheep I have that are not of this fold" (*John*, X, 16).

Furthermore, Christ expressed this love for the sheep that are not of His fold, in a few emphatic words which reveal His firm resolve to find them and to draw them to Himself: "them also I must bring." That is the great purpose of His priestly Soul as Head of His Mystical Body. Today, in the glory of His Father, He ceaselessly repeats those same words, now addressed to all His priests, to all consecrated souls and to all the laity. He appeals to their apostolate, but it is indeed *He* Himself Who leads His sheep to the fold, through this apostolate. For therein is the final purpose of Christ as Head of the Mystical Body: to gather together all souls into one body: "and there shall be one fold and one shepherd." The Head looks always and above all to the unity of His Church.

O Christ, since, by an absolutely free gift of Your Mercy, You have deigned to call all Christians, members of Your Mystical Body, to share in varying degrees in Your priesthood, give to all their souls something of Your missionary concern for all those who are still far from Your Church. Grant that, both in the prayers of all Your members and in all the liturgical acts of the sacramental ministry of Your priests, this missionary intention of the growth of Your Mystical Body may be constantly present, and that it may animate all their dealings with their brethren and inspire their enthusiasm for union with You.

30. THE GRACE OF CHRIST THE HEAD

> *And of his fullness we all have received,*
> *and grace for grace.*
>
> (John, 1, 16)

The absolutely unique privilege of the hypostatic union, by which the Humanity of Christ is perfectly united with the Divine Word, is the source of all the spiritual riches of the Savior. It is the source, in the first place, of the sanctifying grace which abundantly fills the human soul of Christ: it constituted the personal holiness of Christ, and caused the Father to be well-pleased with Him. In the relationships of the Head with His members, it is this same grace which constitutes the "capital" grace—His Grace as Head. This mystery of the Grace of the Head dominates the whole doctrine of the Mystical Body.

1. *The Mystery of plenitude*

What abundance of grace there is in the soul of a Saint—of a Saint John or a Saint Paul! What an absolutely inconceivable wealth of grace in the souls of all the Saints through all the ages! And what of the Blessed Virgin?—whom the angel saluted with the title: "Full of grace."

Now, the sum of all these graces does not add a single degree to the grace of Christ; for there is not more grace in the whole Mystical Body than in Christ alone. The Head can receive nothing from His members, but it is from Him that they receive all. Their holiness can add nothing to His.

This plenitude of the grace of Christ as Head is such that it extends to all the operations which are accomplished in the order of grace in the bosom of the Church. No act of grace can occur except by the grace of Christ. His grace as Head extends to all the supernatural efforts ordained to the building up of the Body of Christ—to the "gathering together" of all things in Him.

2. *The Mystery of unity*

The grace of the Head gives life to the members. This is not to be understood as meaning that such grace works merely as moral cause, as a suppliant intercession with God; but in the sense that it is a real communication of divine life. The grace of the Head is in itself so powerful that it overflows on the members to give them the power to perform meritorious actions.

Now, this life-giving virtue exercised by Christ the Head over the members of His Body, can be explained only by this mystery of the unity which exists between Him and them.

Everything, of course, derives from His Divinity, the Principal Cause of all supernatural activity. Nevertheless, it is not by His Divinity that Christ exercises His grace as Head; it is by His Humanity that He does so, because it is through His Humanity that He is in contact with us and that we are united with Him.

In speaking of this unity of the Head and His members, we must carefully guard against two opposing errors: the first, to say too little; the second, to say too much. It would not be sufficient to regard the Mystical Body as simply a moral union based on feelings and wishes held in common. Such a union must certainly exist, but the Mystical Body is founded on a deeper unity. On the other hand, we would err by excess were we to suppose a kind of physical unity which would produce a fusion of the members and the Head, such that their faults should be reflected back on Him, while they could have the right to enjoy the absolutely incommunicable privileges of their Head (*See Encyclical on the Mystical Body*).

The union which exists between Christ and us is a union of life. It is a mystical unity: "The whole Church, which is the Mystical Body of Christ, forms as it were a single person (*quasi una persona*) with its Head, Who is Christ" (*Saint Thomas,* III, q. 49, a. 1). Christ and we are but one, in the sense that He can enable us to share in all His communicable riches and can give us the power to communicate in His mystery, while leaving us our own personality and even bringing that personality to its final perfection—but by the way of trials and of the cross.

3. *The Mystery of the Intimate Presence*

In order that the Sacred Humanity of Christ should exercise this life-giving activity over His members, it is necessary that Christ should be in intimate contact and mysteriously present with souls. And yet, apart from sacramental Communion and the Real Presence in the tabernacle, the Sacred Humanity of Christ is in Heaven, and infinity lies between us and Heaven.

We must banish from our minds such images and modes of thought as belong only to the material and physical order. Even in this very order, however, does not all scientific progress tend to establish that there is an interdependence between the various parts of the universe, and that distances no longer count? Witness the communication of words and ideas from one end of the universe to the other by waves, and the ever increasing speed and range of such communication. Yet, this is but a faint image of the contacts which exist within the Mystical Body. There, the order is that of grace. Now, in this order, Christ is Sovereign Master: He acts everywhere with the same power and the same efficacy, all distance being completely suppressed. For far superior to all things that seem to our human minds to be separated, there is that mystical union which constitutes, from the active presence of the Head to all His members, a more valid reality than are the material and visible unions of things of this world. It will be the work of faith to make us vividly alive to this intimate presence of Christ in our souls.

O Jesus, we adore Your invisible action in the visible activity of Your Church. Make us understand that to obey the Church is to obey You; and that there can be no more certain sign of a soul's love for You, than its willingness to submit to the guidance of Your Church and to Your Spirit animating the Church.

31. ONE ONLY HEAD

Christ is the head of the church.

(Ephes., V, 23)

During His public ministry, Christ had laid down the first foundations of His Church by the preaching of His Gospel. On Calvary, He brought forth the Church. After His Resurrection, He organized it by constituting the hierarchy. On the Day of Pentecost, He solemnly promulgated its foundation, and, by sending His Spirit, He publicly inaugurated the apostolic Mission of His Church. Today, it is He Who directs His Church and leads it towards its end.

1. *One only Head*

"It is He alone Who leads and governs the Church" (*Encyclical on the Mystical Body*).

He does so, in the first place, *invisibly*. We have contemplated Him in the exercise of His Sovereign Authority over minds and wills, over hearts and consciences, over all mankind. "By this interior direction," writes Pius XII (*loc. cit.*), "He not only takes personal care of each one of us, as *the shepherd and bishop of our souls* (1 *Peter*, II, 25), but He also provides for the needs of the whole Church." It is He Who enlightens and strengthens the bishops and priests of His Church so that they may faithfully and fruitfully fulfill their particular functions. It is He Who, in times of crisis, raises up Saints in order that, by their example, they may promote the growth of His Mystical Body.

He leads and governs the Church *visibly* also, in every-day matters of doctrine and government, through the hierarchy. All the powers possessed by the Church come from Christ and are exercized in His Name. The Pope is the Vicar of Jesus Christ. He has no authority distinct from that of Christ. It is Christ, Who, while continuing Himself to govern the Church in a mysterious manner, directs it *visibly* at the same time through him who holds His place on earth—the Sovereign Pontiff, the visible foundation of unity.

It is Jesus Christ Who governs each particular diocese through the voice and jurisdiction of its bishop. Each bishop feeds and governs, in the Name of Christ and in submission to the Pope, that part of Christ's flock entrusted to him. But it is Jesus Christ Who enlightens the members of the hierarchy, so that they may faithfully conserve the treasury of the Faith, may defend it energetically, may explain and sustain it with piety and with zeal.

It is Christ Who is with the Councils, by His active illumination. It is He Who is with His Church all days, even to the consummation of the world, as He Himself promised His Apostles, to enlighten and sustain and lead the Church to its end.

2. *The qualities of the Head*

Tu solus sanctus: all those who are Saints, are Saints only through Him, by participation in His Sanctity. And what is their sanctity when compared with His?—for the Sanctity of Christ is something of a completely different order. It is a sanctity that is substantial because the Humanity of Jesus is hypostatically united to the Divine Person of the Word.

Sanctity means union with God, but it also means detachment from creatures. Jesus certainly did everything in order to be near to His brethren on earth, to understand them, to love them, to live with them and among them. But His unique Sanctity explains the moral isolation in which He lived on earth. He was alone, terribly alone, as far as this earth was concerned. Even His Apostles misunderstood Him; Mary herself was puzzled and questioned Him, in the Temple and at Cana. He was alone with His Father. *Tu solus.*

Tu solus Dominus. All who possess any authority hold that authority from Christ. He only is truly the Lord, and there is no human authority without His Authority. All human lords and leaders will appear before Him to give an account of their government, even of their temporal government, and of the manner in which they have practiced the virtues of their state.

He alone is the Lord: by His Law, by His Gospel, by His Church.

He alone is the Lord: by His grace, which penetrates the souls of men; by His Spirit, Who enlightens, inspires, guides and strengthens them; and by His Eucharist, Which transforms their hearts and frees them from their own selfishness.

Tu solus Altissimus: He alone is great.

He rules *all mankind.* It is He Who gathers all men together and, with His Sovereign Authority, restores the shattered unity of mankind.

He rules over *time* and *eternity.* Throughout all the centuries, He accomplishes His work, for all things are at His service.

He rules over *death:* He has conquered death by rising from the dead. He is *the Life.*

He has won dominion over *sin,* which He crushed by dying on the Cross; and He uses this victory to ensure the triumph of His Reign.

O Jesus, our Head, give to the members of Your Mystical Body an understanding of the mystery of Your Church. Let them cease to regard it as a purely administrative and human society. May all those who bear pastoral responsibilities in Your Church, draw from You, their Head, the light and counsel they need, so that they may always remember the true nature of Your Church, and the supernatural, eternal, divine End towards which You are ceaselessly directing it.

CHAPTER THREE

The Response of the Living Member to the Call of the Head

Quis es, Domine? . . .
Who art thou, Lord? . . .

Domine, quid me vis facere? . . .
Lord, what wilt thou have me to do?

(Acts, IX, 5, 6)

FOREWORD

As soon as the Christian begins to contemplate the splendor of Christ, our Head, he feels the desire to give himself entirely and on every level of his being, to Our Lord. But, at the same time, he trembles with apprehension, because he knows that he is undertaking an immense, divinely beautiful and terribly exacting work. His whole being is in turmoil, and he is tempted to turn away. He feels within him a threefold tension, so severe at times that it seems to be torturing him.

There is the tension of the visible which so irresistibly attracts him by appealing to his passions; and the tension of the invisible whose beauty and nearness he feels so urgently in Christ, but which eludes him . . .

There is tension between the things of the world which he thinks he possesses; and the things of eternity which attract him because they are the answer to a very profound need of his soul.

Finally, there is the tension between his own selfishness and the needs of others, between his own personal rights and those of the community of which he is a member.

But, in His Infinite Goodness, the Heavenly Father always gives to His children the spiritual strength which enables them to answer His appeal as soon as they themselves have answered His love with theirs.

In the theological virtues, which are at the origin of each of these tensions, Christ our Head has embodied the strength which will enable His members to conquer such tensions and to make use of them in self-oblation to Christ.

THE GIFT OF SELF TO JESUS CHRIST, OUR LORD

32. BY FAITH

> *Now, faith is the substance of things to be hoped for, the evidence of things which appear not.*
>
> (Heb., XI, 1)

Faith is a gift of God, which places in the souls of the believer the principle of a permanent tension of his whole being, torn between the appeal of the invisible and the attraction of the visible world. Tension, too, because, on the one hand, faith brings peace, since it rests on the witness of God and gives the soul a sense of security in the possession of truth; while, on the other hand, it kindles a thirst in the soul, by awakening in the soul a desire to penetrate more and more into the mystery which always eludes its understanding. But faith is also a liberating force, to the extent to which, through faith, the Christian makes a gift of his whole being to Jesus Christ.

1. *Faith is the vivid realization of a Presence*

Faith does not create a Presence, but discovers it, and becomes conscious of it. Faith experiences a Presence as a living reality so close that it seems to be within grasp. This Presence is that of the Holy Trinity within the soul! The Presence of Christ in His Apostles (*Matt.*, X, 40), and in the members of His Mystical Body (*Matt.*, XXV). There is yet another Presence. The member of the Mystical Body knows that Jesus Christ acts in him by His grace and His Spirit. But his love for Christ makes him ceaselessly desire an ever deepening intimacy with the Sacred Humanity of his adorable Savior. Now, apart from those blessed moments when his Eucharistic Christ is present within him in Holy Communion, the soul knows that the Sacred Humanity is in a "place" in Heaven. It is at this point that faith enters in with all its life-giving power. Faith is no mere imaginings, which would only prove to be obstacles in its way. Distance has no part in faith; and, through faith ,the member of the Mystical Body is directly and immediately connected with and incorporated in Christ, the Head. In the Person of Jesus Christ, Head of the Mystical Body, the soul attains to Christ in His Divinity and in His Humanity. Through faith, the member becomes aware of the presence of the Head, leading and forming His Mystical Body.

2. *Faith is a spiritual contact with the Person of Christ*

Faith is an acquaintance with the very Person of Jesus Christ: not a cold and abstract acquaintance, but one which is deep, intimate and personal. Through the words He has spoken to us, faith attains to Christ in His secrets and His desires, in His Heart and in His Soul, and in His plan of love for each one of us and for all mankind as united in His Mystical Body. In proportion as the soul cultivates a generous and ardent faith towards Christ, it discovers the perfections of Our Lord, His attributes and His Personality Itself, because Christ reveals and gives Himself to the soul. Faith thus establishes an extremely powerful "spiritual contact"[1] between the believer and Christ: a knowledge which provokes love, which implies and demands love, which blossoms in love, and reaches its perfection in an intimacy of adoration, of love and of reciprocation.

3. *Faith is a total self-oblation to Jesus Christ*

Through incorporation, Jesus Christ takes possession of the baptized soul; and it is faith which places the believing soul under the effective sway of this sovereign dominion of Christ.

The believer submits his understanding to Jesus Christ. He does so, in the first place, by accepting all the teaching of Christ, by believing on His word those truths revealed by Him which surpass the power of our human understanding. But he also does so in another sense. Faith introduces into the understanding and the life of the believer, a principle of judgment, of appreciation, of direction, which enables him to look beyond the external appearances of events and things, to control his purely natural reactions towards his fellow men, to rise above earthly horizons in order to enter into the designs of God, to see God and God's Will

---

1. "Per contactum spiritualem": St. Thomas, III, q. 48, a. 6, ad 2. See also St. Augustine: "tangit Christum qui credit in Christum": he touches Christ who believes in Christ (*Sermo* 243).

in all visible things, and, finally, to submit himself to the higher designs which Jesus Christ our Head has for the world.

Hence it is that it is not the intelligence only which submits in faith, but the will and the entire personality also. The will must enter actively into the very genesis of the act of faith, in order that the intelligence may accept Christ's words for the sole and only reason that they are the words of God. But because faith is a principle of life, of tension and of action; because it contradicts the tendencies of our nature; because it obliges man to rise constantly above himself, so that he may walk in God's light—faith demands the total oblation of the will to Jesus Christ, at every moment of our spiritual ascension to Him.

O Jesus, since it is true that, in order to love You, we must first know You by faith, how much indeed must we love You if we are to believe in You and shape our entire lives according to Your Teaching? You are the Eternal Word of God, the Word Himself in Person, the Incarnate Truth. Teach us to make our faith in You an oblation of our whole selves to Your Person, so that we may receive Your Life and Your Love, and possess You.

33. BY HOPE

For we are saved by hope. But hope that is seen is not hope. For what a man seeth, why doth he hope for?

(Rom., VIII, 24)

The Christian is subject to another tension during his life on earth. By his human nature, he is a citizen of the world; but by his vocation and the grace abiding within him, he is a citizen of Heaven, being already a co-heir with Christ, a member of the Mystical Body Whose Head is in Heaven. Therefore, while still a pilgrim in the midst of perils, the Christian is already saved through hope in Christ. In proportion as it involves a complete oblation of self to our Savior Christ, risen from the dead, hope will be a liberating virtue for the Christian soul.

1. *Hope is a certitude*

The believer lives in constant fear of not being able to preserve those invisible and eternal benefits revealed to him by faith. When he looks into his own soul, he finds only uncertainty, misery, the knowledge of his weakness, the virulence of his passions, the multiplicity and the force of his temptations, the battle between the flesh and the spirit, and the ever-present immanence of death. All this is indeed calculated to fill his soul with anguish and to make him doubt his perseverance.

But hope brings him giant and unshakable certainty. On God's side, all is sure: the promises of Him Who is the Truth; the Gift of the Son; the existence of the Church; the Infinite Mercy of a Father; the tenderness of a Mother; the merits of the Savior and Head, with the certainty that mankind is already saved in and by the Redeemer; finally, the certainty that the parousia will come at the hour fixed by God, with the triumphant return of Christ.

On the one hand, anguish: on the other, security.

But the interior drama of the Christian arises when, yielding to the temptation to seek in himself the foundation of a more comfortable security in the earthly and the human, safe from all hazards and trials, he undermines the certainty that comes to him from God. The more he seeks to establish himself in self-assurance and in a selfish peace, the less he puts his confidence in God alone, and therefore his whole security is threatened.

The role of hope is none other than to turn the minds of men towards God, so that they will look *to Him alone* for necessary help, unshakable strength and pardon. Hope demands that the believer should give himself entirely to his Head, in order to join with Him in the great battle which must be fought to save the world; in order to prepare the coming of the Kingdom; and in order to share in the infinite merits of the Redeemer and be lifted up, by the power of the grace and living presence of the Holy Spirit, towards the Father of all mercies.

2. *Is hope merely expectation?*

The Christian's dilemma does not consist in the fact that, on the one hand, he is deprived on earth of the possession of eternal benefits, while, on the other hand, he must labor ceaselessly in the expectation of such possession which will be his only in a remote future.

Eternal Life *is already begun* in him by grace. The Christian possesses the Blessed Trinity. God is already his Good—a Supreme Good given to all who seek God. But is there yet a place for hope? Yes; and for three reasons.

In the first place, while it is true that the Presence of God is even now a reality within the reach of the believer, he attains to eternal and infinite treasures "in a dark manner" only, through faith. Only in Heaven, in the possession of the beatific vision, will he attain to their full and glorious realization. He will then discover the infinite abyss which exists between what he expected to receive and what has actually been given to him. What a sincere and intense longing for Heaven there is in many souls! And yet, is not this very longing one of the most powerful means of purification, and one of the most effective encouragements to real holiness? Indeed, this longing has diminished in the world with the weakening of the virtue of hope. It is the property of hope to kindle the desire for Heaven in the hearts of men, that it may become in them a devouring flame; the desire to contemplate the Holy Trinity face to face, to see Jesus Christ in all the glory of His triumph—in the fullness of His Mystical Body, with the Blessed Virgin presiding as Mother over the assembly of all the Saints. If there is stress and strain within the Christian soul, it is because that soul, already possessing those infinite treasures whose splendor it glimpses, suffers because as yet it cannot directly contemplate them, and lives in holy fear of losing them, to which is added its distress at the knowledge that, by so many, these treasures are entirely unknown and ignored.

On the other hand, while God is even now our only Good, He is also the "Good difficult to attain" (Saint Thomas). We must pass through many combats; we must learn, by painful experience, our weakness and our powerlessness to find, in ourselves and in merely human means, the strength which will enable us to attain to our final end; for only thus can we win our way to God so that we regard Him as our only Good. Hope is, therefore, given to us to uphold us in the midst of all these dangers, and to enable us to seek after the Supreme Good without yielding to presumption or to despair.

Finally, like all the Christian virtues, hope is a social virtue, a virtue of the members of Christ. It is indeed concerned with the personal salvation of the individual Christian, but regarded as a member among members, since the object of hope is the fulfillment of the Whole Christ, the extending of the Kingdom of God. That kingdom has already begun: it must grow and develop, despite all the obstacles opposing it. Hope is given to the Christian so that, through this virtue, he may ceaselessly nourish and develop in himself the calm conviction that the Kingdom of God is being advanced through all the trials of human life and through his own personal tribulations; that Our Lord is shaping all things towards the building up of His Kingdom: the successes of His

Church as well as the persecutions which seek to annihilate it; His disciples' faults as well as their virtues; the wars which sunder mankind and the laborious efforts to restore peace and unity among men; one's own personal failures as well as one's successes.

O Jesus our Lord, we are saddened by the thought that so many of our fellow men are torpid with despair in a world which is itself anguish-ridden. Grant that all Your members may feel the heartening thrill of an invincible hope, while they joyfully await that triumphant hour wherein You will present to Your Father, Your Mystical Body—the Whole Christ, in the unity of Love. We place our hope in You alone; and we would make that hope—in all the circumstances of our lives, especially in those fraught with pain—the gift of our whole being to Your Sovereign Power as our Redeeming Head, Who leads men towards their destiny through all the vicissitudes of human history.

34. BY CHARITY

A. *THE LOVE OF CONFORMITY*

> *For I have given you an example, that as I have done to you, so do you also.*
>
> (John, XIII, 15)

The Christian life is none other than the imitation, reproduction and continuation of the life of Jesus Christ in each member of His Mystical Body. The Apostles knew very well that Jesus was calling them to imitate in all things the sublime example of holiness He had given them. "But according to him that hath called you, who is holy, be you also in all manner of conversation holy," wrote Saint Peter (1 *Peter*, 1, 15). This conformity with Christ is demanded, however, by the very laws of love.

1. *The need for admiration*

Admiration is a necessary part of all true love—of the love of husband for wife, of child for parent, of the disciple for his Master.

When the Person loved is Jesus Christ Himself, this love

expresses itself as enthusiastic admiration. The soul is so thoroughly won over by the perfections and the splendor of Christ, by His holiness and His beauty, that it desires at all costs to imitate Him, to walk in His footsteps, to follow along the way that He went, to think and judge like Him, to feel and love with Him. All sincere love, we have said, entails admiration; and the love of Jesus is unique in that it can embody an admiration free from all limits, without being shackled by the fear, as in merely human love, of being checked by the very limitations of the beloved. For our admiration of Christ cannot but increase as we learn to know Him more and more intimately. The Soul of Christ is an abyss of splendor. The more we penetrate that abyss, the greater the wonders we discover in it; but we also come to realize that, though we advance from understanding to greater understanding of Its wonders, there will always be yet more splendid magnificences to be discovered in Christ's Soul.

2. The need for union

In its very inception, all true love presupposes certain affinities between two persons, conducing to union; it creates and develops mutual resemblance, and reaches its full blossoming in a community of life and of goods. Love urges the lover to resemble the beloved in order to establish more perfectly a union of thoughts, of wishes, of hearts, of lives.

The Incarnate Word was bound to submit in some measure to this law of love. He became man and lived a human life among men. He willed to be like unto His brethren: "wherefore, it behoved him in all things to be made like unto his brethren . . . (but) without sin" (*Heb.*, II, 17; IV, 15). But because His love is of a fullness which gives and is given with limitless spontaneity and generosity—swallowing up distance, sweeping over abysses, to bring Divinity and Humanity together in the unity of His Divine Person—His love is a merciful love: "to be made like unto his brethren, that he might become a merciful and faithful high priest."

On the other hand, our love must be a love of conformity, since we ourselves are but miserable in ourselves and utterly dependent on God for all things. This does not mean, of course, that we can claim to reach the heights of the perfection of our Divine Model: the love of conformity means that we must ceaselessly strive to model ourselves on Him by seeking to correct our faults, to rise above our weakness and to imitate Him, in order that we may reach a union of our wills with His Divine Will.

It is this constant effort which pleases Our Lord, and which shows our willingness to love Him in spite of all our weaknesses.

3. *The law of assimilation*

Assimilation is that gradual transformation which the Holy Spirit of Christ, our Head, effects in the member of His Mystical Body. Jesus Christ desires to change into Himself the soul which gives itself sincerely to Him. According to the eternal plan of God, the Christian should become "comformable to the image of his Son" (*Rom.*, VIII, 29). Christianity is completely defined in this assimilation of the sons of God to the Only Divine Son.

That he may thus become another Christ, the member of Christ's Mystical Body must, first of all, imitate his Divine Master in His *sentiments* and His interior dispositions; so that he may have in him "this mind . . . which was also in Christ Jesus" (*Philip.*, II, 5). He must then practise, according to the example and under the guidance of his Head, the *virtues* which Christ has manifested in His Sacred Humanity, with a special care to cultivate the Love which Christ showed for His Father and for His brethren. Finally, and in a yet more profound way, the Christian must enter into the *states* and the *mysteries* of Christ, into His life of Sonship, and into the life of His Mystical Body.

O Jesus, it is above all through a longing to prove our integrity that, if we love You sincerely, we seek with all our strength to imitate You. How could we dare unblushingly to protest our love for You, if we were not making every effort to model our lives on Your life, and to make our hearts beat in union with the beatings of Your Sacred Heart?

35. B. THE LOVE OF SACRIFICE

I came not to send peace, but the sword.
(Matt., X, 34)

Sacrifice is a fundamental requirement of love. All love—whether it is conjugal, paternal, maternal, or the love of friendship for a person or a community—presupposes sacrifice, in order that it may prove its reality by positive acts, but above all because love is essentially the giving of oneself to another and for another's service.

1. Love, in itself, implies sacrifice

He who loves seeks to forget himself, to renounce his selfishness in order to ensure the happiness and seek the good of the beloved. By opposing and rejecting the spirit of sacrifice, men have defaced love and degraded it to the level of selfish pleasure; while, at the same time, they have deprivd it of its very life and power.

How could sacrifice be absent from the love of Christ? If our love for Him is genuine, and not just a mask for self-love, it must indeed be expected that sacrifice will always accompany that love. But the nature itself of our relations with Jesus Christ makes this requirement more imperious still, since it becomes a demand welling up from the very depths of life. Our spiritual purpose is to become really transformed in Christ, so that His life may be substituted for ours, and if we desire to find this life of adopted sonship in Christ, it is necessary that our own personality should cede to the Person of Christ. Saint Paul lays down this law in these words: "It is now no longer I that live, but Christ liveth in me." If we are to open wide to His Life, we must not throw a barrier of selfishness around ourselves.

And, at the same time, this is to seek the good, the glory and the joy of the beloved Christ! For His glory, His good, His joy is to see the growth of His Mystical Body—to find those who offer themselves to His love, that He may fill them with the riches of His Life.

2. The love of Redemption

Because sin has entered into the world, upsetting the divine plan and placing an inclination towards evil in wounded human nature, sacrifice has become inherent in love.

Sacrifice *detaches:* it prevents man from stopping short at creatures to center his aims solely on them. He realizes their frailty, their vanity, their powerlessness to satisfy him, and also the danger and the obstacle they can prove to him in his ascent to God. In proportion as a soul has not personally experienced, through sacrifice, the nothingness of all that is not God, his love is a wavering love and is always liable to eclipse through descent to created things.

Sacrifice *purifies:* sinful man is always liable to introduce an element of self-seeking, even into the most elevated and most spiritual region of the interior life. In seeking their object, his faculties are troubled by the violence of passion, the tyranny of the self, the attraction of what appeals to the senses. Each of his faculties must pass through the purifying fire of sacrifice and through the dark, cleansing night of the soul.

Sacrifice *repairs:* the memory of its own past ingratitudes, and the sight of the blasphemous indifference of men towards Him Who is all Love, are a deep sorrow for the heart that loves Christ. Such a heart feels intensely the necessity for compensation, for reparation, for expiation. Every sacrifice offered by the humble circumstances of daily duty, becomes an occasion for manifesting and renewing its love. The loving heart expects, welcomes and seeks such occasions.

3.   *The love of service*

Christ, our Head, calls upon all the members of His Mystical Body to cooperate with all their strength in the tremendous enterprise of saving all mankind. This is not just another purpose added to the purposes of our life. It is the true purpose of the whole Christian life, whatever may be the particular vocations and the means chosen to attain it.

Now, this enterprise of universal salvation demands the giving of a love which proves itself in sacrifices of every kind. For those who have heard the irresistible call of undivided love, it is the sacrifice of heart, of possession, of will. For all Christians, it should be the sacrifice of comforts, of selfish security, and of supine satisfaction in the possession of the goods of this world.

O Jesus, teach us to understand how Your love comes to disturb our easy ways of living, and to disrupt our plans always centered on the search for a security we imagine to be beyond the reach of tempests and vexations. You have not come to bring a slothful peace, but to bring the sword which cuts, trims and tempers souls for liberating combats.

36.   C.   THE LOVE OF SUBMISSION

> *He that hath my commandments and keep-*
> *eth them: he it is that loveth me.*
> (John, XIV, 21)

Every love naturally demands submission to the being loved. To love someone is to seek to please him and to meet his least wishes—or rather, it is to divine these wishes so as to anticipate them. Love enchains: it binds the lover to the beloved.

1. Obedience to the Commandments of Christ

Jesus Christ teaches us that to love Him is to keep His Commandments. These words of the Divine Master remove two opposing errors. On the one hand, to those who would make the love of God to consist in mere feeling, Jesus points out that His love is essentially an act of the mind and of the will, expressed as the practical observance of the Commandments.

On the other hand, there are those who hold that the love of God is merely submission to His Commandments. Perhaps their attitude could be said to imply that, just as the Old Law was fulfilled by the observance of its precepts, so the religion of Christ is to be defined exclusively as the keeping of the evangelical Commandments.

Our Lord has exactly stated the relationships which exist between obedience and love. He places love at the beginning, at the center, and as the perfection of this whole order. At the beginning, because He wills that obedience should be inspired by love; at the center, because He establishes the law of Love among all the Commandments to which he demands our submission; and as the perfection, because He wills that He should be obeyed in order that Love may triumph. It is a very noble and very practical manifestation of love: it is the expression, proof and guarantee of love. But love is of a higher nature than obedience, and has other ways of expressing itself. There is a clear distinction between the two: love is addressed to the person; obedience envisages only the commandment. There can be obedience without love; but there is no sincere love without submission, when the Person loved is Our Lord Jesus Christ.

2. The submission of our whole being to the Person of Christ, the Head

In addition to obedience to the Commandments, love calls upon us to submit our whole being to the Person of Christ, the Head of the Mystical Body.

First of all, to the Person of Christ as God, as the Divine Word. "All things were made by him; and without him was made nothing that was made" (*John*, I, 3). We are absolutely contingent beings: we owe to a continuous creative act of God, at every instant, not only our existence, but our created substantial being, our activity, all that we have and are. We can ignore this contingence, deny it, revolt against it. But when the human mind has grasped, however gropingly, the extent to which this radical contingence holds man in absolute dependence on Necessary

Being, on "Him Who is," as God is defined in the Old Testament; when, enlightened by faith, a soul has come to understand, in the splendor of a light received as a personal message from Christ, that this same God, Creator and Father, has been revealed as Infinite Love, that "God is love" (1 *John*, IV, 9), and that His whole creative work is a work of love—then, indeed, will the conviction of the soul's dependence on God blossom into a love overflowing with gratitude. Nay more, this very love will urge the soul to proclaim this dependence, and to express it efficaciously by a spontaneous, free and happy submission.

This loving submission is also directed to the Sacred Humanity of the Head, now glorified, triumphant, and rich—through His birthright as Son, and by right of conquest as Redeemer—with all the splendor and all the power necessary to the Head, in order to govern His Mystical Body, to vivify it, to lead it to its fullness as the Whole Christ.

But we must consider this matter yet further. What a change of outlook takes place in a person who has understood his vocation as a member of the Mystical Body! He knows that he has been created *for* Jesus Christ, in order that he may be His with every fiber of his being; that he may become, in a sense, a part of Christ in the unity of His Mystical Body. No longer, therefore, can he do anything without Christ; no longer can he live the true life, apart from Christ; for on Christ alone is his whole life centered, and in Him alone he lives. Christ ceases to be for him simply that Sovereign Master Who, living apart from him and far above him, governs and directs all things. Jesus becomes for him that Master living within him, Who, by the constant influx of His life, sustains him in his supernatural being as a member of the Mystical Body; and Who, by the inspirations of His Holy Spirit, urges him to fulfill, within the Mystical Body, his personal mission in the service of the Whole Christ.

To love Christ is not only to accept, but joyfully to will, a permanent and total dependence on Him, so that the Whole Christ may be realized in all splendor and beauty.

O Jesus, how those are to be pitied who do not realize that, in seeking to safeguard their independence in their relations with You in order the better to do their own will, they stifle love! Love does not just tolerate dependence; it demands dependence. To love You is to renounce one's own will, and to find one's happiness in obediently submitting to Your guidance. Here I am before You! I belong fully and exclusively to You. Dispose freely of me for the extension of Your Mystical Body.

PART TWO

THE LIVING COMMUNITY OF THE MEMBERS OF THE MYSTICAL BODY

One body and one spirit . . . One Lord, one faith, one baptism.

(Ephes., IV, 4-5)

FOREWORD

Jesus Christ speaks: "Come and see (*John, I, 39*) . . . *I did not wish to keep for Myself alone all the riches which I have received from My Father. I called you all to enjoy them with Me. It is as Head of My Mystical Body that I said to My Father:* And all my things are thine, and thine are mine (*John, XVII, 10*); *and therefore they are yours, members of My Body, that as My members you may share in them.*

Yours are the created riches which adorn my Sacred Humanity; yours My grace, My merits, My virtues, My mysteries, My priesthood, My Sacrifice. All are yours, that from them you may draw on the full richness of My life as the Man-God.

Yours the richness of My Sacred Humanity Itself: My Body, My Blood, My Soul.

Yours, the Divine Riches of My Life as Son of God! Yours, My Father, My Holy Spirit, and to welcome you on the threshold of My Divine Family, My Mother. They are all yours, to enable you to share, in Me, the Life of the Blessed Trinity.

Yours, to share, with Me, *the divine treasures and the society of the Divine Persons. I . . . and you—with the perfect distinction of My Person and your persons, but* you with Me *in the most intimate union.*

Yours, that you may share them together, one with another, *not in isolation or in a spirit of selfishness.*

What above all makes the members of My Body a living community, in the unity of One Head, is this communion in the same life, this sharing of the same source of riches, this possession in common of divine and supernatural treasures."

37. INCORPORATED IN THE WHOLE CHRIST

For in one Spirit were we all baptized into one body.

(1 Cor., XII, 13)

Baptism is the foundation of all the riches of the Christian. The first effect of Baptism is incorporation. We may consider, in a logical order, the different effects of Baptism (incorporation, filiation, purification, regeneration), on condition, however, that we bear in mind that all these riches are communicated to the soul *together*, at the moment of receiving Baptism.

1. A *bond of appurtenance*

To be incorporated is to become a member of Christ and of His Mystical Body—"to be baptized into one body" with all our brethren. By incorporation, the baptized person belongs, with all the depths of his being, to Christ and to the Church. In Baptism, Christ, the Head, takes possession of the Christian, whom He incorporates in His Human Nature and whom, through His Sacred Humanity, He brings into relationship with His Divine Person as the Incarnate Word, making him one of His members.

This incorporation attaches the baptized person, not only to Christ the Head, but to His Whole Body which is the Church, and thus to the Whole Christ. It is the authentic and official manner of entering the Church. It is the union with the Christ-Head, in His Body, by His Body, with His Body.

This incorporation is thus the basis of union with Jesus Christ, but also with His Church; it is the basis of the fidelity to all the duties of charity and of community life which are implied in our belonging to the Mystical Body.

This incorporation also inspires us to voluntary repentance after sins of human weakness, since the soul realizes that it is "attached" and "bound" to Christ and to His Body by links which cannot be broken by such passing failures.

Finally, when faith is being tried in the crucible of purification, and the soul imagines that Christ is rejecting or abandoning it, what consolation and peace there is in the assurance that nothing can separate that soul from Christ! "Who can separate me

from Christ?" cries out the Apostle. And what a source of Hope
to realize that, so far from no longer desiring that soul, Christ
has decided to make His disciple a part of Himself, in a sense;
a member of His Body to Which that disciple is henceforward
indissolubly united.

2. *A bond of communion in the same collective life—the Life of
the Whole Christ*

Incorporation is not the act of a single day: it is a grafting
into a life, the life of a Person, of Christ Jesus Who still lives in
His Church. It is because, being all incorporated in Christ, we
live by His life, that we form His Body. Thus it is that Baptism
creates unity.

To be a living member of Christ and of His Church is to be
filled with the life of grace and of charity which springs unceasingly from the Christ-Head and which is spread abroad in the
whole Mystical Body by the Holy Spirit, the Spirit of Christ,
the Soul of the Church.

To be a living member, therefore, is not to fold in on oneself,
but to fling oneself open to this collective life, to share in all the
riches of the Whole Christ, to receive all from Him . . . and each
soul will receive in the same measure in which it opens itself to
Him.

To be a living member, again, is not to seek to have all this
consolation for oneself in a spirit of selfish enjoyment: it is to
contribute one's own personal share of vital activity and of self-
oblation, in order to increase and expand the life of the Whole
Christ.

Finally, to be a living member is not to "diminish" Christ to
the size of the narrow and personal needs of our own spiritual
life; it is to enable Christ to live His life in us, for the building
up of His Mystical Body.

3. *The presence of the Church in Baptism*

The Mystical Body is present at the Baptism of a child. It is
from the community that the life of Christ is communicated to
the baptized person. It is in the community of the Church that
the vital union of the Head with the new member is effected.
Moreover, the whole Church is represented at the ceremony:
first, by its minister who acts in its name by administering the
Sacrament "in the intention of the Church" and according to the
prescribed rites; but also by the godparents, who receive the

mission of guarding the fidelity of the new Christian to the Faith
into which he or she has been baptized. Thus, the whole community is involved in the reception of this new member, as though
to ensure that he or she will be a living member.

Furthermore, "it is the faith of the whole Church which
bestows on the baptized person its beneficent power, thanks to
the action of the Holy Spirit Who creates the unity of the Church
and through Whom the spiritual treasures of each member are
held in common by all the others" (Saint Thomas, II, q. 61, a. 1).
What an admirable radiation of the Faith of the Church—"fides
ecclesiae"—and of community life in the Church.

*Lord Jesus, do not allow your Christians to become hardened
in a pharisaic sufficiency or in an attitude of indifference towards
all those who have not yet received the gifts of Your Redemption;
but grant that the discovery of the riches of their Baptism may
fill their hearts with a searing anguish at the thought of the mil-
lions of souls who do no yet know You, and inspire in them the
desire and the resolution to fulfill without delay their baptismal
vocation in the service of their brethren.*

CHAPTER ONE

The Relations of Christians, Living Members of the Mystical Body, with Christ, Their Head

For we are made partakers of Christ.

(Heb., III, 14)

Our Savior communicates to His Church the treasures which are most suited to it.

(Encyclical on the Mystical Body)

CHRISTIANS SHARE TOGETHER THE MYSTERY OF CHRIST AND THE RICHES OF HIS REDEMPTION

38. HIS GRACE

As the branch cannot bear fruit of itself, unless it abide in the vine, so neither can you, unless you abide in me.

(John, XV, 4)

Our grace, the grace which adorns our souls, is indeed our own and is a personal possession, a quality which transforms the very essence of our soul. It is not a complete substance which could exist of itself with an identity apart from the soul, something which could be added to the soul from outside, as though it were a kind of spiritual fluid: it is a transformation of our soul, such that, through it, our soul is made pleasing (*grata*) to God, is attuned to the supernatural, is adapted to the divine climate and made capable of participating in the very life of God. But our grace cannot be separated from the grace of Christ, nor can we separate them in our thoughts or in our faith. We can therefore say with all truth that our grace is the grace of Christ, not only because He has merited it for us, but because it comes to us *from Him*. His grace is a social grace.

1. *In its origin*

We are drawn together by the same grace—by Christ's grace as Son, by His grace as Head. By His grace as Son, which makes all of us sons of God in the Son; by His grace as Head, which makes us all members of the same Body, of His Body.

In diversifying itself from person to person, that grace does not result in placing the sons of God side by side in mutual isolation, as though each were to sanctify himself on his own account

alone. There is but One Son. Grace joins us to Him, makes us
to be sons by participation in His Sonship, in one and the same
Life, that of one Living Person, of one and the same Body.

Let us avoid the inaccurate images which such current
expression as: "grace derives from Him, flows from Him" . . .
would tend to create. They are accurate in as much as they
emphasize the common origin of all grace. They are inaccurate
in as much as they suggest a phenomenon external to Christ,
whereas grace is a phenomenon of assimilation to Christ. Grace
leads us within. *In Christo;* it makes us to drink at the same
Divine Source.

2. *In its nature*

The grace which comes from Christ to us is the same which
sanctifies the Sacred Humanity of our Head. It is *His* grace which
animates His Soul, and which divinizes our souls. There are not
two different graces in Him—one for Himself alone, the other
for us. It is His personal grace which is His grace as Head; and
because of His fullness, His grace as Head is given to us.

Here we have a new basis for a very profound intimacy
between Christ and our souls. This grace is not only a grace from
God: it carried the mark of Christ. It makes us like unto Christ,
it assimilates us to Him, producing in us those fruits of virtue and
of holiness which will impress more and more upon our souls
the image of Christ. It is a grace of Christ which tends to swallow
up our whole being in His powers and His faculties, and leads
us to think, feel, love and act like Him, so that we may become
like other Christs, made like unto the image of the Son. Our
Lord desires to be able to continue to live His life in each one
of us.

Here, too, we find the basis of a very intimate community of
life among the members of the same Body: a communion of souls
under the action of the same grace which transforms them to the
image of the same Model, and under the powerful force of that
same process of divinization which raises them and urges them
in the same direction and towards the same end.

3. *In its purpose*

The aim of Christ's grace is to divinize mankind, to form the
Body of Christ, to spread itself abroad to all the members so that
they may share the fruits of the Redemption. It is a grace
redemptive of the whole world. The effect which it produces on

our souls is the stifling of our selfishness, the awakening of a feeling for others, of concern for them, of the constant perspective of the work to be done by all together—the building up of the Whole Christ. His grace kindles in us an aptitude for self-oblation, whose flower is charity. When grace begins to live in a person, it unites that person supernaturally with all.

O Jesus, grant that, in ever increasing faith, we may come to realize Your intimate Presence in us by Your grace. It is through grace that we live in You, and You in us. Grant that, by its assimilating action, we may allow ourselves to be gradually transformed into Your likeness, so that we may help You to build up in Yourself the Whole Christ.

39. HIS MERITS

> *Therefore, as by the offense of one, unto all men to condemnation; so also by the justice of one, unto all men to justification of life.*
>
> (Rom., V, 18)

Merit is a right to the possession of eternal life. It is therefore a right to obtain, in Heaven, the reward of the vision of glory. But glory will be the full blossoming of grace, eternal life having already begun here on earth in our souls. To merit, therefore, is to win the right to an increase of sanctifying grace. But, of ourselves, we can obtain nothing: it is in Christ and by Christ alone that we can merit, and it is His merits which are applied to us in His Mystical Body.

1. *Jesus Christ has merited for Himself and has taught us to merit*

The Incarnate Word could have been the source of supernatural life for His Mystical Body, without having to merit for Himself. As the Only Son of God the Father, He had the right to glory and He need not have suffered and died. But, through love for us, He wished to merit in a mortal flesh and a body subject to pain. "Wherefore it behoved him in all things to be

made like unto his brethren, that he might become a merciful
and faithful high priest" (*Heb.*, II, 17). Towards this end, He
suspended, during His earthly life, the outward manifestation of
His beatific vision and the exercise of those rights to glory which
His human virtue possessed because of the hypostatic union. He
willed, through suffering, to merit His glorification, the Resurrection of His Body, His spiritual reign over mankind, and His role
as Head of His Mystical Body.

Thus, His life can become the model of all meritorious life.
There is, of course, a vast difference between His merit and ours.
In the first place, His actions and His sufferings were those of the
Man-God, and had therefore a merit of infinite value. Further-
more, our merit has value only through His: we merit only by
Him and in Him.

But, however, Christ has shown us how we can merit. He has
shown us that the secret of great merit is the charity with which
we adhere to the Divine Will in our everyday actions, and the
generosity and filial love we show in accepting and offering up
the trials and crosses of our lives, for the Redemption of the
world. By His personal example, He has taught us to carry our
cross.

2. *Jesus Christ has merited for us*

By meriting for Himself His exaltation, Jesus has merited for
us our justification. It must even be said that it is the same merit
which reaches out to us. Jesus has merited all the graces whose
disposition as Sovereign Master, was to constitute His Mission of
life-giving Head; and it is these graces which, as Head of the
Mystical Body, He disseminates in our souls that He may fill them
with His life.

But how could He have merited for us? Merit is personal,
and no one can merit sanctifying grace except for himself. The
answer is that He and we are but one: our life and His are joined
together in a real unity, in the reality of a single Body wherein
His life becomes ours. His merit, therefore, can become our
merit: "He extends Himself to men, in so far as they are His
members" (Saint Thomas, III, q. 19, a. 4). All that Christ has
done, He has done as the Head Who bears us within Himself;
as He Who, knowing in advance the whole spiritual life of each
one of us with each one's personal needs, already lived that life,
meriting in us all that would be necessary to enable us to live
it in our turn.

Of course, on the Cross where He became our Redeemer, it was Christ Who *alone* offered Himself to His Father in a supreme oblation of His love. But, since He was meriting in our name and was representing us as our Head, there is a sense in which it can be said that we were already present in Him and sharing in His Sacrifice. The Father already saw us all in His Son, and Jesus was already bearing us all in His soul. From that hour, we were redeemed souls.

3. *Jesus Christ, as Head, applies to us His merits in the solidarity of His Mystical Body*

The merits of Christ must now be applied to our souls, in order that we may benefit from their efficacy. It is in Baptism, which incorporates us in Christ, that the first application of these merits occurs. When we have thus become members of Christ, we are ourselves able to merit, since our human nature is now associated with the work of its own restoration in the spiritual life. The application of the merits of the Redemptive Sacrifice does not take the form of a sort of automatic and individual distribution. Certainly, this application depends upon our good will, our personal generosity, our obedience to grace; but it also depends on our union with the community of the Church. It occurs in the Holy Sacrifice of the Mass, through the Sacraments and all the treasures of the Communion of Saints, in prayer and through our meritorious action, in the form of all the graces which Jesus bestows upon us. But this is so only because Jesus Christ, after having merited for us and in our name, gives, through His grace and through our union with Him, the strength to merit for ourselves.

For the solidarity of mankind in the fall, the New Adam has substituted the solidarity of mankind in the Redemption. But Jesus calls upon each person to labor with Him and in Him for the Redemption of His brethren, by actions which ensure his own Redemption.

However, Jesus does not invite them to join their merits to His because His merits would be insufficient and would need to be supplemented. On the contrary, indeed, it is because His merits are beyond measure sufficient and superabundant to Himself, that He wills that men's good actions should in their turn become meritorious.

O Jesus, give us an unwavering and unshakable confidence in the power of Your merits. Each one of us can say with all certainty: "Your merits are mine . . . they belong to me." If our souls sometimes falter, it is because they have not yet understood to what an extent we are united with You, and how inexhaustible are the riches which You have ceaselessly at Your command, to bestow according to the measure of our faith in Your redemptive role and of our willingness to cooperate in a spirit of love.

40. HIS VIRTUES

> But of him are you in Christ Jesus, who of God is made unto us wisdom and justice and sanctification and redemption.
>
> (1 Cor., 1, 30)

Our virtues are those of Jesus, not merely in the sense that Jesus Christ has practiced all virtues in perfection, and that, without His example, we ourselves would not know how to practice them. Our virtues are those of Jesus, in quite a *literal* sense, because it is He Who infuses them or forms them, by His Spirit, in His Mystical Body.

1. *Our virtues are not our own*

The Apostle forbids us to glory in ourselves as if our virtues were our own.

One of the greatest obstacles in the spiritual life is this self-sufficiency, this complaisance of the proud self in what it regards as its virtues.

People imagine they have virtues which in reality they entirely lack. They regard as virtue, qualities which are not at all virtuous. Thus, mere timidity is promoted to the virtue of humility; weakness of character is taken for the virtue of meekness; violence or authoritarianism is hailed as virtuous strength of will; while what is regarded as affability, is just vanity hungering for esteem and for praise.

Finally, there are those who, even granted that their virtues are authentic, give themselves the credit for them, as if they had acquired or were practising these virtues by their own unaided strength.

"For who distinguisheth thee? Or what hast thou that thou

hast not received? And, if thou hast received, why dost thou glory, as if thou hadst not received it?" (1 *Cor.*, IV, 7).

2. *Our virtues are, in a sense, those of Jesus our Head, the Mediator of holiness*

Every virtue certainly demands personal cooperation, an effort of the will, an act of self-oblation.

Jesus contains in Himself all holiness

But, at the outset, it is not for us, properly speaking, to sanctify ourselves, since we are not able to do so. "Without me, you can do nothing . . ." It is not within our power to acquire wisdom, to establish justice, to work out our own redemption. All this has already been done: all this is in Christ. He incarnates this whole order of holiness: He contains it within Himself, since He is, as Saint Paul says, "wisdom and justice and sanctification and redemption." And He adds that Christ is all these *for us*, to be *our* wisdom, *our* justice, *our* sanctification, *our* redemption. Why is this? "That, as it is written, he that glorieth may glory in the Lord." (1 *Cor.*, I, 30-31).

It is therefore from Christ, from that Unique Source, that we must derive all those virtues. It is *His* Sanctity which contains in an eminent manner all the virtues of the Mystical Body. It is *His* Sanctity which is manifested in the virtues of the members of His Body and in the whole of that Body.

Jesus establishes His Sanctity in His Mystical Body

Furthermore—since Christ is the unique Mediator of Sanctity and of Life, as He is the one and only Mediator of Truth—it is He, the Head, Who establishes all His virtues in His Mystical Body.

Our personal effort should be directed towards enabling Christ to establish, fashion and increase His virtues in His members. We must be "clothed with Christ"—but not as though the Head covered His members by simply casting the mantle of His virtues externally about them. We must understand the phrase as meaning that, being united with Christ in the Mystical Body, we are *interiorly* changed in Him, that we are assimilated to Him by the transforming action of His Spirit, that we are made participators of His justice, His sanctity, His redemptive life.

It is *His* grace which, becoming the very essence of our soul, shines in our faculties through the virtues, and engulfs our entire being.

It is *His* charity which animates the charity of the members, so that it becomes the soul of all their other virtues. It is He Who, by His Spirit, gives an increase of charity in our hearts.

It is *His* Spirit Who inspires, sustains, directs and fructifies each one's efforts to practice the moral virtues; Who infuses in our souls the theological virtues; and Who makes His gifts to bear fruit within us. It is His Holy Spirit Who exalts the whole Mystical Body to holiness.

3. *The virtues of the Whole Christ*

There is a further reason why it is impossible for any of us to glory in his personal virtues. These virtues must be judged in the perspective of the unity of the Mystical Body. Our sanctity is that of members of the Mystical Body—of members who have already received much, and who are receiving at every moment the prayers, merits and examples of the other members. We are continually upheld by the whole Body; we are continually renewed, stimulated and completed by it. Each of us is but a tiny ray in the sun of the Sanctity of the Whole Christ; and it is this Sanctity which alone counts with God. Each of us is but a tiny portion of the Mystical Body, and it is in union with our brethren that we must reproduce the Sanctity of Christ, by faithfully filling the place allotted to each of us in the building up of that Body. No one can presume to reproduce of himself alone, the full Sanctity of Christ.

We have a solid foundation of humility in the fact that our weaknesses and our failures are our own. Our virtues and our meritorious actions are of the Whole Christ.

We have also, in this doctrine, a solid foundation of charity: that if we judge another, it will always be with the charity we owe to a fellow-member of Christ; and that we will cooperate, with all our powers, in the sanctification of the Mystical Body.

O Jesus, do not permit us to be in the least complacent about any of the poor efforts by which we seek to reproduce Your virtues. But since You live in us and work the works of holiness within us, grant that we may adhere with all our soul to the sanctifying action of Your Spirit, in order to advance the growth of Your Mystical Body.

41. HIS MYSTERIES

God . . . even when we were dead in sin,
hath quickened us together in Christ . . .
and hath raised us up together and hath
made us sit together in the heavenly places,
through Christ Jesus.

(Ephes., II, 5, 6, 7)

So intimate a community of life exists between Jesus, the Head of His Mystical Body, and His members, that there is a sense in which it could be said that the Gospel is not His story only, but is also by anticipation already ours; and that the Church's liturgy is not only the ensemble of our feasts, but the application to ourselves of His mysteries celebrated in them.

1. *We were present in Christ's mysteries when He was living them for us*

When Jesus was living the mystery of His Birth in the poverty of the manger; the mystery of His humble and hidden, laborious and obedient life in Nazareth; the mysteries of His apostolic life in the towns and villages of Palestine; the mysteries of His suffering during His Passion and Death; and the glorious mysteries of His Resurrection and His Ascension—we were present at each one of them. We were present, not only as a whole, but as each holding his own personal place, as members of Christ's Mystical Body.

We were present at these mysteries, first of all, *because Jesus, in living them, carried each and every one of us in His soul, as Head of the Church.* He saw us, by reason of His beatific knowledge. He saw how we, in our turn, would be called to live these same mysteries, by passing along the way that He Himself was taking. He saw the graces of which each and every one of us would stand in need, in order that we could make truly our own the spirit in which He Himself was living His own mysteries.

But His own Mysteries were not exclusively His, but were already ours also. For Christ was living them, not for Himself alone, but for us. Since He is the Son of God, Christ had no need to live a life of poverty, humiliation and suffering: as Son,

He had the right to a glorious and triumphant life. But He willed, "for us and for our salvation," to take a mortal body which could feel pain. He willed to practice the virtues which we ourselves would have to cultivate, in order that He might leave us an example. Whatever happens to us, and whatever the form which the mystery of our lives may take, we should always say: "Jesus has lived this before me . . . He has lived it for me, to show me how to sanctify it and to obtain for me the grace to live it when my turn came."

Moreover, we were present in the Mysteries of Jesus *because, in the mind of God, we were there.* When the Father was rejoicing in His Son at Bethlehem, in the waters of the Jordan, on Thabor, on the Cross, He saw us all in Jesus. He made no distinction in His Mind between Jesus and us; for He saw only one Christ, the Whole Christ, in Whom we were all present, making but one with Him.

For the Father saw the Head of the Church, the Son Whom in love He had sent into the world to save the world through the Church. In the plan of God, the public function of the Redeemer was inseparable from His personal title of Son.

2. *The mysteries of Jesus are a present reality for us*

Jesus lives in His Church. In the cycle of her liturgical feasts, the Church carries us through the succession of the mysteries which comprised the human life of Christ. We re-live, in the Church, the very life of Christ. But this liturgical cycle is more than the moving evocation of a historical event which occurred two thousand years ago. Under the visible sign of a liturgical feast, it is an actual reality which takes place in our soul, provided we enter, with faith and love, into the spirit of the mystery, opening our souls to it, seizing upon it, and making our own the interior dispositions of Christ when He was living it.

Through His Church, and through the action of His Spirit Who animates the Church, Jesus actually distributes to us, at the very time when we are taking part in the liturgical celebration of each mystery, the special grace which He had merited by living that mystery for us. We receive the grace of a new birth into His Divine Life on the blessed Feast of Christmas; the grace of a new manifestation of Christ in us and of an increase of faith, during the Octave of the Epiphany; the grace of interior renewal and of spiritual renovation, during the purifying period of Lent, in preparation for the great Paschal meeting with the Eucharistic Christ; the grace to detest sin and to cultivate a spirit of sacrifice, during the shadowed week of the Passion; the grace of joy, of peace, of liberty, on the triumphant Day of the Resurrection and during the whole light-filled period of Christ's apparitions; the grace to lift up our souls, with an intense thirst for Heaven, on the glorious Feast of the Ascension; the grace to cooperate more generously in the life of the Church, during the long weeks after Pentecost.

Each of the holy anniversaries of the life of Jesus marks for us, therefore, a more intimate participation in one of the states of His Sacred Humanity, in His actual life, in His Divine Life. But this participation is effected for each and all of us, only in the Church and with the Church.

O Jesus, how happy indeed is that soul which, by remaining ever open to the action of Your Divine Spirit, allows itself to be formed by Your Church! It receives in the words of the liturgy, all the spiritual nourishment which it needs for every day. It thus unceasingly renews itself, tastes the very pure interior joys of living its life in Your life, and finds, through participation in Your mysteries, a light and a strength which transforms its whole existence.

42. HIS PRAYER

> . . . *always living to make intercession for us.*
>
> (Heb., VII, 25)

The whole life of Our Lord was a prayer. The Gospel records some instances of Christ's lifting up His Soul in intimate colloquies with His Father.[1] This is to enlighten us about prayer and to encourage us to pray. We see in the Gospel how Christ would retire into the mountain, and there pass the whole night in prayer. But, apart from those times spent in silence, Jesus preserved a permanent state of prayer and of constant self-oblation to the Will of His Father, in the midst of His Apostolic Life. In what way does our Head now make us participate in His prayer in Heaven?

---

1. *Luke*, X, 21—before the grave of Lazarus, *John*, XI, 41—on the Cross, *Luke*, XXIII, 34 and 46.

1. *Through Him: "Per Ipsum"*

Our prayer has not of itself the power to reach God. It rises
to God through the prayer of Christ, and must be founded in His
prayer, if it is to be pleasing to the Father Who is in Heaven.

The reason for this is that Christ's prayer is the prayer of
the well-beloved Son, the prayer of Him Who has said: "Father
. . . thou hearest me always" (*John*, XI, 42). He Who prays is
indeed the Incarnate Word, the Only Son in and by His Sacred
Humanity. That is why Jesus always speaks to His Father when
He prays.

Today, the Church, the Spouse and the Mystical Body of
Christ, lifts up her prayers and supplications to the Father and
to the Holy Trinity, "through Jesus Christ, Our Lord, Who liveth
and reigneth with Thee, O Father, in the Unity of the Holy
Ghost."

This liturgical formula is very rich in significance and light.
If we learned to understand its richness, we would no longer use
those mediocre prayers which we sometimes vainly attempt to
say as from ourselves—barren prayers, because they come from
a soul which is still too rooted in its own sufficiency. This formula
puts an end to that great discouragement and weariness which
makes so many Christians turn away from prayer, because their
prayer has not been answered. "*Per* Christum Dominum . . .*"*
Humility, the indispensable condition of our pleasing God by our
prayer, will find its solid foundation in this certainty that our
prayer must be united with the prayer of Christ, must be assumed
into His prayer—must, in a word, become the prayer of Christ,
the Sole Mediator.

2. *In Him: "In Ipso"*

But, above all, if our prayer can truly be called, in a sense,
the prayer of Christ, or if His prayer can be called ours, it is
because Jesus Christ is the Man-God Who, as Head of the
Mystical Body, contains all of us in Himself, prays with us in
His prayer, and draws unto Himself the whole of His supplicat-
ing Church.

It is He Who prays in us, His members. It is His Spirit Who
inspires the prayer of the Mystical Body. "And, because you are
sons," writes Saint Paul, "God hath sent the Spirit of His Son
into your hearts, crying: Abba, Father" (*Gal.*, IV, 6). It is He
Who guides the Mystical Body in its supplications: "Likewise,
the Spirit also helpeth our infirmity. For we know not what we

should pray for as we ought; but the Spirit Himself asketh for us with unspeakable groanings" (*Rom.*, VIII, 26). It is He Who animates the Mystical Body with His charity, and gives to it by His grace, value and fecundity in the sight of God.

Happy indeed is the soul which has, even once, experienced the benefit of prayer truly established in Christ! Such a soul throws off the shackles of time and of the ephemeral, to participate in the prayer of the Eternal Priest. It is transported by the surgings of adoration, of love, of thanksgiving, which spring from the Heart of Jesus and rise up to the Father. It comes to understand that, by this prayer, exalted and unified in Christ, it attains in this very moment the End for which it was created: it realizes the "One Thing Necessary."

3. With Him: "Cum Ipso"

The prayer of Christians, members of Christ, cannot be an isolated and individualist prayer. To pray with Jesus means to pray with the other members, with the Whole Mystical Body. It is to make our prayer Catholic, universal.

The first essential, therefore, is to rid ourselves of selfish preoccupations in our prayer. Each of us has, most certainly, the right and the duty to confide to God his personal concerns and needs, and those of his family and friends. But in doing so, he must always bear in mind that he is a member, that his prayer is that of a member who derives his life from the Mystical Body, and that his prayer should aid him to fulfill more perfectly his life of membership.

As long as a Christian fears that his prayers will cease to benefit him personally if he sets aside his own little intentions in favor of the great intentions of the Head and of the Mystical Body, he does not yet know what it means to be Catholic . . . He does not yet know the Whole Christ. Furthermore, in this as in everything else, the words of the Master hold good: "he that shall lose his life for me, shall find it" (*Matt.*, X, 39). Whoever says a Catholic prayer, receives an increase of grace, of charity and of holiness.

To pray with the Head in a Catholic prayer, is also to unite oneself with the official prayer of the Church, praying as a Body, as a visible and hierarchic society. Even when we cannot enjoy the splendors of the liturgy, we should pray in the spirit of the liturgy, by uniting ourselves spiritually with all those who, night and day, in monasteries and churches, in presbyteries and chapels, are lifting up to God the praise and supplication of the Church.

How good it is to know that we are thus in union with the whole
Mystical Body, with all the Saints in Heaven and on earth; that
we are carried by the mighty movement of adoration and of love
which, in the breathing of the Holy Spirit and the guiding impulsion of the Head, lifts up the world to God! How rewarding it is,
then, to have realized in what sense our prayer is a prayer of
members! On the one hand, we learn why we need not wonder
at the poverty of our prayer or be discouraged by its deficiencies.
On the other hand, this doctrine reveals to us the grandeur and
power of our prayer. It is the prayer of the Whole Christ which
counts in the sight of God and glorifies the Father: by uniting
itself with that prayer, by assimilating itself to that prayer, the
prayer of the members shares in the efficacy of that of the Whole
Christ.

*O Jesus, our Head, You expect of us that—by conforming our
heart with Your Heart, and by making our own the intentions,
desires and aspirations of Your Sacred Heart—we will enable You
to continue in us and in Your Mystical Body, by the power of
Your Holy Spirit, Your eternal mission of prayer for the advancement of Your Father's Kingdom on earth, the spread of Your
Church, and the redemption of all mankind.*

43. HIS PRIESTHOOD

> But you are a chosen generation, a kingly
> priesthood.
>
> (1 Peter, II, 9)

It is by the sacramental characters that Jesus Christ, Head
and Sovereign High Priest, causes the members of His Body to
share in His priesthood. This is a splendid dignity, of which, alas,
so many Christians have no due appreciation. If they but understood this immense dignity, their whole religious life would be
thereby transformed; their reverence for what is sacred would be
powerfully increased; and their understanding of the grandeur
of the sacramental order in the community of the Church, would
be enlightened and deepened profoundly.

1. *What is the sacramental character?*

The sacramental character or mark is a spiritual reality which is impressed on the soul by three of the Sacraments: Baptism, Confirmation and Holy Orders. It is an ineffaceable *sign* which marks, for all eternity, the members of the Mystical Body, and indicates that they belong to the Christ-Head and are joined in one Body with Him. It is the imprint of the Head, the seal of Christ, which marks the members as belonging to His Body.

It is an interior sign, and yet one which designates the members of that exterior and visible Society which Christ has established in the world in order to transform the world from within itself. Records and statistics can show the number of the baptized, the confirmed, the priests.

But the grandeur of this sign is within, in the depths of the soul. It is a *consecration* which reproduces in the members something of what constitutes the dignity of the Head, of the Man-God. To get some idea of it, we must contemplate the mystery of the Incarnation. Christ's human nature has been substantially consecrated by its union with the Divine Person. In an analogous way, the souls of the members of the Mystical Body are consecrated by their participation in the dignity of the Head, the Incarnate Word, in His priesthood, in His Sacrifice; and thereby made like unto the Christ-Priest. The sacramental character introduces the members into the visible religion of Christ—into that great movement of perfect religion and of holiness which springs from the soul of the Sovereign High Priest, to render due homage of adoration and love to the Holy Trinity, and to offer the Divine Sacrifice to the Father.

Finally, being a Sign, a Consecration—a Consecration to the worship of God—the sacramental character creates in the soul an *aptitude* for fulfilling sacred functions within the Mystical Body, and the power to exercise them. It gives to the soul's acts of worship, an objective value of holiness which makes them pleasing to God, by reason of this consecration itself, and of the imprint of the Beloved Son which they carry.

2. *The community aspect*

Religious individualism is abolished, and the subjectivism which originates in feelings of self-sufficiency is conquered. Personal religion has authentic value only if it is assimilated with the religion of the whole Mystical Body: it is that of members. What has value in the sight of God, is the religion of the Whole Christ.

It is the community which welcomes and incorporates a new member, in order to make him participate in its collective life, in its redemptive mission and in its worship, by the baptismal character which gives him the right and the power to receive the other Sacraments. It is for the defense of the community and of its faith, threatened on all sides, that the bishop makes a baptized person a soldier of Christ, with the mandate to bear witness to the Faith that is in him. It is "for the others," for the Christian community, that the deacon is clothed with the character of the priesthood, to produce sacramental rites destined for the sanctification of the faithful, and for the uniting of the community in a love centered on the Holy Eucharist. He offers the Sacrifice of the Mass and consecrates the Sacred Host for the Whole Church. He presides at the public prayers of the community.

But there is One—the great High Priest, Our Lord Jesus Christ—Who rules this whole sacramental order. He imprints in His members the sacramental characters, which enable them to participate, in different degrees, in His Priesthood, and which are derived from His own sacerdotal power. He causes these different sacramental characters to manifest themselves, by vivifying them through the influx of actual graces. Here, everything comes from Christ—from His Sacred Humanity, that prodigiously powerful instrument of the Blessed Trinity; from His Mediation; from His Priesthood. Everything is transmitted through Him, that it may rise up to the Blessed Trinity. He is the Sole Priest: the others are His ministers. Through their ministry, it is He Who really continues to baptize, to consecrate the Host, to forgive sins, to give life to souls. It is He Who incorporates in His religion, the religion of His priest-members and of all the baptized; it is He Who incorporates the liturgical offering in the offering of His Sacrifice, to make it the resplendent oblation of the Whole Christ.

O Jesus, Eternal Priest, I adore You and I beg of You to accept my thanksgiving for having deigned to permit us to share in Your priesthood. How often we are overwhelmed at the thought of the lamentable poverty of our personal acts of religion, while we long to live a religion "in spirit and in truth." And You calm our distress with the certainty that, because of You and Your character impressed on our souls, our acts of worship have an authentic value with the Father and are pleasing to Him. But, at the same time, what a call to true holiness and to Your grace, this sacramental consecration maintains constantly within us!

44. HIS SACRIFICE

*. . . that Jesus should die . . . to gather
in one the children of God that were
dispersed.*

(John, XI, 51, 52)

At the Last Supper, Christ preserved His Redemptive Sacrifice of the Cross in a sacramental rite, so that He might extend the saving virtue of that Sacrifice through all ages and in all places. The Mass is this sacramental rite, which figures, expresses, contains in a symbolic manner, makes present and efficacious in its actual application, the one Redemptive Sacrifice of the Cross, so as through it to constitute the Mystical Body of Christ.

1. *The profound meaning of the Sacrifice of the Mass*

a) What is *presented again figuratively* in the Mass, is a *past occurrence*—the immolation of Christ upon the Cross by the shedding of His Blood. This event was not to be repeated or imitated: it occurred once only. Furthermore, it was a hideous crime committed by executioners. The separate Consecration of the Bread and of the Wine on the altar, symbolizes Christ's violent death on the Cross, when, by His immolation on Calvary, the Blood of Christ that had been spilt upon the ground was separated from the Body that hung lifeless and drained upon the gibbet. It was fitting that this drama should be represented for us, in every Mass, so as to recall ceaselessly to us the love of Our Savior, and that Sacrifice of the Cross on which our whole Christian life depends; but also to teach us that "Jesus Christ is in the condition of a victim" upon the altar (Encyclical of Pope Pius XII: *Mediator Dei*).

b) What is *signified* is a mysterious and sublime reality which was accomplished in the Soul of Jesus Christ, during His Passion and throughout His whole earthly life; but which is continued *now* in the Soul of Jesus Who is made really present through the Consecration in the Mass. This reality is the mystery of love, whereby Our Lord has made to His Father the complete oblation of His life, for the salvation of the world. It is in this oblation that the Mass continues the Sacrifice of Christ.

The mystery signified in the Mass is not, therefore, that of a corpse laid upon the altar, or that of a new execution, or that of a simple offering . . . It is the mystery of Jesus Christ, as Head and Sovereign High Priest, offering Himself even unto death for the redemption of men, in order to gather together into the living unity of His Mystical Body, the successive generations of mankind dispersed by sin.

c) Finally, what is *signified,* but also *accomplished efficaciously,* is our deep and intimate participation in Christ's Sacrifice and in the mystery of His love. This efficacious accomplishment is no longer, of course, in the natural Soul and Body of Christ, now the Glorified Victim Who cannot suffer or die; but *in us,* the members of His Mystical Body. The sacramental sign takes on its full meaning only if we understand clearly that it indicates, in order to produce within us, the *dispositions* which our cooperation in the building up of the Whole Christ demands of us, in our souls and in our lives.

On the other hand, the significance of the sacramental sign becomes fully clear only if we view it as directed *towards the future,* towards a purpose now being pursued and progressively realized in the Church since Calvary: the formation of the Mystical Body.

3. *The dispositions which our Mass demands of us*

In the Mass, Jesus gives us the graces which enable us to enter into the mystery of His Redemptive Sacrifice and to cooperate in the formation of the Whole Christ.

First, there is the special grace which helps us to remove from our lives the obstacles which oppose the mighty working of Christ's love within us: the selfishness of our whole nature. This grace is, in a word, the grace of *the spirit of sacrifice;* that is to say,. the spirit of personal participation in the Sacrifice of the Head, as offered for the redemption of the world. It is necessary that each one of us should be personally initiated into the great mystery of the Cross, if we are to cooperate in the formation of the Whole Christ. The mystery of the Cross must be part of our lives and must penetrate our souls, since it is through this mystery that redemption is continued. The Mass is "the Sacrament of our Redemption": *Sacramentum Redemptionis.*[1] "Every time it is celebrated, the work of our redemption is accomplished."[2] In the

---

1. Cf. Saint Thomas, III, q. 83, a. 4: "The whole mystery of our salvation is contained in this Sacrament."
2. Secret of the ninth Sunday after Pentecost.

Mass, it is the same Christ Who, through the ministry of His priests, offers the same sacrifice of adoration and of praise, of reparation and expiation, of prayer and thanksgiving, as was offered by Him on the Cross. It is the same Victim, the same Priest Who offers Himself; but, this time, with us, the members of His Mystical Body. When we seek the significance of our oblation and our Communion in the Mass, we find it in the oblation of immolation by which Christ was offered up to His Father "for the salvation of the whole world,"[1] all mankind being gathered into the unity of His Body. The Victim of Calvary is indeed present on the altar, but alive: He is no longer subject to humiliation and pain. He is in the triumphant glory of His Resurrection and His Ascension. The Sacrifice, the immolation of our selfishness, the Cross, the humiliation, are now *for us,* His members.

Furthermore, the proper grace of the Sacrament of the Eucharist is that of *an increase of charity,* which, on the one hand, purifies the soul from its former self-centeredness, and, on the other, kindles the fire of love for others and the flame of zeal, and develops the sense of devotion to the whole Mystical Body.

Moreover, the whole Church is present at each Mass, offering the Sacrifice of Christ and offering itself with that Sacrifice: the Church in Heaven—"Communicantes"—the Church on earth, the whole Mystical Body. The Mass is the Sacrifice of the Whole Christ, offering Himself to the Father, through the Holy Spirit; it is the Sacrifice of the Head and of His members who participate in His Charity.

O Jesus, our Redeemer, when, at the Last Supper, You had just celebrated the world's first Mass, You offered up Your great prayer for unity: "For them do I pray . . . that they all may be one" (John, XVIII, 20, 21). In doing so, it was surely Your intention to teach us the profound meaning of the Eucharistic Sacrifice; to show us the dispositions we should bring to our participation in it; and to reveal Your great design of forming Your Mystical Body through the Sacrifice of the Mass which You were giving to Your Church. Is it not indeed the Mass which symbolizes and produces the unity of all Your members among themselves, in Your love?

---

1. "Pro totius mundi salute," as the priest says when offering the Chalice.

45. HIS EUCHARISTIC PRESENCE

*And behold, I am with you all days, even
to the consummation of the world.*
(Matt., XXVIII, 20)

With the Blessed Eucharist, it is no longer created gifts alone
which are given to our souls: it is Our Lord Jesus Christ Himself
Who comes into our souls, giving Himself to us. It is no longer
grace alone, but the Author of Grace Himself. It is the Head Who
comes to form, constitute and develop His Mystical Body through
His union with His members.

1. *A presence*

Love desires the presence of the beloved, and to be separated
is a great trial for those who love one another. On the eve of His
departure from His beloved Apostles, the Divine Master deigned
to feel in His Heart the sorrow which those suffer who are leaving
their dear ones. He had an ardent desire to return to His Father;
but He also wished to remain among His own on earth. His love
found a way to reconcile these apparently contradictory desires:
He instituted the Holy Eucharist, which would enable Him to
remain with those He loved on earth. Through this Sacrament,
He would continue to live among them "all days," to console them
always with His Presence. He would receive their visits, would
enlighten and sustain them, would draw them together and unite
them in a unity with Himself.

The soul which loves Christ feels also an intense need of His
Real Presence. It finds its happiness in being with Him, in being
near to His Living Presence in the tabernacle, in remaining—
like Magdalen—for long periods of silent worship at His Feet.
Such a soul has no need of words: it kneels in silence, happy to be
in His Presence, happy to feel itself engulfed and entranced by
the reality of the Presence of its Divine Master. He is there: the
soul is content with this, and desires nothing more. Having Him,
it has all. His presence is fullness and complete satisfaction.

But there are two ways of enjoying this Presence. In the first,
the soul is spiritually self-centered, and forfeits an enrichment of
life. It is concerned with itself only, and seeks its personal consolation for itself alone. The second way is that of a *member* who
seeks, through this contact in faith with Christ, the means of
living more intensely his life of membership, so that he may give
himself more perfectly to Christ and to His brethren.

2. An exchange and a community

"And all my things are thine, and thine are mine" (*John*, XVII, 10). These words from the prayer of Jesus to His Father, can be regarded as addressed by Him to every soul in the state of grace; and they take on their full meaning for such souls, in the Blessed Eucharist.

"All my things are thine" . . . "Through My Holy Eucharist, I give you all that I have, all that I possess, and all that I am. *All that I have:* My grace, My light, My strength, My merits, My holiness, My Blood, My Soul. *All that I am:* I, the Son, come into your soul, with the Father and the Holy Spirit, in order to introduce you more and more profoundly with each of My Eucharistic visits, in our Divine Family; I, the Head of the Mystical Body, come to incorporate you daily more and more into the life of My Body.

"To love is to enjoy together a shared happiness. It is to this community of goods, of life and of happiness that I am calling you. All these I desire to possess in common with you and with each one of your brethren—with all of you, gathered into one family. For, if I am calling you to receive My gifts, it is not in order that you may enjoy them selfishly, but that you may share their possession with Your brethren.

"To love is to desire the happiness of the beloved, and his perfection in its full plenitude. It is this happiness and this perfection of your being that I seek in giving Myself to you and to your brethren, and also in helping you to give yourselves one to another."

The soul is, as it were, annihilated before such riches and such a wealth of love. It feels that it can but receive the outpouring of these gifts of Christ, and open itself wide to them. "How, Lord, can I dare to say in return: *and all my things are thine?* I have nothing but my misery and my sins. All in me that is worthy of being offered to You, has already come from You. This very love which urges me to make a full return to You, has been kindled in me by You. I know my own powerlessness. And yet, I desire intensely to prove my good will and my love."

Jesus answers: "It is your good will I expect from you; it is for your love that I ask. It is yourself I seek, with all your misery and all your nothingness, because I love you for all that I can give you and make of you. It is your state of grace that I love, because it is this state which makes you a member of My Body, and through which I can develop My life of sonship in you, can use you as the channel of My action, and can make My love shine forth for the glory of My Father and for the redemption of all your brethren. For you do not come alone before me; you are united with the other members of My Mystical Body, and I see you in My Church."

O Jesus, my Savior, was it not still self-centeredness which made me discouraged by the feeling of my personal impotence? I am strong with all Your strength, with the strength of Your Church. And this is indeed a source of profound peace to me. "O Lord Jesus Christ, Who said to Your Apostles: Peace I leave you, My Peace I give unto you: look not upon my sins but on the faith of Your Church; and deign to grant her that peace which is agreeable to Your will: Who lives and reigns God, world without end." (First Prayer for Holy Communion, in the Canon of the Mass).

46. HIS BODY, HIS BLOOD, HIS SOUL

> *. . . and the bread that I will give is my flesh, for the life of the world.*
>
> (John, VI, 52)

The Blessed Eucharist is the center of the whole sacramental order. While Baptism incorporates us in Christ, it does not do so directly, as of itself, but by reason of its connection with the Blessed Eucharist, which alone is the source itself of life, because it contains Him Who said: "I am the Life."

1. *The purpose of the Blessed Eucharist*

The purpose of the Blessed Eucharist is to communicate to our souls the very life of Jesus Christ, in order to make us "other Christs." But what is this life of Christ which the Blessed Eucharist gives us? The life of His now glorified Humanity—the life of the Victim Who was immolated on Calvary, and so entered into the glory of the Father. But that is not all. Jesus has willed to unite us, not only with His Sacred Humanity, but, through that Humanity, with His Divine Life.

Jesus has said: "As the living Father hath sent me and I live by the Father; so he that eateth me, the same also shall live by me." (*John*, VI, 18). These words are rich in light, and we must ponder them well. Jesus is not just laying down two terms of comparison: on the one hand, the Son living by the Father; on the other, the communicant living by Jesus. The two terms are joined together by the intrinsic link of the Person of Jesus Christ. "He that eateth" the Eucharistic Christ, will live, through Christ, by virtue of that same life in which Christ lives "by the Father." This life that has been given in fullness to the Sacred Humanity of Christ, the life which comes from the Father to the Son, was that Life which was eternally in the bosom of the Father, the original source of the Divine Life, and which the Father eternally communicates to His Son. And it is this life which we receive in Holy Communion: the very life of the Son. We are called to participate in the life of the Son, in order that, in Him and through Him, we may become other sons of the Father. It is Christ's wish, therefore, that we should contemplate and understand this connection between the Blessed Eucharist and the mystery of His Eternal Generation as Son of God.

But it is possible to conceive this life of sonship through the Holy Eucharist, only within the Mystical Body: first, because it is as Son of God that Jesus Christ has become the Head of the Mystical Body; again, because it is only through incorporation in the Only Son of God, that we become sons of God; finally, because the Blessed Eucharist is the nourishment, the center and the bond of the Mystical Body. And, therefore, this life which the Blessed Eucharist communicates to us, is the life which the Christ-Head possesses in order to communicate it to His members, and to establish between Himself, the Head of the Body, and His members, the closest possible union, It is this union which makes His members live by virtue of His life, and which incorporates them together in His Mystical Body through the life which goes out from Him as the Head.

2. *The means*

The means by which the Blessed Eucharist exercises this life-giving action in the soul, is none other than the union which it establishes between the soul of the communicant and Jesus Christ: the spiritual union through the sacramental union.

Let us consider well the implications of that beautiful word: *to communicate.*

To communicate means, in the first place, to communicate in the Body and Blood of Jesus Christ—in His Sacred Flesh, immolated for the salvation of the world; but it also implies communication in His Mystical Body, in the life of His Church, in the Whole Christ.

To communicate means also to communicate in the Soul and in the very Heart of the Divine Victim, and therefore in the dispositions of that Soul and in the sentiments which filled the Heart of Jesus, in His life of charity when He was offering His Supreme Sacrifice for the salvation of the world; those sentiments and dispositions which are still His when He comes to make us share them through the communication of His Eucharistic mystery.

Finally, *to communicate* means to communicate in the sanctifying and transforming action which the Sacred Humanity of Christ exercises within us during those blessed moments when, as communicants, we possess Him in our souls. It is not we who sanctify ourselves: it is the Sacred Humanity of Christ Which sanctifies us. Those blessed moments after Communion are not, therefore, a time for anxiety, for multiplying words, for reciting vocal prayers, for becoming preoccupied with minor intentions; they are the moments for uniting ourselves with the sanctifying action of the Divine Host of our soul. Through faith, we must enter into direct and intimate contact with His Divinity and His Humanity. With a will free from all obstacles, we must offer ourselves to the embrace of His love, so that He may have full liberty to act within us and to introduce us into the secrets of His Soul.

3. *The manner*

The manner in which the Blessed Eucharist becomes the vital nourishment of our souls, is an action of transformation through assimilation, whereby the soul of the communicant is progressively changed in Jesus, to the point where all that is within it—thoughts, desires, intentions, sentiments—tend to become fully conformed to the thoughts, desires, intentions and sentiments of Christ.

Here is indeed a mysterious application of the law of assimilation, according to which it is the stronger, the more energetic, the more living, which masters the weaker. The fire devours the wood, and changes into fire the metal cast into the furnace. So, too, with the fire of the Blessed Eucharist: in that Sacrament, it is not Our Lord Who is clothed with our weakness; we bring to Him those weaknesses, as so much dust to be cast into the furnace of His Sacred Heart, that they may be consumed in the fire of His Love. It is not we who change Christ into our substance: it is we ourselves who become participators of His perfections and of His virtues. It is He, the Head, Who changes His members in Himself, Who gives to them an increase of His life, Who unites them one with another by His charity. In Him, "In Christo," they are able to love one another.

If we are to submit to this law of assimilation, we must, therefore, forget ourselves more and more. We must not seek, through unconscious selfishness and a misunderstanding of this mystery of love, to narrow Christ within the limits of ourselves, our own personal life, our own preoccupations. On the contrary, indeed, the action of this mystery of love is to make us penetrate more deeply into the life of Christ, in order that we may be associated with His Redemptive Mission, may taste the fruits of the Redemption, and may be led, united together in Him, to the Father through the Holy Spirit.

"O God, Who in this wonderful Sacrament, has left us a memorial of Your Passion, grant us the grace so to reverence the Sacred Mysteries of Your Body and Blood that we may always feel within us the fruits of Your Redemption" (Prayer of the *Tantum ergo*).

47. HIS LIFE OF SONSHIP

> But as many as received him, he gave them power to be made the sons of God, to them that believe in His name.
>
> (John, I, 12)

The expression: *child of God,* conveys very well our dependence on our Father in Heaven and our littleness in His sight. The title, *adopted son of God,* emphasizes the quality of Christian virility, since it signifies a magnificent reality—our participation in the Sonship of Christ, the Only Son of the Father.

1. *Our filiation*

To be a son, is to be incorporated in the Son, not directly in the Word—because there is only one hypostatic union, which is incommunicable—but in Christ's Human Nature, and, through that Nature, in the whole Person of Christ. We thus receive from the Incarnate Word, not our natural birth, but our birth to sonship in grace, and our supernatural activity.

Extremely intimate and indissoluble bonds link, therefore,

the adoptive filiation of Christians with the Mystical Body of Christ. They are sons because they are members. They are "all sons in the Son,"[1] and, furthermore, the more they are members of the Son, the more are they sons in Him.

To be sons, therefore, is to have within us the life of the Son, that we may participate in it. To have within us the life of the Son, we must have received that life through Baptism, which incorporates us in Christ, and through faith, which opens our souls to the gift of Christ, and through faith, which opens our souls to the gift of Christ's life. He gave "power to be made the sons of God" to all those who had received Him through faith.

Finally, to be a son is to imitate, reproduce and continue the life of the Son, by enabling Christ to live His life in us through a progressive assimilation to His Divine Sonship. To understand more clearly how deeply our adoptive filiation is plunged in Christ, we must view the matter, not from the earthly standpoint, but from the heavenly. In His final prayer to His Father, Our Lord invited us to contemplate the mystery of His eternal Sonship, so that we might trace in it the model and the source of our filial life. At the same time, the Divine Master cast an abundance of light on the whole meaning of the Mystical Body. "That they all may be one, as thou, Father, in me, and I in thee." (*John*, XVII, 11 to 21).

Saint Thomas, that faithful echo of Scripture and of Tradition, points out that there is a resemblance between the eternal Filiation of the Word and our own adoptive filiation; a certain participation in, and assimilation to, the natural Son.[2]

2. *How the Filiation of Christ differs from ours*

There are, of course, infinite differences between our adoptive filiation, and Christ's eternal Filiation.

In the first place, the Word is the Son of God *by nature*. He receives from the Father the Divine Nature, by right and in Its full plenitude, through a necessary generation due to the infinite Perfection of the Divine Nature and to the infinite Love of the

---

1. This is the title of some remarkable articles written by the eminent theologian, Father Mersch, *Filii in Filio*. (*La Nouvelle Revue théologique*, 1936).

2. "The adoptive sons are formed in the likeness of the natural Son" (III, q. 39, a. 8, ad 3). "The adoptive filiation is a certain participated likeness to the natural filiation of the Word." (III, 2, 3, a. 5, ad 2). "By the act of adoption, a resemblance to the natural filiation is given to the soul." (III, q. 45, a. 4). "We are made sons of God through assiliation to the natural son, according to Rom., VIII, 29." (*Gent.*, IV, 24, 1).

Father, Who willed to communicate His infinite Perfection. On the other hand, we are the sons of God by adoption, *through a grace* of His Mercy: "For of His own will hath he begotten us" (*James*, I, 18). We become sons, but without having the *natural right* to sonship.

Finally, from the point of view of *unity*, it is not the Holy Ghost Who unites the Son with the Father in the bosom of the Holy Trinity. The Holy Ghost is the fruit of the mutual love of the Father and the Son, and the consummation of Their unity. He intervenes in the extension of the natural filiation of the Word to the Humanity of Christ. For our part, it is through the Holy Ghost that we are united to the Father in the Son.[1]

3. *The resemblances*

The eternal filiation of the Word is the model and the examplary cause of our filiation. How can one dare to speak of resemblance in such a context? The words of Jesus throw light on the matter: it is the unity of the Son with the Father which our adoptive filiation should reproduce and copy.

The unity of the Son with the Father is a *unity of nature* in the Divine Nature. For our part, we must strive for *a union of grace and of charity* with the Father, but in the Son and through the Holy Ghost. As the Son is One with the Father, by nature, so we must, in the Son, become sons with Him, and must seek by grace a union with the Father in the Holy Ghost. Our souls are dazzled with the mighty perspectives of this sublime vocation: they shrink from the conviction that all this is indeed a reality. We had glimpsed a splendid mystery of unity and of love, when Christ said to us: "I and the Father are One." And the fundamental attitude of Christ's humanity towards His Father, during

---

1. In the fourth century, St. Athanasius luminously explained this great difference between the Son by nature and the sons by adoption: "It is through the grace of the Holy Ghost that it is given to us to be in God and He in us . . . We are not, therefore, in the Father in the same manner as the Son is in the Father; for it is not through the necessary intervention of the Holy Ghost that the Son is in the Father and He does not receive the Holy Ghost. Rather, it is He Who dispenses the Holy Ghost to others. And it is not the Holy Ghost Who unites the Son with the Father, but the Holy Ghost Who receives from the Son. The Son Himself is in the Father, as the Father's Word and the Glory of the Father; while we, without the Holy Ghost, are strangers to God and remote from Him. It is through the participation of the Holy Ghost that we are united with the Divinity, in such a way that our being in the Father is not a right we possess ourselves, but comes from the Holy Ghost dwelling with us." (Saint Athanasius: *Third Discourse against the Arians*, cited by Bouyer: "L'Incarnation et l'Eglise corps du Christ dans la théologie de St. Athanase, p. 116).

His earthly life—His filial submission, His generous self-renunciation, His total oblation to the Father—had revealed to us the true Son in His union with the Father. And, behold, our souls are called to contemplate this mystery as the ideal of their own life; nay more, it is in this very mystery that our adoptive filiation causes us to participate!

When studying the sense in which our adoptive filiation bears a certain resemblance to the eternal Filiation of the Word, Saint Thomas writes: "The creature is made like to the Word of God, according to the pattern of the very unity which the Word has with the Father" (II, q. 23, a. 3).

Having taken possession of us by Baptism, Christ unites us with Himself to make us participate in His life of grace and in all His gifts, which it pleases Him to give us; in His personal qualities; in His Filiation; and He assimilates us to Himself according to His own eternal Filiation. Thus associated with His eternal Filiation, we are therefore joined in Him with the Father, through the Holy Spirit. It is to the Father of Jesus, become our Father in Him, that we are united, because we are the members of Him Who is the Son.

O Jesus, adorable Son of the Father, we thank You for having given us the incomparable gift of Your most personal riches, communicated to our souls. We thank You, also, for having willed, through Your merciful grace, to draw all the members of Your Mystical Body into the rapture of Your filial love for God, Your Father. Come unto us, that in You we may be one among ourselves, in the bosom of Your Church, in the unity of Your Spirit of Sonship; come and live in us Your filial life, for the glory of the Father and for the Redemption of souls, so that in You we may all form but one Christ—the Whole Christ.

48. IN THE LIFE OF THE HOLY TRINITY

And my Father will love him; and we will come to him and will make our abode with him.

(John, XIV, 23)

At the same time as he becomes a member of the Son, and because of this incorporation in Jesus, the baptized person is adopted by the Holy Trinity. He enters into the family of God, and participates in the life of the Divine Family.

1. *A real Presence*

At the very moment when the water is poured on the forehead of the baptized and the sacramental words are spoken, Our Lord's promise is literally fulfilled.

We will come to him. This is a new Presence of the Holy Trinity—new, not on the part of God, Who is Immutable, but because new relations are established between the soul in grace and the intimate life of God: the Presence of the Three Divine Persons.

My Father will love him. This Presence is not cold, abstract, colorless, but a loving Presence. Together, in the same movement, the Three Divine Persons love the regenerated soul, by their Spirit of Love, the Holy Ghost.

We will make our abode with Him. This Presence is not passing or intermittent, but remains stable and permanent as long as the soul itself continues in the conditions necessary to make it a worthy dwelling for the Divine Host.

When, in the light of faith, the soul begins to know this gift of God, all its relations with the Holy Trinity are illuminated by this knowledge. Thus, therefore, in order to find God, the soul will no longer be content to seek Him outside itself and remote from it, in a nature which speaks to it unceasingly of its Creator; but it will seek within its own depths to find God in itself, living His life in the soul. To be called to the honor of being able to converse with God and know Him so intimately; to be able to approach, in the secret recesses of his soul, Him Who rules by His Sovereign Majesty all the vastness of the universe; to be able to adore Him, pray to Him, thank Him in the "temple" wherein He deigns to take up His abode; to know that he is enveloped and penetrated with an infinite love; to have the right to warm his soul at this ever burning fire of love, whenever he chooses to do so—such are some of the privileges enjoyed by the baptized person.

2. *The entry into the Divine Family*

The Presence and Indwelling of the Three Divine Persons are a first form of the gift of the Holy Trinity to the soul. There is a second form which is intimately connected with the first: the union with the Blessed Trinity, the communication in the life of the Three Divine Persons. The Presence and Indwelling exist for this union. "That they all may be one, as thou, Father, in me, and I in thee; that they also may be one in us" (*John*, XVII, 21).

These words of Christ free the soul from three misapprehensions to which it is exposed at this stage of its spiritual life:

1) The illusion that the soul is the *container* and God the contained. Here, above all, the imagination can lead us wildly astray. To imagine that our soul contains the Blessed Trinity within itself as in a tabernacle, is to contend that the Infinite can be limited—which is, of course, a contradiction in terms. This is to reduce the idea of God to the limits of our own imagination. How foolish it is to suppose that the soul could impose on the Infinite, the restrictions of its individuality! The reality is very much the opposite: it is God Who contains the soul ... "In ipso vivimus, movemur et sumus" ... "For in Him we live and move and are" (*Acts*, XVII, 28). When it has been laid bare to the Infinite, the soul is able to rise up eagerly towards Him, to adore the Divine Transcendence. Considered from the standpoint of the object towards which it is orientated, grace leads finally to God such as He is in Himself—to each One of the Three Divine Persons.

2) The second illusion is for the soul to imagine that it could itself be the *term*, as if the coming of the Divine Persons should find its complete purpose by the mere fact of such indwelling. Here, again, the divine order is reversed; for God alone is the Term, the Supreme End (*Finis Ultimus*). If the Father comes of Himself, and the Son and the Holy Ghost are sent into the soul, it is to take possession of that soul, to draw it to Themselves, to adopt it—in other words, to introduce it into the Life of the Blessed Trinity and into the Divine Family.

3) At the same time, the soul discovers that its divinization is not effected at a distance from God, apart from the society of the Blessed Trinity—that is, *ad extra;* but is effected *within*, through an introduction into the bosom of the Divine Family. "*In nobis*" ... "In us." God's purpose in creating us is to draw us to Himself, to attach us to Him, "in communion" with His Holy Trinity.

But here again, it is impossible to consider all this as related merely to the *individual* soul. In Christ's conception, it is His Mystical Body which ceaselessly intervenes. "That they *all* may be *one* ... in us," was His prayer. *May be one,* most certainly, in the great reunion in Heaven; but these words of Christ are followed by others which clearly indicate that this entry into the Life of the Divine Family is not postponed to the Hereafter, but is commenced *here on earth.* For Christ adds: "that they also may be one in us; that (i.e. *so that*) the world may believe . . ." (*John*, XVII, 21). It is the sight of the unity of Christians which will convert the world, but of a unity founded on the pattern of the unity of the Father and the Son in the Blessed Trinity . . . "That they may be one, *as Thou, Father, in me and I in thee*" . . . while also being a unity founded on participation in the unity of the Divine Family . . . "that they also may be one *in us*." Herein is the whole mystery of the Church.

O Blessed Trinity, grant that we may taste, in a prayer wholly illuminated by Your Presence, the happiness of living in one family with you. Help us to understand that, even in the midst of our humdrum daily occupations and in the discharge of the duties of our state, our master concern should be to live with Your Divine Family; in order that, at every moment, we may be ready to extend to our relations with our brethren, that fraternal charity which the Holy Ghost communicates to our souls, and which is nothing less than the perfect blossoming of the family spirit.

49. HIS FATHER

I ascend to my Father and to your Father.
(John, XX, 17)

When we seek God and desire to unite ourselves with Him, we encounter the Divine Nature. But this Divine Nature exists only in the Divine Persons; and, beyond this barrier, there is the mystery of the intimate Life of God, the Life of the Blessed Trinity. The Father dwells there in a light which is not accessible to His poor creatures, no one of whom can of himself attain to Him. But the Son has come, and all is changed.

1. *Through Jesus, we have access to the Father*

Without the Revelation of Christ, Who is One of the Three, we would never have known the Father or the other two Persons of the Blessed Trinity.

Without the Redemption, we would never have been permitted to enter into relationship with each of the Three Divine Persons. We would have remained outside the Divine Family. We could have known, of course, through the teaching of Jesus, that God is One in Three Persons; but this sublime mystery would have remained cold and abstract for us, and would not have become a living, personal reality in our lives. We would have received it, through faith, as indeed a very lofty truth; but this Truth would not have become for us a Life.

What Christ willed was none other than to bring life to us through a participation in Him Who is "the Life"; and, that, in Him, we should participate in the Divine Life Itself, in the Life of the Three Divine Persons, in the possession of All and of Each One of Them.

Thus, we possess the Father of Jesus. Through Christ and in Christ, "we have access . . . to the Father" (*Ephes.*, II, 18). We know, by faith, what the Father is in Himself, in the bosom of the Trinity: the eternally springing Source of the Divine Life. We can love and adore Him as the Father, as the Principle of the Blessed Trinity, as the Father of Jesus. Because our minds are lifted up to Him, we gain a better understanding, within the limits of our finite intelligence, of the mystery of the unity of Life in the Divine Family. We have the right to keep in contact with Him Who is at the origin of the whole Life of the Trinity. We are called to enjoy His Presence, to enjoy His Person, to rejoice in the Infinite Love which carries Him towards the Father and makes Him give Himself to the Father. We are called to honor the Father through His Son, in the mystery of His Paternity. In enjoying this possession of the Father, we will in no way tend to separate Him from the other Divine Persons, such separation being absolutely impossible. On the contrary, indeed, since it is as Father that we know and love Him, He Himself will lead us to the knowledge and love of the other Two Persons, Whose Principle He is: the Principle of His Son, and the Co-Principle, with His Son, of the Holy Ghost.

To learn to know the Father, is to learn to know the Son. Jesus has said: "No man can come to me, except the Father, who hath sent me, draw him." (*John*, VI, 44). That the Mystery of the Trinity may become for us Light and Life, we must contemplate long and often, the Mystery of the Paternity of the First Person.

2. *In Christ and with Christ, we can possess and love the Father as our Father*

It is not by ourselves and of ourselves, that we possess the Father: it is with Jesus, in Jesus, and through His Holy Spirit. It is Jesus Who gives us the Father, that with Him we may possess this Infinite Good. He wishes us to communicate in this very unity with His Father, and not only in the created qualities which adorn His Sacred Humanity. It is with His Divine Filiation that He associates us. On the one hand, it is in Him, the Son, that we receive the life which is given to Him in its plenitude by the Father; on the other hand, He carries us with Him in the upsurge of filial love and of total abandonment which bears Him to the Father.

There is, undoubtedly, nothing more moving or worthy of our loving gratitude and generous response, than this ineffable gift of the Father which is given to us by Christ; and wherein we participate in His unity with His Father. Jesus seems to say to us: "I could not give you a more profound share in My own intimate Life. I could not offer you a greater proof of My love than by giving you My Father, and by making you adhere to Him through My Spirit. I was not content that I alone should enjoy the Presence and the Infinite Tenderness of the Father. Together, we shall all enjoy Him. Together, we shall love the Father and shall remain united with Him, adhering to Him. Together we shall possess Him." Thus, the family community which the Divine Savior came to found, is established in a unity of unshakable faith: every son in the same Son, because all have the same Father.

Here we have indeed the perfection of that dual possession, of that possession in common with the Son, wherein is our Redemption. To possess with Him; to possess in common; to both possess the same life, the same riches; to enjoy together the same treasure—such is the master law of friendship and of love, through which two persons are brought together, are united, and merged so as to be no longer two, but one.

Jesus has formulated this law for us all—for the members of His Mystical Body. He has willed that all that is His should be ours, so that all that is good in us should be given to Him in return, and should become His. By right of nature, the Father is His and His alone. But He gave us the Father, in order that, through the grace of Redemption, we also could become the members of the Son, and could love His Father, with Him, as our Father.

O Father, Who dwells in Light inaccessible, Father of Infinite Majesty, Father Whom so many Christians dare to approach only with fear and trembling, You are ours, You belong to us. We taste that happiness with Jesus. According to the degree of our union with Him and the intensity of our lives as His members, Jesus reveals to us what You are and how much

*You have loved us, even to giving us Your Son. Therefore, an
immense and irresistible paean of gratitude rises from our hearts
to You, O Father, Author of all the gifts in the Supreme Gift,
Your Blessed Son. Our soul has now no other desire than to be,
like Your Son, a permanent oblation to Your adorable Person,
through the Holy Ghost.*

50. HIS HOLY SPIRIT

> *. . . But if I go, I will send him to you . . .
> he shall receive of mine and shall show
> it to you.*
>
> (John, XVI, 7, 14)

In sending us the Holy Ghost, His Spirit, Jesus has made us
an incomparable gift. He has not sent His Paraclete once only, on
a solemn day of our Pentecost, the day of our Baptism and the
day of our Confirmation. For the member of the Mystical Body,
life is a continual Pentecost.

1. *Why could Jesus claim that the Holy Ghost is His Spirit?*

In the first place, because, *as the Divine Word,* Jesus is,
together with the Father, the Principle of the Holy Ghost, Who
proceeds from the mutual love of the Father and the Son.

Furthermore, because, *as Man,* Jesus has been filled with
the Holy Ghost. His Sacred Humanity has been taken over by
the plenitude of the Spirit, and was led by the Spirit in all its
aspirations and activities, through every facet of Christ's Apostolic Ministry.

Finally, because, *as Head,* Our Lord leads His Mystical
Body by the Holy Ghost. It is to the Christ-Head that the mission
has been confided of organizing the work of our salvation, and of
leading all men, in unity, towards the true purpose of their lives
—union with God.

Now, Jesus accomplishes all this work through the Holy
Ghost. He sends the Holy Ghost, and dispenses the graces and
gifts of the Holy Ghost, for the animation of His whole Mystical
Body. He is the depository of those gifts and graces. It is He Who
communicates and distributes the riches of the Spirit to each
member and to the whole Church.

2. *The possession in common of the Holy Ghost*

The Father and the Son send the Holy Ghost to the soul, that the soul may enjoy Him. The soul enjoys Him for what He is in Himself—the Bond of Love between the Father and the Son. It is He Who comes to take possession of the soul, in order to introduce it into the life of Light and Love which is the Life of the Blessed Trinity.

The soul enjoys the Holy Ghost for all the light which He pours out upon it. It looks to Him for that light, in order to be directed in all its ways, in order to remain always in the paths of righteousness, and in order to enter more profoundly into the Light of God.

The soul enjoys the Holy Ghost for all the love which He kindles within it, and which makes it participate in the very Love with which God loves Himself and with which He loves mankind.

But, above all, what fills the soul with peace and joy, is that this Holy Spirit is the Spirit of Jesus; that it possesses this Spirit in common with Jesus and with the other members of His Mystical Body.

With Jesus: let us understand the phrase accurately. It implies possession in common by Jesus and the soul, but with the vast difference which exists between the possession of one who gives, and the possession of one who receives; between the Person Who possesses as a *right*, and the person who possesses as a *grace*. It would be even more exact to say that the Christian who is faithful and obedient to the action of the Holy Ghost, is possessed by the Spirit of Jesus. It is this possession by the Spirit which we admire in the souls of the Saints, just as we admire it, throughout the Gospel story, in the actions and undertakings of the Man-God. "Then Jesus was led by the Spirit . . ." (*Matt.*, IV, 1).

But it is quite true to say that it is the same Spirit Who is in Jesus and in the members of His Mystical Body. They live by the same life as their Head. When communicating His Spirit, Jesus does not divide what He possesses in plenitude: He causes the soul to enter into the participation of this Supreme Good.

The Holy Ghost, we have said, is possessed by the soul in common *with the other members of the Mystical Body*. It is this, indeed, which, rising superior to all divisions of races and of peoples and sweeping together all space and all time, forms the profound unity of the Mystical Body. When the Christian who believes intensely in the Holy Ghost, meditates on the Epistles of

Saint Paul, the Confessions of Saint Augustine, the spiritual history of the Saints in every age, he realizes that it is the same experience which he finds, in varying qualities, in these imitators of Christ; and that, with all the difference of degree consequent on their heroic sanctity, it is the same experience which he perceives in his own soul. When, in darkest pagandom, missionaries have had the joy of giving Baptism to fervent catechumens, it is the same effects of peace, joy, charity, humility and the spirit of sacrifice, which they discern in these souls. The Apostle has indicated the profound reason of these mysterious phenomena: under "the diversities of grace . . . of ministries . . . of operations" (1 Cor., XII, 4-6), it is the same Spirit, the Spirit of Christ, Who communicates to the members of the Body, the same Life—the life of the Head. The Spirit is given to them, in order that they may be united with the other members, to form with them the temple wherein God takes up His abode: "In whom you also are built together into an habitation of God in the Spirit" (Ephes., II, 22)—that is to say, the Christian Community.

O Jesus, our Head, increase our faith in the Presence and in the action of Your Divine Spirit in the depths of our souls and of those of our brethren. "Send forth Your Spirit, and He will renew the face of the earth." Give to the members of Your Mystical Body a vivid appreciation of the power they can exercise over the world, if they sincerely believe in the transforming strength of Your Divine Spirit dwelling within them.

51. HIS MOTHER

Behold thy mother.
(John, XIX, 27)

The Divine Redeemer has not only restored the possibility of our intimate relations with God, but has willed to render them easy, agreeable and attractive, by making them family relationships. He had given us His Father; but He had yet another gift to bestow—a gift very near and dear to our hearts—the gift of His Mother. On the threshold of the Divine Family into which He was introducing the members of His Body, He willed that there should be the tenderness of a Mother to welcome them—the tenderness of His own Mother.

First phase: the origin and foundation of the spiritual maternity of Mary

It is in Mary's connection with the Mystery of the Incarnation that her spiritual maternity in relation to us finds its origin and foundation. The source of this maternity is in the generous and unreserved *Fiat* which she gave to the Angel of the Annunciation, who had come to ask her consent to God's wish that she should become the Mother of His Son. In the plan of God, the salvation of the world had been made dependent on Mary's decision at that moment. Her intervention in the redemptive Incarnation was not solely indirect: she not only consented, she *willed. Fiat.* And she willed with a clear understanding of the object and the meaning of the mission which was being confided to her. She had long meditated the Scriptures, and had penetrated the depths of the Prophecies in the light of the very special graces given to her. What was being asked of her was not only that she should conceive and bear the Man-God, Who would be a man among men, though the greatest of all men; it was that she should become the Mother of the Savior of mankind, the Mother of the Redeemer. She understood that this Son was being given to her for us, for the others, for the Redemption of the human race.

In that moment of her decision, was she conscious of all of us individually? We have no authority for thinking so. But why linger on this hypothesis? How much more illuminating is our certainty that, in her great moment, the human race became but *one* for Mary; that she saw all men gathered together into a new People of God, reconciled with the Most High through a New Alliance, saved in solidarity with Him Who was to become her Son. To this plan, Mary did not give a timid, embarrassed, almost shrinking consent, as the scene has been painted for us by the great artists who sought to interpret her humility. She gave herself entirely by that act of will and of love, which formally constitutes her Maternity and in which her whole person is expressed. She willed to become our Mother, in becoming the Mother of Christ the Savior.

Second phase: the promulgation on Calvary. Mary is appointed to be our Mother

"Now, there stood by the cross of Jesus, his mother . . ." (*John*, XIX, 25). She united herself with her Son's immolation, sharing in that oblation of love—in the total giving of His life which Christ accomplished for the Redemption of the world. The context of this union was not that of the private relations between a son and a mother. On the Cross, Christ exercised His public function of Mediator of the New Alliance—the essential act of His Supreme Priesthood. In that hour, the Church was created. Then, the agonizing Christ found the strength to utter those overwhelming words: "Behold thy mother." He said them to John, who, at the foot of the Cross, represented all men whom Christ loves—all of us of His Mystical Body.

At the Incarnation, Mary gives Jesus to us. On Calvary, it is Jesus Christ Who gave us His Mother. It is He Who, acting as the One Mediator, fixed the new plan of the Redemption. As Master, He assigned to His Mother a place near to Him, and still of a secondary order subordinated to Him; but this place, in relation to all mankind, is exceptional, all-powerful, unique. For she is appointed, by the Head Himself, to be the Mother of the Whole Christ. She has been made our Mother, and this in virtue of her function as Co-redemptrix.

Third phase: the actual exercise of the Maternity of Mary

To make all men participate, in the most intimate possible manner, in the life of Him Who is at once her Son and the Son of the Father—such was to be henceforward the purpose of Mary's maternal mission. This purpose, then, is to make the Whole Christ's grow to His full stature, to increase the number of the sons of God, and to nourish the life of grace and of charity within them.

The *means* by which Mary exercises her maternity towards us at all times, are of different kinds: her prayer, the offering up of her past sufferings, the radiation of her sweet presence. But there is one act which contains them all. As at the Annunciation—but now for each of the members and for the Whole Mystical Body—Mary exercises *an effective action of Her maternal will.* From the place that has been assigned in the name of God to her by her Son, she intervenes as a Mother, she dispenses as a Mother. In the light of the Word, which is now the very element in which she lives, she knows the needs of each of her children, she presents them to her Son, and, with Him, to the Father. She does all this with full submission to the Divine Will, but with all the tenderness, all the warmth of heart, all the compassion, all the urgency of supplication, which only a mother can command who desires, at all cost, the salvation and the holiness of her sons. Thus, on an efficacious act of Mary's operative will, the Holy Ghost works within the soul, giving it His graces, increasing sanctifying grace, inspiring virtue and actuating His own gifts bestowed on the soul.

Above all, what constitutes the power of Mary's maternal will over the Heart of God, is the fact that hers is a soul completely filled with graces, possessing the plenitude of the Holy Ghost, and enjoying ineffable relations with Each of the three Divine Persons. This is, indeed, her whole life. Now, it is this whole life which she enlists in her act of maternal will. So it is that, as a real Mother, it is not only life which Mary gives us: she gives us *her* life.

O Jesus, we thank You for having given us Your Mother to be our Mother. You have called us to share with You the incomparable joys of Your filial intimacy with Your Mother. She loves us with the same affection as she loves You. She brings the same love to the Whole Christ—to You, as Head; to us, as members. With You, we have the same Mother. Teach us to know, through Your Holy Spirit in the silence of prayer, the splendor of our Mother, her holiness, her beauty, her maternal tenderness, her exquisite purity of soul, her constant concern and her inexhaustible compassion for us.

52. THE GIFT OF GOD

If thou didst know the gift of God . . .
(John, IV, 10)

That one should dare to envisage a communion in the very life of God, would seem to be a gross impertinence and a kind of insult to the Divine Majesty and Transcendence. And yet, this is the most classic definition of sanctifying grace in the most authentic doctrine of the Church. How is it, therefore, that this definition remains purely abstract and a mere matter of words, for so many souls? If it has pleased the God of Infinite Mercy to give us this incomparable gift, do we glorify God by not adhering to His plan? And yet, on the other hand, how is the Majesty and Transcendence of God to be safeguarded?

1) When the soul enters into communion with the Father and the Son, through the Holy Ghost and in Christ, the disposi-

tions which animate it and the sentiments which take possession of it, plunge the soul into a state wherein it acquires, to a remarkable extent, the sense of the Divine Transcendence.

First of all, *in throwing itself wide to the Infinite, the soul feels intensely its own insignificance, feebleness and powerlessness.* It acquires, in that moment, a consciousness of its nothingness, more intense than could be given by years of meditation on the misery of men. Like Peter, glimpsing the Divinity of Jesus, the soul is tempted to cry out: "Depart from me, for I am a sinful man, O Lord."

In the light of God, it sees in itself nothing but darkness and corruption: reviewing its past, heavy with sin, infidelity and resistance to Love, it realizes with pain that it stands before God, holding out empty hands. There is no more efficacious and painful purification than the soul's conviction of the presence, nearness and possession of the Blessed Trinity, of the One God in three Divine Persons, Who calls the soul to come to Him and to unite itself with Him in love.

2) Furthermore, it is in this moment that *the soul realizes that the gift of God is an absolutely free gift.* Until then, it knew intellectually that, in the supernatural domain, it has no rights, and that everything in that domain is a gift of the Infinite Mercy. In practice, however, when it had to pass through trials of a purely spiritual kind, and found itself in a sad state of spiritual dryness, the soul would come near to reproaching God for allowing it to continue in its aridity, not always succeeding in curbing a kind of resentment and bitterness towards God on that account. And if, indeed, some light came to pierce the darkness of its spiritual exile, it seemed to the soul quite natural and in the ordinary course of events that God should give it this consolation. It had not yet understood that, in Christianity, all is given; "every best gift and every perfect gift is from above, coming down from the Father of lights" (*James,* I, 17). It had not understood what is meant by "the gift of God."

But now it is plunged in the life of God! It submits to the divine embrace in a passive manner, realizing that it can but throw itself wide to the gift of God, receive from Him and allow itself to be utterly possessed by Infinite Love. It remains silent, no longer daring to speak. It trembles at the thought that, by a disordered movement of its nature, it might see that Love departing from it. If, in the moment when the soul has the impression that it could reach out and take possession of God, were it to seek to do so of itself, then, indeed, it would very quickly learn to its confusion, that it has no right of itself to reach God at will, and that God hides Himself from the presumptuous. God will give Himself to the soul, when *He* wishes and in the manner which suits *His* own good pleasure. There is undoubtedly no other domain wherein the soul can acquire with greater intensity, the sense of the Divine Transcendence. "If thou didst know the gift of God . . ."

3) Finally, and perhaps supremely, it is in this moment that the soul becomes convinced that its whole ascension to God can be accomplished only by *Jesus Christ, in Jesus Christ* and *with Jesus Christ*. The soul knows that of itself it is powerless: that it is Christ Who has transformed all things within it.

It is He Who has raised up the soul to the level of the Divine Life, in order to introduce it into that Life; for it is by Him that this extraordinary grace has been merited for the soul, and is constantly applied and communicated to the soul.

It is He, Jesus, who, having incorporated the soul in Himself, associates it with His own life in His Mystical Body. It is in Him that the soul presents itself on the threshold of the Life of the Blessed Trinity: in Him, as one of His members, united with all the others, with all the Saints, with the whole Church—triumphant, militant and suffering—and, dominating all this union in Christ, united with Mary, the Mother of Jesus, become the Mother of the soul.

It is in Christ that the soul now dares to address itself to the Father, communicating in the prayer of the Son, in His oblation, in His filial love; and inspired by the Spirit of Jesus, Who teaches the soul to know the Father and the Son, and to speak to Them simply and with immense trust. The soul fears no longer. It feels that it is of the Divine Family; that it is a true son of the Father.

O Jesus, our Head, the more we are called to participate in Your riches and in Your splendor, the less we are tempted to glory in ourselves. The more we realize the generosity with which the Father has lavished all His gifts upon us, the more conscious we become that of ourselves we have nothing and that we have received all. But, in a special way, we then realize that the Father's supreme Gift—the Gift which is the irrefutable proof of His Infinite Love—is You Yourself, O adorable Savior, Who contain within Yourself, and are Yourself in Your own Person, the Plenitude of all riches.

CONCLUSION

53. IN A UNITY WITH ALL

> . . . that, being rooted and founded in
> charity, you may be able to comprehend,
> with all the saints, what is the breadth
> and length and height and depth; to know
> also the charity of Christ . . .
>
> (Ephes., III, 17, 18, 19)

If it is true that each member of the Mystical Body finds his
joy and his fullness in the possession of the riches of Christ, in
what way and to what extent could his personal happiness be
increased by the fact that he possesses all these riches in common
with the other members of the Body?

1. *The person*

In the Church, the Body of Christ, no conflict need be feared
between the person and the community. Each person is in the
service of the whole Body, to aid it to fulfill its mission—the
formation of the Whole Christ. On the other hand, the whole
Mystical Body is at the service of each person, to help him to
reach his supernatural destiny and to fulfill his vocation of
belonging to Christ.

The individual person is not in himself a self-sufficient being
shut within himself. Not only has he need of others to fill up his
deficiencies, even in the natural order, but he is essentially an
open being, because he is a spirit: open to God of Whom his
soul is the image; open also to his fellow men, with whom he
desires to be able to communicate in the order of knowledge
and of love, so as to enrich, improve and perfect himself. Furthermore, the individual person should enter into relations with
his fellows, in order to collaborate in the same collective task
demanded by the unity of the human species.

The natural plane gives us a glimpse of how things are
ordered on the supernatural plane. "God is faithful; by whom
we are called into the fellowship of His Son, Jesus Christ our
Lord" (1 *Cor.*, 1, 9). All are called to belong to Christ; all are
made for Him, to be the members of His Mystical Body. It is in

Christ that each person realizes himself in his personal vocation to membership. It is in Christ that he perfects himself, while forming, with the other members, the Whole Christ, and while sharing with them, in Christ, the life of the Blessed Trinity. The individual person ripens to perfection, only within the community of the Mystical Body.

"God . . . all in all." (1 *Cor.*, XV, 28). When Saint Paul wrote those words, he was envisaging the unity of the Mystical Body. God will be all for each person, but also *all in all, forming but one:* in other words, this unity of the Mystical Body will become a reality when all shall together possess the same Supreme Good, and participate together in the same life.

Now, it is here on earth that this eternal life begins. Here and now, therefore, the joy of the Christian should be to build, with all his brethren, the Kingdom of God. It is indeed true that this joy of the Christian soul is always mixed, during its earthly life, with a certain sorrow and often with immense sorrow; but the reason for this is none other than the sight of the great number of his brethren whom the Christian sees to have no taste for these higher joys.

2. *Charity for the other members*

This charity makes us seek the joy of tasting these pleasures in union with our brethren. To love the other members is not merely to give to them or even to give ourselves to them: it is to desire their essential good in the participation of the same Supreme Good, and their true happiness in communion with the same Source of Beatitude—God. It is to desire their full personal perfection, by helping them to cooperate in the collective task and to give themselves for their own part; so that, in union with all, they may contribute their personal share of collaboration in the formation of the Whole Christ. By thus giving themselves, they receive aid from the other members towards their perfection and the fulfillment of their personal vocation.

3. *Love of God*

Finally, it is our love for God Himself which demands that we should taste the joy of sharing with all the other members, the riches of Christ. For joy is the fruit of love.

Our true happiness should be a participation in the happiness of God. The Blessed Trinity finds Its intrinsic and sufficient happiness in Itself, and in Itself alone; but the Goodness and Mercy of the Heavenly Father have willed, by an absolutely free act of Love, to delight in the unity of the human family of mankind, in order to associate all men with the work of the creation; and in the unity of the Mystical Body, in order that they may become, in Christ, His cooperators in the work of the Redemption.

Our love of God demands our adherence to His whole plan, and our conformity with His entire wishes. Our joy should be derived from the joy of God. Charity, in us, is a participation in the same love with which God loves us and loves all men: therefore, if we wish to live by charity, we must find our joy in praying with the other members of the Mystical Body, in working with the others in the same work, and in rising up together into the Light and Charity of God.

O Jesus, Our Lord, You Who have willed to gather together in one body—Your Mystical Body—all our fellow men, grant that, even here in the midst of the trials of this world, we may together taste the happiness of sharing with You that life of Charity which will continue through all eternity.

CHAPTER TWO

IN A HORIZONTAL LINE:

The Relations of Christians, Members of the Mystical Body, Among Themselves and with all Others, According to the Unique and Universal Law of Charity

> *But, doing the truth in charity, we may in all things grow up in him who is the head, even Christ; from whom the whole body, being compacted and fitly joined together, by what every joint supplieth, according to the operation in the measure of every part, maketh increase of the body, unto the edifying of itself in charity.*
>
> (Ephes., IV, 15, 16)

THE UNIQUE AND UNIVERSAL LAW OF CHARITY

*The unique and universal law of charity governs and ani-
mates entirely the relations of the members of the community
among themselves and with other men. We must understand this
law, and all the demands it makes upon us.*

First, there are its ascetical *demands. The asceticism of
charity, like that of the other two theological virtues, is very
severe. Fundamentally, it implies the practice of self-abnegation;
and there are some who would hold that the human ego should
be condemned, despised and utterly suppressed. However, in
this work of weaning the soul from its own selfishness, it seems
perhaps more humble and even more efficacious that the rank
and file of Christians should seek quite simply to forget themselves and their own concerns in order to serve others. In this
way, they avoid temptations to spiritual pride, the illusion that
they are self-sacrificing martyrs, and the danger of bringing their
ego into even greater prominence, under the pretext of analyzing
it more minutely in order to break it more effectively. The forgetting of self for the sake of others, is a liberating asceticism.*

*   *   *

*However, though the purification necessary for the blossom-
ing of charity is such a powerful force, it is not sufficient merely
to satisfy all the requirements for such purification. For as soon
as we enter into relationships with others and seek sincerely to
live our everyday social life, we find that there are obstacles to
be overcome, and therefore virtues to be practiced. There are
the rights of others to be respected, according to the virtue of
justice. There are the things which oppose us and upset our plans:
these we must learn to put to good use by rising superior to them,
that we may be governed in the duties of our state, and in all
the major and minor events of our life, by the virtue of prudence.
There are the trials which we must arouse ourselves to meet and*

conquer, or they will conquer us. There is all the inner agitation in the depths of our unconscious, which we must know how to curb and control. It would be both vanity and illusion to make a pretence of practicing self-oblation without first learning self-mastery in the midst of these interior and exterior trials. Charity overcomes these obstacles by leading the soul to do "whatsoever things are true, whatsoever modest, whatsoever just, whatsoever holy, whatsoever lovely, whatsoever of good fame," as Saint Paul counsels us (Phil., IV, 8). A person who sought to give himself to others without having faced up to the task of self-oblivion and self-mastery, would run the very grave risk of merely seeking himself, even in circumstances where he imagines, and perhaps sincerely imagines, that he is giving himself to others.

* * *

Of course, there can be no question of doing all this merely stage by stage; nor of preventing the soul from hastening on to another stage until the purpose of the previous ones has been solidly attained. The life of charity cannot be divided into precise categories; for this life wells up in the soul which is animated by grace, as soon as that soul manifests a right intention, good will, and a readiness to strive generously for that ideal of love which it has chosen—or rather, which the Master Himself has given us and towards which we are "pressed" by charity (2 Cor., V, 14). Charity, therefore, puts on all its shining beauty and radiating power, in self-oblation for others, in all the forms of goodness, patience, long-suffering, mercy, sweetness and service, which such oblation can assume.

* * *

Is this, then, the final summit of charity? By no means; for charity has no limits. "Sursum corda, semper . . ." The disciple of Christ will not rest in this. The very law of love demands that, in and through this self-oblation, the disciple should seek to induce others to throw themselves wide to light and love, to surrender themselves in their turn, and thus to fulfill their personal mission of service to the whole community, in the Mystical Body of Christ. It is this which the disciple desires and seeks. Charity, therefore, extends to the mutual communion of souls, *of minds, of wills, of hearts, of persons: it extends to the "Communion of Saints" in the Church, with the whole Church—militant, suffering and triumphant.*

I.

SELF-OBLIVION THROUGH HUMBLE AND SELFLESS CHARITY

54. THE CONDITIONS OF SELF-OBLIVION

> *If any man will come after me, let him deny himself . . .*
>
> (Matt., XVI, 24)

Every spiritual doctrine which is not based on a solid asceticism, exposes the soul to dangerous illusions. The forms which this asceticism can take are various, and there is one form which the doctrine of the Mystical Body invites us to draw from the Gospel. *Our Lord ceaselessly preached the forgetting of one's self.* But we must first of all clearly indicate the conditions in which the practice of this asceticism will bear its full fruit.

1. *The forgetting of self is primarily a gift of God*
There are many devout souls who, in all good faith, set out to wage bitter warfare against themselves, and are surprised that they find victory so hard to gain. Too often, they imagine that self-renunciation should be their own unaided task in the climb to holiness; and that this preliminary and painful period of asceticism will be followed by one in which they will taste the sweetness of intimacy with Christ, all their wrestling with self being then at an end.

This is a mistake, which is the cause of much spiritual ineffectiveness. The Divine Master Himself must give this grace of self-oblivion, for it is essentially a gift of His love. He will suddenly set the soul free, at the moment He Himself has chosen, but on two conditions: the soul, understanding this truth, must pray humbly and perseveringly for the gift of selflessness; and it must have a firm conviction of its own utter dependence on God, so that it no longer relies on its own unaided efforts at self-mastery. The self will not disappear, but it will no longer be an obstacle: it will take its proper place, as a nonentity in the sight of Him Who is All. It can even become an instrument of real sanctification.

2. *In the warfare against self, it is first necessary that the mind should be enlightened*

Another case of error is to make interior purification depend, primarily and above all, on an austere effort of the personal will. The will has, of course, its part to play—and a very important part indeed! But it is a blind faculty. There are many insufficiently enlightened souls who grope their way blindly forward through efforts of the will alone—efforts which are indeed meritorious, but very severe and meagerly rewarding. In the spiritual life, as in all human activities, God wishes that the intelligence should come first, and that it should be guided by the light of reason, of faith, and of the gifts of the Holy Ghost.

The human reason has the power, of itself, to convince a man that he is very limited indeed. Genuinely learned savants and thinkers are modest men. But authentic humility is a specifically Christian virtue; and human reason cannot, unaided, lead to the forgetting of self.

To attain to self-oblivion, the light of faith is a first necessity. Through it, the soul discovers the grandeur, the perfection, the rights of Christ; the transcendence of God, and the littleness and misery of man. This light shines forth and shows the way that is to be followed. The life of Jesus can grow within us, only if the self does not usurp us entirely.

Furthermore, the virtue of faith implies a very purifying exercise of self-oblivion. To live by faith, it is first necessary to lay aside one's imagination and one's feelings; but also to rise superior to one's reason.

Finally, the Holy Ghost, through His gifts, floods the soul with clear and penetrating light, through which it gains an extremely acute and sometimes painful consciousness of its nothingness and its misery in the sight of the Holiness and the Transcendence of God.

3. *The forgetting of self is the condition for living as a member of the Mystical Body*

A third source of error is ignorance or practical disregard of the doctrine of the Mystical Body. There are souls who, without ever realizing what they are doing, make themselves in some way the center of the universe; and this, not only in the sense that they see all else revolving around themselves, but also in the sense that they imagine God as guiding the events of the world for their own personal good. They even go to the length of supposing that God alters the natural order of things, so that their own little projects may be successful.

This is a reversing of the divine plan. Every soul has, most certainly, its own personal value in the sight of God, Who takes account of the prayers which each soul offers to Him, in that eternal plan by which He guides the events of the world. But He sees each soul as a member of the Mystical Body of His Beloved Son. In the divine plan, each member is for the service of the Mystical Body: his own sanctification should contribute to the extension and to the sanctification of the whole Body. Furthermore, since each receives from the entire Body—and, primarily, from the Head of the Body—all the life which is the essence of his holiness, each member will receive that life only in the measure in which he opens his soul, through charity, to the collective life of the Body, and participates in it through his own generous self-oblation to the whole collective plan of the Divine Head.

This giving of self emerges, therefore, as a logical requirement for this life of membership. Yet again, the doctrine of the Mystical Body will free the soul from its religious individualism.

"O my God, O Trinity Whom I adore, help me to forget myself entirely in order that, changeless and at peace as though my soul were already in eternity, I may establish myself in You. May nothing be able to trouble my peace or make me depart from You, O my Immutable One; but may every minute carry me yet farther into the depths of Your Mystery." (Prayer of Sister Elizabeth of the Trinity).

55. SELF-OBLIVION

A) *IN OUR INTERIOR DISPOSITIONS*

> *Each one not considering the things that are his own, but those that are other men's. For let this mind be in you, which was also in Christ Jesus . . .*
>
> (Phil., II, 4, 5)

In a body, each member lives from the vital movement

imprinted on it by the head. The Christian, as a member of Christ, should find his source of life in the Life of his Head, and should therefore imitate Him interiorly, model himself on Christ, make his own the mind of Christ. Now, when the sincere Christian searches, with deep respect, the Heart of the Divine Savior, and compares what he finds there with the sentiments of his own heart, he discovers sorrowfully what a difference, and often what an opposition, there is between the movements of the Heart of Christ and those of his own.

1. *The facts*

What rules the heart of a man who has abandoned himself to his nature, is very often an attachment to self—egoistic, sensual, proud self.

Egoism does immense harm in the human heart, which has been made for love. It breaks up marriage, paralyzes and disturbs the whole of social life, and destroys the peace of communities whose very life-blood is reciprocal communication among souls.

The *egoistic* self is at the center of its own universe, all else being in relation with it to serve its interests. It is of itself powerless to turn towards others in love or service.

The *sensual* self seeks its satisfactions and its pleasures in created beings and created things. It demands that these should be at the service of its passions. The sensual self profanes and kills love.

The *proud* self takes various forms. On the one hand, it is expressed in exaggerated self-esteem which makes it impose itself on others, in displays of presumption, self-complacency, boasting and domineering. It criticizes others, and lowers them so as to exalt itself. In an incisive, stubborn and harsh manner, it imposes its own will, and seeks to get its own way in all circumstances. It is never in the wrong. It treads ruthlessly on other people's feelings and ideas, being contemptuously indifferent to them.

On the other hand, the proud self shows itself in vanity, in an exaggerated desire for the esteem of others, a desire for the limelight and to be the center of attention, to be liked, approved of, praised—even when the praise is patently insincere and calculating. For vanity is self-conceit. It shows itself initially in a person's readiness to assert himself in no uncertain fashion against others. Then the fear of losing ground in the esteem of the others, causes him to be timid, pusillanimous and discouraged. The next stage is that self-conceit puts on the mask of exclusiveness, by cultivating a tendency to monopolize—to pass everything off as his own; or a tendency to take root in his own opinions and plans, refusing to admit when he is clearly wrong; or a tendency to an independence which prevents him from submitting to any rules. Or again, self-conceit becomes demanding, so that the person grows touchy, testy, suspicious and jealous of the success of others. He becomes the prisoner of his own envy, spleen and spite, because others have not understood him or recognized his worth.

2. The sentiments of the Heart of Christ

In contrast with the chaos which lays waste the human heart, what strikes a person who contemplates the Heart of Christ is that this Heart beats only for Another and for others.

The Heart of the Son beats only for His Father, for His Heart is animated and filled solely with that filial love which urges him to seek only the glory of the Father. "My meat is to do the will of Him that sent me," said Christ (*John*, IV, 34): His happiness is to make Himself pleasing to the Father, so that the Father may proclaim Him His "beloved Son" in Whom He "is well pleased" (*Matt.*, III, 17). Whether in His silent hours of prayer on the mountain, or in His long and arduous hours among the people, Christ preserved the most intimate union with the Father, because His Sacred Heart was always given completely to the Father.

For the Person of Christ is the Person of the Divine Word, being that of the Person of the Son Who lives entirely for His Father in the bosom of the adorable Trinity.

On the other hand, the Being of Jesus Christ is that of a Redeemer. He has come for the sake of mankind, to enlighten them, to love them, to save them. His whole mission is directed to the salvation of His brethren; so that, here also, it can be said that He lives only for others. It is for them that He will lay down His life (*John*, X, 15).

3. For a member of Christ, who wishes to live his whole life as a member of the Mystical Body, the axis of all his thoughts is completely displaced and altered. He no longer finds his center in himself, but in Christ and in the Whole Christ.

a) He lives through Christ and in Christ. He must also live for Christ. The dominating idea which should constantly shine through all his other thoughts and feelings, is the extension of the reign of Jesus Christ, the desire that Christ should be known, loved and served. The self no longer counts for him. Its only importance lies in being given to Christ, that His Spirit may reign absolutely in his soul. Its only values lies in being now "Christ's" (1 *Cor.*, III, 23), so as to be the free and docile instrument in the hands of the Savior and of the Beloved Son, for the accomplishment of His supreme design—the glory of His Father by the redemption of souls in the Whole Christ.

b) The thoughts of the member of Christ are habitually centered on the Whole Christ, on the Whole Church, and on all the other members of the Mystical Body who participate with him in the same life. His thoughts are habitually directed towards all those souls who, desiring to live to its full reality their life as members, give themselves generously to all the inspirations of the Holy Spirit, thereby exalting the whole Body by the enthusiasm and eagerness of their love; but his thoughts are equally concerned with all those who, although incorporated in the Church, do not share its life, and with all those who as yet are not part of the Mystical Body of Christ. These matters are what should obsess the thoughts of the true Christian. When the Christian has adopted this ideal "mind . . . which was also in Christ Jesus," he will gradually come to regard the least purely selfish thought or act as utterly miserable—or he may even come to realize this quite suddenly, in the light given to him by the Holy Spirit; and he will learn to look upon all the self-seeking of mere egoism—whether individual or that of a family or human group—as paltry and as opposed to the Divine Plan.

O Divine Savior, give to all Christians the grace to understand that the forgetting of self is not a superior asceticism reserved to certain select souls who hunger and thirst for perfection, nor a form of sacrifice befitting only great trials. Teach them to realize that it is the normal and permanent state of mind of Your disciple who desires to live, in a consistent way, his life as a member of Your Mystical Body.

56.   SELF-OBLIVION

B)   *IN OUR JUDGMENTS*

> *Wherefore, thou art inexcusable, O man, whosoever thou art that judgest. For, wherein thou judgest another, thou condemnest thyself. For thou dost the same things which thou judgest.*
>
> (Rom., II, 1)

Jesus Christ has reserved to Himself the ultimate judgment of all mankind. It is to the Head alone that the right belongs of judging the members of His Body. And yet, judgment is a necessary act and a noble prerogative of the human mind. How, then, can it be possible to pronounce judgment on others without running counter to the law of Christ and to His prerogative as Judge! Judgment must be made as a member of the Mystical Body; and the exclusion of self from judgments will render them more pure and more free.

1. *The judgment must be purified from all evil passion, which necessarily vitiates and falsifies it*

It must be purified from pride, therefore, because the proud man has an exaggerated idea of his own superiority, and hence also a tendency to underestimate the worth of other people. Similarly, an undue assurance about one's own shrewdness, leads to precipitate judgments pronounced on uncertain evidence or to a snap decision . . . Envy and jealousy are a cause of trouble through the irritation or the depression they cause on account of qualities which give others an advantage in some way . . . Anger destroys the calm of mind which is indispensable to objective judgment . . . In a word, the judgment must be freed from all the passions—hate, rancor, vengeance, simple antipathy, secret aversion—which are contrary to justice and to charity.

Any person who, knowing himself, makes no effort to forget the self with its tangle of passions, is incapable of making a true and equitable judgment. And what is to be said about those who have never taken the trouble to examine themselves sincerely! We can be immediately certain that the passions of which they are the blind slaves, will occasion and inspire all their judgments. Saint Paul's words should, however, be a salutary warning to them; for the Apostle declares that what they judge and condemn in others, is precisely what they do themselves. The people they judge are, as it were, so many mirrors in which they are unconsciously see and judge themselves. All unknown to ourselves and by a natural inclination, the deepest tendency of our subconscious mind makes us seek out in others the defects which are creating chaos within ourselves. A knowledge of this fact of experience should lead us to be discreet in the judgments we pronounce publicly; and it should prove of very great assistance to us in laying aside our selfishness and in getting to know ourselves as we really are.

2. *The judgment should be freed even from the simple egoism of nature, apart altogether from any question of evil passion*

To judge in truth, we must strive to forget ourselves, to go out from ourselves, to lay aside our own personal views and the outlook they dictate in us, so that we may be able to put ourselves in the place of the others and see the matter from their angle. This discipline is necessary, first of all, in our relations with our fellow men, if we are to understand them, and if we are to try to discern the hidden motives which have urged them to act as they did—while we are at the same time convinced, however, that the deepest springs of their motives and their intentions escape us entirely. God alone sees into the depths of the human heart. Self-oblivion and this effort to be charitable will enable us to avoid summary, superficial and hasty judgments, as well as those which rest only on what we call our "intuition about a person"—often mere self-flattery—or on almost groundless suspicions.

Self-oblivion should equally lead each of us to be on his guard against the influence which his particular type of temperament can exercise on our judgments, by inclining them in the direction to which the temperament itself leans. There are various classifications of temperaments, according to anatomical, physical and chemical constitution; but each classification will indicate temperaments which are particularly susceptible to external influences, or especially impressionable and subject to physical reactions. And it is quite certain that a natural tendency to emotionalism, or to activity, or to fickleness, can have dangerous repercussions on the judgments made by people of such temperaments. But phlegmatic temperaments are not immune, because a natural tendency to stolidity, to apathy, to indolence, to indifference, has its own pitfalls. However, whatever the temperament, this watchfullness over it should be exercised calmly and peacefully; for each one of us must humbly accept his temperament such as it is. Furthermore, it is quite certain that, while it can be an obstacle, the temperament can also be a great help in our judgment and our intuitions, if it is properly orientated.

We must also bear in mind that, not persons only are submitted to our judgment, but events themselves. How difficult it is, therefore, to approach them with an open mind! We are so often led to view these events in the light of the unfortunate or happy consequences they can have for ourselves; or to consider them, not as they are in themselves, but as we would have them to be. Thus, our imagination intervenes, to affect our observation and the objectivity of our judgments.

Again, it is not merely a question of being on our guard against influences which our natural defects, or our constitution,

or the deficiences of our temperament can exercise on our judgments. Certain virtuous inclinations can also play their part.

A person who is kindly will be ready to shut his eyes to the
defects and shortcomings of others, in circumstances where his
duty demands that he keep his eyes wide and observantly open.
A naturally sweet-tempered person should take care not to repress
his reactions of righteous anger against error or evil, when it is
his duty to protest against either of these. A tendency to self-
effacement is in itself a virtue, and can be the genuine virtue of
self-oblivion. But when duty demands that we should shoulder
our responsibilities and assert ourselves, self-oblivion demands
that we speak out resolutely; for, in this context, the forgetting
of self must take the form of setting aside our own natural
tendency to self-effacement and eniency.

*O Jesus, I tremble when I consider that, when I appear
before You as my Head and my Judge, on the Last Day, You
will remind me of the judgments I have passed on my brethren
during my lifetime. Help me henceforward to reach such judgments only in the spirit of a member, completely void of deceptive individualism, anxious to safeguard always the unity of
Your Body, and with a zeal for justice and for truth, animated
with love for my brethren. By doing this, I shall, in Your Mercy,
secure Your approval on that awful Day for all the judgments
I have made on men.*

57. SELF-OBLIVION

C) *IN APOSTOLIC ACTION*

> *He was not the light, but was to give testi-
> mony of the Light.*
>
> (John, I, 8)

Every Christian should be an apostle. The apostle is not himself the light. If he believes in his own light and trusts in it, he
deceives himself, and his action is useless—indeed, often harmful.
His role is to be a witness, to efface himself before Him Whom
he announces, like the Precursor Saint John the Baptist, who
"decreased" and disappeared when he had given his testimony
concerning Him Who is the Light.

1. *When preparing to deal with souls*

The attitude of the apostle must be one of profound respect

for, and great delicacy towards, the souls with whom he is to come into contact: respect for their person, for the mystery that is in each one of them, for their liberty. He must prepare himself for such meeting, by a generous effort at self-effacement. The laying aside of his own self and his own selfishness will protect him against two conflicting errors:

On the one hand, *an excessive confidence in his own personal worth and in the effectiveness of his means of action.* This is a clear indication that he has not prayed; that he has no due appreciation of his own powerlessness; that he does not yet know that the grace of God is alone capable of touching the consciences, enlightening the minds and moving the wills of men. He is excessively assured of himself and of his own ideas, and imagines that he can meet from his own spiritual and moral resources all the needs of those with whom he has to deal, and answer all their questions. He makes rash pronouncements about highly complex subjects and about difficult problems which call for enlightened knowledge and balanced judgments. Because he has never studied, he is unaware of his own ignorance, so that he is in a permanent state of mental and moral presumption—of "conceit sublimed by ignorance"—whose consequences can be very serious when it comes to bearing witness to a doctrinal truth.

On the other hand, self-oblivion will protect the apostle against *the error of an inferiority complex which paralyzes his action.* He cannot free himself from a feeling of his powerlessness and personal incapacity, to an extent which will enable him to rely *only* on the *grace* of Christ. At the root of this faint-heartedness, is an excessive preoccupation with the self and a lack of self-detachment, which are all the more dangerous for being subtle and concealed. Because a person is timid, he imagines he is humble; because he shirks his responsibilities and evades a task which demands considerable effort, he deludes himself that he is modest; because he is overwhelmed by his own incapacity, he imagines that there is not a hint of proud self-sufficiency in his soul. The apostle who relies only on Christ, conquers his shortcomings. No longer surprised at them or disturbed by them, he detaches himself from them, so that he may be an obedient instrument in His hands Who leads and inspires him.

2. *When dealing with souls*

This is indeed the moment when the apostle should "empty" himself. When a person, seeking God, asks the apostle to reveal God to him, and finds in that apostle simply another self-centered person, he will merely be irritated. Why should he exercise self-oblivion at the instance of another who is but his equal—and often his inferior—in human qualities? On the other hand, how powerfully such a person will be attracted by the mysterious presence of the living God, which he senses in the soul of an apostle whom he sees as representative of Christ.

He that seeks to be truly the precursor, does not stoop to human ways of winning the esteem and the praise of others. He avoids over-eagerness, because it is so easy to be swept away with one's own activity and to pin one's faith on it. Very rarely indeed is there a really disinterested action, in which there is no admixture of the self. The signs of such admixture are readily seen. The apostle is disturbed, over-anxious and somewhat feverish in his activity, so that he loses his sense of proportion. He begins to be satisfied with the ideas he thinks up, with the judgments he reaches, with the virtues he is practicing. Gradually, he begins to lose ground, and very soon he is usurping to himself the credit for a work which depends on God alone.

The more completely the apostle is selfless, the more effectively does the grace that inspires him pass unadulterated to others through his words, and the more luminously does it shine in his whole life. God then finds in the heart of His apostle, His own authentic design of doing all things for the Divine Glory. He blesses this apostolate, takes delight in it and makes it fruitful.

The precursor has prepared the ways for the coming of His Lord; and the souls with whom he has dealt open the doors of their souls to Him Who knocks, seeking entry.

3. *Afterwards*

The encounter between the apostle and the soul is ended; but the apostle, who passes on to other tasks, must continue to the utmost his effor at self-renunciation. He must carefully avoid the temptation to look back complacently on what he has done or to be complacent about what he is now achieving: "Brethren, I do not count myself to have apprehended. But one thing I *do:* forgetting the things that are behind and stretching forth myself to those that are before, I press towards the mark . . ." (*Phil.*, III, 13, 14)—words which should be the motto of every apostolate.

The apostle must not linger to gloat in any way over the results which he believes, and often quite wrongly believes, he has attained. He must cut short any feelings of vain glorious satisfaction and complacency, as well as any temptation to speak to others about a success, or attribute it to himself. Our Lord's words about the Pharisees who, in the most noble of acts—

prayer, almsgiving, penance—sought only their own glory, are already a lacerating verdict against those who follow their example: "Amen I say to you, they have received their reward" (*Matt.*, VI, 5). It is thus that the merits of so many apostolic actions are lost, which had nevertheless been undertaken with a generous intention.

Equally, on the other hand, self-oblivion forbids the apostle to dwell on some failure, thereby indulging his wounded vanity; or to be disturbed by some humiliation to which he has been subjected or some awkward mistake he has made in dealing with a soul. In such circumstances, he must calmly and humbly abandon all into His hands Who has no need of our assistance, and Who knows how to make "all things work together unto good" (*Rom.*, VIII, 28), when He so pleases—even the errors and faults of our instructions.

O Jesus, make us know the joy of giving ourselves to others in a total renunciation of ourselves. Burn into our souls the conviction that of ourselves we are but "unprofitable servants"; and that if, in Your immense Goodness, You have deigned to call us to become Your cooperators in the establishing of the Reign of God, we can be so only in the measure to which we enable You Yourself to use us as Your instruments—which we can do only by stripping our souls of self, by the help of Your grace, thus making them genuinely apostolic souls.

II.

SELF-MASTERY

58. THROUGH THE RULE OF CHARITY OVER OUR SENSES

> *For what doth it profit a man, if he gain the whole world and suffer the loss of his own soul?*
>
> (Matt., XVI, 26)

No other words of Our Lord could be quoted as affirming with greater emphasis the primacy of the soul. All the conquests of the universe are worthless to a man, if he does not succeed in conquering his own soul, in making himself master of his soul in order to subject it to His sovereign dominion Who alone has the power to save it.

1. *The Holy Scriptures*

While Saint Paul utters severe words of condemnation against impurity, emphatically declaring that "neither fornicators . . . shall possess the kingdom of God,"[1] the Divine Savior promises beatitude in eternal light to the clean of heart. These, Christ declares, "shall see God" (*Matt.*, V, 8). They shall see Him even here on earth, by the pure and limpid glance of their souls, in the souls of their brethren and in the interior temple of their own bodies wherein dwells the Blessed Trinity.

The Gospel affirms the superiority of the spirit over the senses and the flesh. Whereas the Pharisees gave to exterior actions the place of first importance, Jesus taught that what counts above all else is what is within a man (*Mark*, VII, 15), his spirit, his soul. This is the center of men's responsibility, and their subject. Jesus seeks from every man an account, not only of even his most secret actions, but also of his desires, his thoughts, the dispositions of his soul, because it is his soul which should make itself mistress of the body and rule over the flesh. It is the soul which is at the root of all that occurs in a man and of all that he accomplishes: "For from the heart come forth evil thoughts, murders, adulteries, fornications, thefts, false testimonies, blasphemies" (*Matt.*, XV, 19).

Saint Paul has described the conflicts between the flesh and the spirit: "But I see another law in my members, fighting against the law of my mind and captivating me in the law of sin that is in my members." (*Rom.*, VII, 14-25). The Apostle goes on to point a contrast between "the things that are of the flesh"—"the wisdom of the flesh" being "death"; and "the things that are of the spirit"—"the wisdom of the spirit" being "life and peace" (*Rom.*, VIII, 5-12).

2. *The doctrine*

Why must a man gain the mastery of his senses and of his flesh?

1) *Because the dignity of the human person demands this mastery.* A chaste person is one who gives to the spirit, to the human reason, the place which properly belongs to it. In such a person, the reason rules the senses, and the spirit rules the flesh, so that the spirit is given the primacy. By contrast, what worse slavery can there be than that of those unfortunate people who

---

1. I *Cor.*, VI, 9—*Ephes.*, V, 5-7—1 *Cor.*, XV, 50.

become slaves to their passions, are incapable of resisting the tyranny of the senses, are no longer able to think, to reflect, to make a free decision—in short, to accomplish those properly human acts which are the nobility and the grandeur of the human person. They can no longer do these things, because their minds are darkened, their reason disturbed by the imperious demands of the flesh, the violence of temptations, the craving for sensual satisfaction. The animal in them has gradually killed the human being, and has atrophied in them the life of the spirit.

By bringing into the world the beautiful virtue of chastity, together with humility and charity, Jesus protects the dignity of the human person and gives man back to himself in the rightful perfection of his nature. Christ's divine teaching lifts human wisdom to its full slendor, and fixes the conditions which ensure the equilibrium and the happiness of men.

2) But however noble in itself, this care for human dignity *must itself be subjected to the higher law of charity*. We must avoid falling into a kind of proud pharisaism which would make us proclaim that we are "not as the rest of men," and would stifle all pity in us for the unfortunate victims of the war of the flesh against the spirit. We must guard equally against developing an attitude of pagan stoicism, which would make us shut ourselves away in the ivory tower of our own egoism, in order to shun the great highway of human life where the battle of flesh and spirit is being waged.

A man must be master of his senses, in order that his heart may be free to become engrossed in the apostolate, and that his soul may be generously responsive to all the appeals constantly made upon his fraternal charity. The slavery of the heart stifles generosity and delicacy of feeling. It folds a man selfishly in upon himself, so that his only attraction is towards created beings and created things wherein he can find the selfish satisfaction of his carnal appetite.

Those who belittle the celibacy of the priest and the vowed chastity of the religious, have no conception of the power of devotedness, the depths of sacrifice, the enthusiastic warmth of the holy immolations, which chastity ceaselessly inspires and animates in the hearts of Christ's apostles, for the service of their brethren and the growth of the Mystical Body.

3) Saint Paul has shown that, if the victory of the spirit must be ensured in the war against the flesh, it is, in fine, for a higher reason: *in order to establish the reign of the Holy Spirit* in the members of Christ's Mystical Body, so that, led by the

Spirit of God, they may be truly sons of God.[1] Having been made sons, and participating ever more intimately in the filiation of the Son, the members of the Mystical Body wish to be like to their Head in all things, to belong to Him without reserve, to love Him for His own sake with an exclusive love; and, with Him, to love God above all things, as Pure Spirit and Infinite Beauty. Herein is the final reason of Christian chastity—that *chastity is dominated by love for Him Who is Infinite Love.* The Apostle Saint Paul has emphatically shown the perfection of chastity and the superiority of the chaste person who gives himself completely to the Lord. Such a one is not "divided," but "is solicitous for the things of the Lord; how he may please God" (1 *Cor.*, VII, 33, 32).

O Jesus, grant unto all the members of Your Mystical Body to understand that the meaning of their incorporation is that of an indestructible attachment to Your Adorable Person as Head. May the magnetism of all that is in You of Beauty, of Purity and of Holiness draw them away from the attractions of the flesh and of the senses. Give unto them Your Divine Spirit so that they may be assimilated, by a gradual process of spiritualization, to Your ineffable chastity.

59. THROUGH CHARITY INSPIRED BY JUSTICE

> *Blessed are they that hunger and thirst after justice; for they shall have their fill.*
> (Matt., V, 6)

Justice is the moral virtue which leads us to respect the rights of others. Because he is a disciple and brother of Christ, a member of the Mystical Body, and because he should be animated by charity, the Christian must cultivate an impassioned zeal for justice, which will lead him to wage grim war against all injustices, but first of all against himself and the tyranny of his own selfishness. It is charity which will kindle, feed and control this virtue of justice.

1. *Respect for the essential rights of the human person*

The right to life and to the working conditions befitting a human being; the right of the human person to respect for his

---

1. "But you are not in the flesh, but in the spirit, if so be that the Spirit of God dwell in you . . . For whosoever are led by the Spirit of God, they are the sons of God . . . For the Spirit Himself giveth testimony to our spirit that we are the sons of God" (*Rom.*, VIII, 9, 14, 16).

dignity, reputation and vocation; the right to man's fundamental liberties as a rational and social being—these are the rights which the Christian is bound to respect in others, if he wishes to live with God and with his brethren, in that peace which is the tranquillity of order, whatever the human, family, social or religious community to which he belongs.

Justice is exercised at every moment in our relations with others. It requires self-mastery in order to conquer the fundamental egoism of sinful nature.

The egoism of a domineering pride, which takes satisfaction in making its superiority over others felt in the person's manner of speaking and of dealing with others, of judging them and making use of them.

The egoism of negligence and of indolence, which is incapable of making the effort required to pay a debt at the proper time, to return a borrowed object or to order one's affairs and one's correspondence.

The egoism of class, of social conformity or simply of a way of life where one takes more than sufficient thought for the morrow. This is the kind of egoism which makes a person insensible to the miseries of others, indifferent to the needs and the anguish of those who live insecurely from day to day and which leads a person to be harsh and unjust in judging others for whom life is a constant struggle.

The egoism of ambition, which causes a person to ignore or to transgress the rights of others whose competition he fears or of whom he is jealous to the extent of injuring their reputation and of attempting to besmirch their good name with their neighbors.

The egoism of habit and routine, which makes a person neglect to be thoughtful for others, in the midst of a community life where he is constantly meeting the same people. Such neglect is a failure to respect their human dignity, their individual personality, their greatness as creatures loved by God, their nobility as children of the Father and their vocation as consecrated persons.

The egoism of a hardened heart, which is utterly unmoved by anything which does not intimately concern itself, or its own affairs, and in which the revelation of unjust oppression kindles not the least spark of interest as to the source of such injustice or the place where it is occurring.

The egoism of sloth, which makes a person refuse to enter into difficult or dangerous strife, however just and holy may be its cause.

Christians should be in the vanguard of those who are resolved to join forces for the establishment of a social order which is more just and more worthy of human dignity.

2. Respect for other people's right to the truth

The right of others to know the truth by the plainness of our speech, the frankness of our attitudes and the sincerity of our feelings, is one of the solid foundations of social relationships and of all community life. Love of the truth, for its own sake, will prove of very great assistance to the Christian in respecting this right of others; as will also, and above all, the love of God and of the neighbor. But this respect for justice implies a vigorously ascetic attitude: it demands very considerable self-mastery.

1) Self-mastery in making the laborious effort of *choosing our words* so as to convey the truth, or at least to do so as nearly as we can. The Divine Master has laid down this law concerning frankness and openness in speech: "But let your speech be: Yea, Yea: No, No. And that which is over and above these is of evil" (*Matt.*, V, 37).

Self-mastery in order to control a natural tendency to imprecision, to invention, to dissimulation. We must avoid all falsehood, all exaggerated language, all embroidering of what we have to say, all twisting of facts to fit a story, all ambiguous phrases, all wriggling evasions.

Self-mastery in order to resist the speciousness of a public opinion led astray by tendentious propaganda, and to maintain the truth about men and events, even when one is alone in defending it.

2) Self-mastery in *the frankness of our attitudes* towards others. Here, also, Our Lord has indicated where our duty lies. He condemned the Pharisees for their duplicity, for their false and deceptive attitudes. Self-mastery is required if we are to cultivate this fine frankness, by which we show ourselves to others as we really are, without attempting to present a mask which deceives them into supposing that we are something quite different.

Self-mastery in order that we may escape that worldly spirit and those pharisaic attitudes of circles wherein only the external, the appearance, the superficial, the conventional, is regarded as of any importance; and, furthermore, in order that we may not yield to the temptation of those flatteries, praises and obsequious attitudes and words, together with all those evil tricks and cunning insincerities, by which one seeks to ingratiate oneself with others. Unless care is exercised to exclude it, this spirit has a tendency to insinuate itself, in various subtle ways, into every human community. There is always the temptation to win the esteem of others by disingenuous means, by accommodating airs, by studied attitudes, and by various ruses designed to secure the sympathy of our companions.

3) Self-mastery in *the sincerity of our feelings.* Our external relationships with others are absolutely futile, unless our subjective disposition itself is sincere and true. Sincerity condemns lying, and even the intention to deceive. Such condemnation is indeed necessary, but still very negative. Others have the right to our positive assistance in seeking for the truth, and it is as a body that we should seek to communicate in the truth. Our Lord formulated this need for sincerity, in His Sermon on the Mount. "Your Father who is in secret . . . your Father who seeth in secret," Christ said, knows your most intimate thoughts, and you will not deceive Him. What He expects from you in your relationships with your brethren, is precisely what He expects from you in your relation with Himself: uprightness, limpidity of soul and purity of feelings.

O Jesus, grant to all those who desire to love you in a practical way, the grace to understand that their relations with You are intimately connected with the manner in which they behave towards their brethren; and that, in their interior life, they cannot regard as foreign to their purpose, those rules imposed by the virtue of justice on all human relationships and on affairs of the most material nature. Teach them to understand that, in their interior life as in all else, they must be animated by an ardent zeal for justice. Fill their souls with Your charity, so that they may ceaselessly hunger and thirst after justice.

60. BY PATIENT CHARITY IN SUFFERING

Charity is patient . . . beareth all things . . .
(1 Cor., XIII, 4, 7)

Patience is not a purely passive resignation, as some people think. Christian morality regards it as one of the aspects of the virtue of fortitude. It can be a very fruitful exercise of self-mastery—provided, however, that it is animated by the charity of Christ.

1. *In the trials deriving from our nature*

Under this heading, we include the crosses of our physical constitution, of our temperament, of our humors; the crosses of our character, our habits, our passions, our sins and their consequences; the cross we must bear when, ceaselessly urged on by our appetite for knowledge, we discover the limitations and deficiencies of our mind, in all fields of research; the cross of our sensibility, tortured by real or imaginary trials; crosses laid on us by the weakness and the failures of our will; crosses of weariness, of monotony and of failures in our daily work; crosses from matters which are utterly beyond our power to control—sickness, bereavements, financial ruin, national disaster.

When he is faced with all these crosses, there is one attitude which must be alien to the Christian: to resolve all these matters by an indolent defeatism, crumpling under them and becoming discouraged. There is also the proud attitude of the stoics who, running counter to the truth of human nature, act as though they despise suffering and refuse to allow themselves to show any reaction at all towards it.

The disciple of Christ takes up his cross. He accepts it such as it is—small, if it is small; considerable, if it is so—simply and sincerely, without exaggeration and without regarding himself as a martyr. He meets it and carries it courageously, using it to raise himself to greater spiritual heights, and controlling it with a self-mastery which is fostered and purified in his soul by the charity of Christ.

By charity towards his brethren, in avoiding anything which might make them feel the weight of their own crosses. Through love for them, he remains silent, arresting on his very lips the complaint that comes from his heart, and not showing the least indication of the effort it is costing him to do so.

Through filial charity also, as a member of the Son, the Christian seeks to imitate Christ's complete oblation of will to His Father when the chalice of His Passion was presented to Him: "Not my will, but thine be done." Some of these crosses originate for the Christian in his own nature: he has received them at his very birth. Others are but the reverse side of gifts given by God. Others, again, are there by the permissive will of the Heavenly Father, as part of a plan for maintaining His son in an attitude of humility and dependence.

2. *In the trials that come to us from others*

Others have their own crosses to bear, just as we have ours.

If they take forms different from ours, their causes are the same. Relations with others—especially in circumstances where contact is of daily routine—can become an occasion for the practice of Christian patience, sometimes in a heroic degree. It is sufficient to consider how the crosses of each person can become a testing of the patience of those who are in contact with them. Everything in others can become a source of irritation for us: their way of thinking, of getting in a nervous state before some event, of judging; or even, quite simply, the way they do the most ordinary things of every day, their idiosyncrasies and their manias, their garrulity or their dumbness. All of these things in others can become insupportable to us, without any fault necessarily on their part or any deliberate intention to annoy.

Christian patience emerges, therefore, as an eminently social virtue which is the very condition on which community life depends. Philosophical and moral systems which aim essentially at exalting the self, admit their bankruptcy when it comes to sustaining a man who is faced with the contradictions of life, and to leading him to acquire self-mastery in conquering and enduring them. On the other hand, Christian charity knows how to be patient. Through love for others, it prevents us from letting them feel that they are a burden in any way; it stifles within us our complaints, recriminations and grumblings; it controls our waves of instinctive anger or our irrational irritation. Through love for Christ, and in order that we may cooperate in the extension of the Whole Christ, it changes what could have been a fault into what is certainly an action of redemptive merit. Charity can reach to even greater heights: it will not hesitate to offer up, for those very people who are the source of irritation and suffering, all the satisfactory and impetratory value of this victory of love.

Finally, without seeking any return, patience inspired and sustained by charity will have its own reward even here, in the consolation it brings of helping our suffering brethren by our example and our collaboration, to support one another with greater forebearance and understanding, and to bear their crosses together in the spirit and with the patience of Christ their Head.

O Jesus, Who has taught us, by Your contacts with men and Your silence during Your Passion, to make the virtue of patience an essential element of Redemption, grant us the grace to accept our everyday life without complaint or revolt, in a patience wherein humility, sweetness, faith and trust are united, in order that our soul may be at peace under the transforming action of Your charity.

61. BY COURAGEOUS CHARITY

*For God hath not given us the spirit of
fear, but of power and of love and of
sobriety* (i.e., self-mastery)

(2 Tim., I, 7)

In the religion of Jesus Christ, there can be no place for soft-
ness, half-heartedness and cowardice. Christianity is the religion
of virility, of fortitude and of courage. For the Head of the
Mystical Body calls His members to a daily ascent towards
holiness, by the way of virtues genuinely practiced and of charity
heroically exercised. He demands that they should be witnesses
unto Him even unto the uttermost parts of the earth.

1. *Warfare for the truth of Christ*

There are nations that claim that they can organize mankind
without considering God in any way. This is both vain and
blasphemous; because "unless the Lord build the house, they
labor in vain that build it" (Psalm 126). Such nations sin against
mankind; because, unless men are guided by a moral law superior
to themselves, they will be torn by their own passions and there
will be endless strife among them. How many are there who are
intelligent and clear-sighted enough to realize the catastrophe
that must attend the exclusion of God from human affairs; and
who, by their personal, family and social life, have the courage
to proclaim these essential truths, and their belief in One God,
in His Transcendence and His Justice?

In the midst of a world which has not only forgotten God,
but which seeks its happiness according to principles that are
the very negation of those of Christianity, it needs courage to
bear testimony to the Truth of Our Lord Jesus Christ and to His
universal Sovereignty.

Many indeed seek God in a vague way; but they want Him
to preside over a religion of humanism from which the spirit of
sacrifice has been banished as something uncouth. Courage is
needed if we are not "to make void" the Cross of Christ, and if
we are to present the Whole Christ to the world, in all His
mysteries, and especially in the Mystery of Sacrifice.

Others tend to distinguish between Christ and the Church,
in their hearts and in their outward attitudes. In certain circles
and atmospheres, courage is needed to speak, not only of Christ,
but also of His Church; and to maintain that the Church belongs

to Christ, and Christ to the Church. Courage is needed, in such
circumstances, to defend the hierarchy, the clergy, and the laws
of the Church.

In places where the Church is hated, it takes courage to go
to Holy Mass and to fulfill every public act of Catholic worship.
Where there is danger of religious indifferentism,[1] because by
tradition and custom complete freedom of worship exists for all
denominations, courage is needed to bear witness to Christ and
to the Church by a life which is in conformity with the social
doctrines of the Catholic Faith and with the spirit of the Gospel.
To lack this courage is to be ensnared by that "human respect"
which insinuates itself subtly into all situations; and, to describe
it bluntly for what it is, human respect is pure cowardice in face
of public opinion, and slavish capitulation to the ideas of other
people. It is so subtle that it can infiltrate even souls which, by
their vocation and their mission, have consecrated their lives to
Christ.

2. *The Christian's sources of strength in his combats for the
   Faith*

The Christian's strength is, in the first place, his love for Jesus
Christ. He who loves his Divine Master with a virile and tender
love, will not stand indifferently by when he sees that Master
attacked in His Person, and His work of saving mankind utterly
paralyzed. To prove to his Savior the sincerity of his love, the
Christian is ready to enter the lists in His defense, to compromise
himself, to sacrifice his interests and his reputation and even to
lay down his life.

This charity of the Christian extends to the whole Mystical
Body of Christ. It does not consist simply of an active love for
each member of the Mystical Body, individually regarded: it has
for its object the common good of the Church, of the Mystical
Body as a corporate whole. As a member, the Christian feels himself to be responsible for the whole Body: he has the courage to
defend the Church and to fight for the Church.

However, though in itself so powerful in urging the Christian
forward in his combats, charity needs to be reinforced by spiritual
energies which enable the Christian to maintain his self-mastery
in the midst of perils. He may have great and ardent good will,
but his human nature, with its weaknesses and its cowardice in the

---

1. (This word is to be read in the sense given to it, for example, by Cardinal
Manning who writes of "the *indifferentism* which equalizes all religions and gives equal
rights to truth and error"—Translator).

face of sacrifice, still cries out to be left in peace and still shudders at the efforts demanded of it. But the Christian has at his disposal, first and foremost, the supernatural virtue of fortitude, which enables him to stand firm and to show courage in the difficulties encountered in his life as a Christian and in the public profession of his Faith. Natural strength of character acquired by natural means is an excellent thing, but here it is not enough. For the warfare is on a different plane and of another order.

Moreover, in certain circumstances, this type of combat is so dangerous that we must fear the weariness of our nature, always prone to go slack through the continued effort required of it. The Christian is armed for such moments of human collapse; for he has received the supernatural virtue of fortitude. In such moments, the virtue of charity living in the Christian soul, becomes anxious and seeks from God alone the necessary assistance; and in answer to that call, the Holy Ghost covers this weakness with a divine strength infused into the soul. This is the gift of the Holy Ghost which is the secret of the heroism of the martyrs.

O Jesus, what a cold fear numbs my heart when I recall Peter's denial, Judas's betrayal, and the flight of Your Apostles! But they had not yet received the Holy Ghost, nor had you yet risen from the dead. By "the power of Your resurrection" (Phil., III, 10), *give unto all the members of Your Mystical Body, a participation in Your own Fortitude as their Head.*

62. BY CHARITY STRONG IN FIDELITY TO THE DUTIES OF OUR STATE

> *Not every man that saith to me, Lord, Lord, shall enter into the kingdom of heaven; but he that doth the will of My Father who is in heaven, he shall enter into the kingdom of heaven.*
>
> (Matt., VII, 21)

Genuine courage is not always the kind which suddenly comes out in exceptional circumstances; it is the type of courage which is quietly and constantly exercised every day in the faithful discharge of the humble duties of our state in life. This fidelity indicates that the person has a sense of duty—that is to say, he is acutely conscious of the imperative nature of his duty, but also loves it.

1. *The role of the supernatural virtue of fortitude*

In the resources of his own natural energy, and in such purely human motives as a feeling of his personal dignity, the will to success, a taste for his work, and so forth, a man very often finds the strength to fulfill the duties of his state. But he is at the mercy of such natural motives and resources; and he faces a serious problem when his nature, instead of being a help and a stimulus to him, wilts before the austerity and rigor of the duties of his state, and becomes for him an obstacle to fulfilling them.

The Christian possesses, in the supernatural virtue of fortitude, all the resources of strength which will sustain him in the midst of difficulties. This virtue will enable him *to stand fast*, without yielding to discouragement, when the task becomes painful, onerous and exhausting.

It will help him *to accept calmly* the tediousness of "the daily round, the common task," and the monotony of a work whose pattern never varies from one day to the next. It will aid him *to conquer and control* the feeling of weariness, of repugnance and of disgust, occasioned by the contrarieties, the failures, the inadequacy of his most stubborn efforts, the complete collapse of some undertaking—all incident to every walk of life, and all threatening to submerge the soul in the muddy waters of despondency.

The supernatural virtue of fortitude will help the Christian *to persevere to the end* in his devotion to duty, despite temptations to be remiss at times, and despite his natural inclination towards ease and indolence, towards instability and personal whim. It will help him to cultivate a strong soul, capable of ruling itself and of disciplining the impulses of a nervous, emotive and impressionable temperament. It will assist him in controlling the movement of a character which is active, prompt in getting things done, but inclined to fold up before an obstacle or to fret impatiently at any delay. Fortitude will enable the Christian to acquire self-mastery, serenity, due measure and dignity, in the accomplishment of the duties of his state in life—qualities which are made more precious by the fact that the Christian is today drawn more and more into the vortex of a society where everything occurs with feverish agitation and is carried out at soul-searing speed.

2. *Charity strong in fidelity to the duties of our state*

In the soul of the Christian, the supernatural virtue of fortitude is animated by charity, which also inspires in the soul fresh and powerful motives of fidelity to duty.

First of all, the duties of his state take on for the Christian an imperative character, because he sees in them the expression of God's Will. He would regard the shirking of these duties as the shunning of a Living Person, of One Who rules over him and on Whom he is dependent at every moment. To go to the performance of his duties is for him equivalent to going to meet a loved Person Who gives Himself through faith, or rather Whom faith seeks out. To remain faithful to the duties of his state is, for the Christian, to remain in the loving glance of the Christ-Head, of the Master to Whose eyes all things are "naked and open."

And because he loves, he does not regard these duties as a yoke of slavery imposed on him from without. On the contrary, they are for him the occasion and the means of showing to God that his love is not just a babbling of pious words, but is proved by actions. "Not every one that *saith* to me, Lord, Lord, shall enter into the kingdom of heaven; but he that *doth* the *will* of my Father . . . shall enter into the kingdom of heaven."

Religion is not something apart from life: it is life itself lived in that filial spirit which makes the Christian adhere lovingly to the Will of the Father; and in that charity which makes him unite himself with the infinitely loving and infinitely good Divine Will, whose expression is the duties of his daily work, even when they become most irksome and least rewarding.

At the same time, in communicating to the Christian soul a new and higher strength, charity exercises its transforming power, through the person who acts, even in the action itself which constitutes the duty of his state. The disciple of Christ accomplishes this action with his heart and with his mind, with his love and with all his will; and therefore he takes pains to do it as perfectly as possible. This concern for perfection penetrates the very matter of the task itself—acting in it, so to speak, like leaven—so that the manner in which the work is done will be positively marked by it: that is to say, it will be carried out conscientiously, carefully and with technical perfection, so that it is completely transformed from within its own nature by the spiritual motive-power of the person doing it.

However modest this task may be, and however secular it may seem, it is, for the member of Christ, his manner of cooperating in the creative action of God, and his way of making his own little contribution to the building up of a human society wherein all the functions are marked by solidarity and contribute to the common good. On a more exalted plane, it is by the faithful fulfilling of the duties of his state that the Christian collaborates in the formation of the Whole Christ, and shares in the Redemptive Mission of Christ and of the Church.

O Mother most powerful, you have shown us to what summits of greatness Christian patience can rise, when you stood bravely at the foot of the Cross, and when you went about your humble daily tasks in the home of Nazareth. Teach us to acquire, under your maternal protection, the mastery and control of our own souls, in the fidelity with which we carry out the daily duties of our state in life.

63. BY PRUDENT CHARITY

Charity . . . dealeth not perversely.

(1 Cor., XIII, 4)

Prudence is the virtue which rules our actions, and it therefore plays a very considerable part in our lives. It is through this virtue that a man can achieve real self-mastery. It is this virtue which preserves a healthy equilibrium in the other virtues, and protects them against the dangers of their extremes by excess and by defect.

1. *The role of prudence in God's plan*

Divine Providence governs the world and all that is in the world, according to a plan whose ultimate purpose could only be the glory of God. All created beings and things are called to glorify God, in their own fashion. Inanimate objects and the plants and animals, says Saint Augustine, "cry aloud that they have not made themselves . . . If we listen attentively to what they say to us, we shall hear them proclaim: It is You, O Lord, Who have made us; it is You Who are Infinite Beauty" (*Confession*, XI, 4-5).

But, in this harmony of the creation, man has a unique place distinct from all else, and has his own way of giving glory to God, which is in conformity with his nature as a rational and free creature. It is by his faculties of intelligence and of will that he glorifies God, his Creator and His Father.

Although man, through the radical contingency of his created being, is in a condition of complete and absolute dependence on God, he nevertheless has the unique distinction that God, in creating him, has made him master of his own destiny. This certainly does not mean that anything done at any moment by a person, can be entirely independent of the supreme sovereignty of God. It means that it is quite freely, by a personal act, by a positive exercise of will leading to certain deliberate behavior, that a man enters into the divine plan, conforms his will with the Divine Will, and carries out the designs which Divine Providence has for him. To put this more accurately, Divine Providence has willed to give man the honor of being personally involved in his own conduct. Thus, by an act of infinite delicacy, God permits a man to cooperate with Him in governing his own human life and in securing a mastery over the whole creation.

Now, it is by the virtue of prudence, that a man thus freely governs himself. It is by practicing this virtue that he becomes the captain of his soul, in order to steer it safely through the reefs and shoals of life. The virtue of prudence guides his mind by leading it to select the best means of achieving the particular purposes he proposes to himself, and to secure his destiny as a man and as a Christian. It forms his judgment and orientates his will.

Among all the motives which the virtue of prudence offers to the Christian as a son and as a member of the Mystical Body, the place of honor is given to charity—the virtue which urges the Christian to behave always as a son of God, and to seek to achieve the ultimate purpose of his creation by promoting the glory of God, his Father, through his active cooperation in extending the Mystical Body of the Son. For a member of the Mystical Body, the supernatural virtue of prudence is the surest means of remaining in dependence on the Christ-Head, by Whom God governs the whole world.

2. *Prudence, the virtue of self-mastery*

The first act of prudence is *to deliberate* with oneself, in order to decide what are the best means to be adopted, in each particular case, to fulfill the duties of one's state. This act calls for self-mastery to enable the Christian to "keep" his soul in the midst of preoccupations and activities, in order that he may be able to preserve that inward calm in which he can reflect and take counsel with himself. Self-mastery is required, moreover, that the Christian may be able to control his natural tendencies to precipitation, to presumption or to temerity, which make so many people act as though they were animals governed only by instinct, or unresisting victims of their own habits, or slaves chained down by their own passions. Already from the point of view of self-mastery, prudence is a liberating and peace-creating virtue.

On the heels of deliberation, comes the necessity of *judging* —of choosing, among several possible solutions, the one best suited to achieve the purpose sought. Self-mastery is necessary here, to purify the motives which can influence one's judgment, to control impressions, to discipline the passions, to set aside personal or social prejudices and to guard against everything else which is capable of vitiating one's judgment.

The last and most important act of prudence, and in accordance with which it is defined as the virtue of action, is *effective decision*. How many fine projects there are which end in vapor; how many good resolutions degenerate into vague and insipid wishes!

The Christian requires self-mastery if he is to plan and carry out effectively what he has purposed to do, without becoming entangled in useless delays and evasions. This quality is also demanded if he is not to be discouraged by the obstacles he meets; if he is to face up to them directly, and not attempt to compromise with them in a cowardly fashion; if he is not to take refuge in lazy evasion or abstention, behind pretexts which are mere cowardice.

Self-mastery is needed to dominate a phlegmatic or an impulsive temperament, a natural incapacity for exerting himself or a feverish haste in doing so. Self-mastery, too, in order to preserve his sense of values when he acts, so that he will know when to yield to the truth instead of opposing it, and humbly to adapt his ideas to the truth, despite deceptive and specious appearances which are calculated to lead him astray. Also, in order that he may preserve his feeling for what is possible and opportune, without, however, capitulating, compromising or indulging in low cunning and immoral opportunism. To preserve, as well, a sense of measure, by always attempting to strike a golden mean which avoids the exaggerations of defect, at one extreme, and of excess at the other. To preserve, in his action, a sense of his responsibilities, not shirking them or laying them on others. Thus, in all these matters, self-mastery will ensure that the virtue of prudence is at the constant and positive service of fortitude and of charity.

Finally, the Christian needs self-mastery in order to rise superior to existing circumstances, not allowing his outlook to be darkened by a too narrow horizon, but looking calmly into the future by calculating the consequences of his actions for himself, and their repercussions on others.

O Jesus, our Head, give us Your light so that, when we are preparing to do any work, we may seek calmly and deliberately, without presumption or temerity, to discern the best means of fulfilling the duties of our state as perfectly as we can. Make us carry out, with constancy and vigilance, our program of life, so that, in all things and above all things, You, Who have willed to take the initiative in our conduct by Your prevenient grace, may be able to recognize Your own thoughts in our deliberations, Your own designs in our decisions, Your own wishes fulfilled in our actions—by all of which You ceaselessly draw us towards the Father, in Your Spirit of Love, for the triumph of Your Charity and for the extension of Your Mystical Body.

III.

THE GIVING OF ONE'S SELF TO OTHERS

64. BY CHARITY FULL OF KINDNESS

> *Charity is . . . kind . . . thinketh no evil; rejoiceth not in iniquity, but rejoiceth with the truth.*
>
> (1 Cor., XIII, 4-6)

Kindness is not, as some think, a sign of weakness: on the contrary, indeed, it is a very positive and combative virtue. Its essence is the strength of a person's self-control, and the conquest of his egoism. Like the other virtues, it too presupposes self-oblivion, but it has for its object the giving of self to others. It is this interior disposition which inclines a person to think kindly, to wish well and to do good.

1. *To think kindly*

"Charity . . . thinketh no evil." Kindness excludes malevolent and suspicious thoughts; thoughts which ascribe evil intentions and vicious purposes to others; thoughts which put an evil interpretation on the gestures, actions, words and even silence of others.

Kindness inclines a person to think favorably about his brethren, to give them the benefit of the doubt at all times, to trust them and to maintain towards them an attitude of easy and cordial benevolence. A kind soul always harbors kind thoughts about others.

However, kindness is not synonymous with naivety or with stupid susceptibility to illusion and fraud. It does not mean that we are to read into others, qualities which they clearly do *not* possess. Kindness sees things as they are: the bad as well as the good. Where there is evil, it does not regard that evil as other than evil. Indeed, a person who lives by faith has a marked aptitude, even for discerning evil—an aptitude given to him by his knowledge of Original Sin and of its consequences in man even after the Redemption. He knows the limitations and the miseries of mankind, and is therefore not surprised to meet them in others, as he has met them in himself.

But if he is kind, this clear insight into the shortcomings of others gives him no pleasure: he "rejoiceth not in iniquity, but rejoiceth with the truth." Now, the truth is that, side by side with these deficiencies and this evil, there are, in the other members of the Mystical Body, splendors, richness and excellent qualities, which are the fruits of grace. For the loving glance of Christ rests on all men, and He wills that they should be saved. Side by side with error, and often in the error itself, there is truth in every man, and defects may be but the reverse side of the good qualities not so easily discerned. The kind person rejoices in all this "truth": for kindness prompts him to see with the eyes of faith the luminous truth that those around him are sons of God, brethren of Jesus Christ and temples of the Holy Ghost. These magnificent wonders shine splendidly for him in all his fellow members of the Body of Christ, and he is content to leave their defects unnoticed.

2. *To wish well*

For the Christian who has a proper sense of values, to wish well to others means, first and foremost, to desire their true and unchanging happiness—their eternal salvation.

There are some people who, knowing nothing about the religion of Christ or having very distorted ideas about it, hold that this eternal happiness is won by the endurance of unhappiness, as such, on earth. This is not the case; for there are trials and crosses which are received in a bad spirit and which provoke blasphemy and rebellion against God in some souls. Eternal happiness is won by the cultivation of virtue, and particularly of the virtue of charity. If we are to be admitted into the eternal Kingdom of Love, we must already have loved here on earth.

Faith will then have passed into Vision, and hope into Possession; but "Charity never falleth away" (1 *Cor.*, XIII, 8), since
it is the very breath of Heaven.

To wish well to others is, therefore, to wish for them a life of
love. It is to desire that the Charity of Christ may grow in them,
that the Holy Spirit may breathe more fruitfully upon their
spirits, and that the life of Christ may become more intense in
their souls, so that they may fulfill with ever increasing perfection, their vocation as members of Christ.

To wish well to our fellow brethren in Christ, is to desire with
an ardent desire that they should participate more intimately in
the life of the Mystical Body, and draw more deeply from those
supernatural and divine treasures which are the very substance
of their peace, their strength and their freedom as sons of God.
And, in this hierarchy of good, it is to desire for them the legitimate happiness of those who love one another on earth, according
to God's will: the joys of home, of family, of friendship, of art, of
knowledge and the pursuit of knowledge, the joys of the mind
and of the heart. To wish well to others, is to find one's own joy
in the happiness of others.

3. *To do good*

This does not mean simply to give alms or to do a good deed
or to perform some good works, in a passing and occasional way.

To do good, as members of the Mystical Body, is to create
about ourselves—in all our day-to-day relations with others—a
constant atmosphere of kindness, of cordiality, of fraternal and
helpful solidarity, which makes it a pleasure for others to work
with us, and creates warm bonds of friendship and of union of
hearts. An atmosphere, too, of peace, of joy, of tolerance and
expansiveness, which helps the others to blossom, to open their
hearts to good and to fraternal love, to improve, to find within
themselves and to spread around them a wealth of good qualities
which had previously remained latent and unsuspected. To do
good is to leave a warm glow of happiness wherever we have
been—or at least to add our little share to the stock of the world's
true happiness by maintaining an attitude of sincere affability
which seeks disinterestedly to give pleasure to others, to avert
from them all that would cause sadness and pain and to lead
them to where they will find joy in the peace of God.

Kindness involves a constant giving of ourselves to others, in
a wealth of thoughtful attentions which anticipate wishes before
they are expressed, of very tactful deference, of exquisite polite-

ness, of cheerful amiability, and of heartening words which encourage, sustain, invigorate and inspire to greater effort and more heroic endurance. A kind person knows, when necessary, how to offer sincere praise to others, not in order to flatter them or to win their esteem, but because they are worthy of such commendation. On the other hand, when genuine charity demands that he should take another person to task for that other person's good, a kind person does not hesitate to do so, because he desires above all the good of the soul. He shows thereby that he loves with a true love. Kindness, therefore, demands energy, courage and strength of will, especially in parents, teachers and all those who exercise authority.

O Jesus, Who has revealed to us the Infinite Kindness of the Father, help the members of Your Mystical Body to bear one another's burdens in the midst of the difficulties of life. Grant that, to the dark forces of malice and of hatred, they may together oppose the radiant and conquering power of kindness and of love.

65.　BY CHARITY WHICH FORGIVES

> *Bearing with one another and forgiving one another, if any have a complaint against another. Even as the Lord hath forgiven you, so do you also.*
>
> (Col., III, 13)

The charity which forgives is undoubtedly one of the summits of Christianity. In such charity, the transforming power of the grace and of the charity of Christ is vigorously manifested; and this power is made more compelling by the fact that it helps the Christian to conquer and overcome obstacles which are tenaciously reinforced by his own legitimate feelings of resentment at injuries done to him.

First obstacle: Our own nature

To forgive is, first of all, to stifle within us our natural feelings of resentment and anger, and perhaps even of hatred, as well as our desire to be avenged. Then, we must promptly forget and not let our minds dwell on the affront or the injury which has cut us to the heart. Finally, we must carry our generosity to the point of giving ourselves to those who have offended us. We do so by being friendly and courteous towards them, as we are to other people; by speaking to them, because there is a silence which freezes and which can be eloquent with bitterness; and by being ready and willing to do them any service. For is not forgiveness the perfect giving of one's self?

But, beneath all this effort of magnanimity, there is a legitimate feeling which we cannot smother—our desire for justice. We have been the victim of an injustice, and we cannot resign ourselves to enduring it without voicing the protest of an indignant conscience. To respect one's own rights as a human person, is a duty.

There · certainly can be occasions when a higher common good demands that we should seek legitimate reparation. But, when Jesus requires his disciples to forgive "till seventy times seven times" (*Matt.*, XVII, 22)—that is to say, always—He calls on them to rise superior to the plane of the individual and his rights, in order to consider their role as members of His Mystical Body.

The life of the Mystical Body, since that Body is a community of human beings with Christ as Head, would suffer constant debilitation and a slowing down of its very life-blood, if each member were wrapped up in himself and in a hungry concern for vindicating his rights. The charity of Christ desires to find no obstacle to its animation of the whole Body; and Jesus regards as acts of His members, only those acts on which He can set the seal of His Charity—of that Charity which pardoned His executioners and which works Redemption.

Second obstacle: public opinion

This objection springs up with a great show of logic and compulsion, in a wounded heart: "But this is not a matter which concerns myself: it concerns others. If life in society is not to become utterly impossible, the rules of morality must be respected. Have I the right to sacrifice them, and to flaunt public opinion which is judging me and which will brand me a coward?" A very legitimate concern for one's honor, immediately awakens the instinct of self-defense.

But to follow public opinion and to allow one's whole pattern of conduct to be dictated by it is not freedom. The Christian is free, when he dominates public opinion by seeking to enlighten it. One of the relics of paganism is this very concern for one's "honor"; but higher values have been brought into the world by Christianity. The greatness of soul shown by forgiveness, is to be measured in accordance with these values. Superior to all my rights is my right to love all my brethren, because I have a duty to do so—a duty and a right which makes me include among my brethren those who have injured me. Jesus has pointed to this spirit of forgiveness as the real touchstone of His true disciples. "For, if you love them that love you, what reward shall you have? Do not even the publicans this?" (*Matt.*, V, 46).

Third obstacle: the judging of the sin

No sooner have the legitimate feelings been conquered which stem from justice and honor, than a third obstacle presents itself —this time in the name of the truth. "This offence which strikes a blow at my reputation, is a sin. I have no right to seem to ignore or minimize it, or to act as though it had not occurred. It *has* occurred. It has also offended Christ, and He demands of me that I condemn it."

Here, the Charity of Christ demands, not only a generosity of heart which can sometimes be of heroic measure, but also and above all a clearness of mind sufficient to distinguish between two elements which seem to be indissolubly united: the sin and the sinner. The judging of the sin belongs to the true Judge—to Him Who sees the hearts and reads the most secret motives of men. But this life is the time for His Mercy; and Jesus, my Head, demands that I keep my judgment of others untainted by my passions and free from my personal prejudices, so that, animated by faith, it will be marked with something of His own Mercy and compassionate understanding.[1]

For, on earth, it is with His merciful Charity that He associates me. He desires that I share in the love and spirit of forgiveness that fills His Sacred Heart, by finding in Him the forgetting of the injury and by seeing the offender as a member of Christ's Body—by seeing him in the Person of Christ.

O Jesus, our Redeemer, how could it ever have been said that Your religion is alien to the life of the earthly city and without influence on that life? How greatly indeed would this earthly life be transformed if—amid the injuries, the misunderstandings and the injustices which set one against another in

---

1. (Cf. Cardinal Newman: "Whatever is right, whatever is wrong, in this perplexing world, we must be right . . . in learning patience, meekness, purity, forgiveness of injuries, and continuance in well-doing."—*Sermon One* in *Sermons on Subjects of the Day.—Translator's note*).

the heart of families, professions and communities—something of Your Divine Compassion were to become a real force in the world, through the members of Your Mystical Body.

66. BY PRACTICAL COMPASSION

Amen, I say to you, as long as you did it to one of these my least brethren, you did it to me.

(Matt., XXV, 40)

The scene of the Last Judgment throws exceptional light on the doctrine of the Mystical Body. As it is related to us by Saint Matthew, it links up with Christ's whole teaching about the vine and its branches, recorded by Saint John, and with Saint Paul's doctrine of the Body of Christ. It reveals the eschatological aspect of Christianity; but it also manifests the profoundly human and universal aspect of the Mystical Body.

1. *The Mystical Body and the actions of our everyday life*

Because the Mystical Body is an essentially spiritual reality, some are inclined to think that acts of the spiritual life—prayer and the offering of merits—are alone relevant to it. From this point of view, the communion of members within the Mystical Body, would consist solely in the reciprocal exchange among themselves of their prayers, their merits and their satisfactions. The whole life of the Mystical Body would thus remain on the plane of intention. And, undoubtedly, we have in this conception, one of the most touching and most efficacious forms of the Communion of Saints.

In the scene which He paints of the Final Judgment, however, Christ's words imply much more than this. All the actions of our human life, even the most material and the most temporal, appertain to the life of the Mystical Body. Indeed, Christ appears to have designedly and precisely chosen such actions—of eating, drinking, clothing, imprisonment, sickness.

The life of the Mystical Body is not something extraneous to human life, imposed from without, so to speak, on the daily life of men, while not being an intrinsic part of that life. On the contrary, these very humble and ordinary actions are the materials that must be permeated with the life of grace and of charity, in order to give a redemptive value to such actions. For the Church, the Mystical Body of Christ, takes to itself all that is human, sin alone excepted, in order to give eternal value to every one of our human thoughts and actions. At the Final Judgment, in the sight of all men, Christ will solemnly and definitively ratify the eternal value of our acts of practical compassion. It is not in that dread hour, however, that He imparts this value to them; for He already does so here on earth, in His Body which is the Church.

2. All men are called to become members of Christ

It is not human *actions* only which the Church transforms: she seeks to gather to herself all *men* and to transform them into members of Christ's Mystical Body. Who, then, are those presented, in Christ's account of the Final Judgment, as "ye blessed of my Father?" Are they those who were Christians from the very outset? It is quite clear that the Gospel teaching concerning the Final Judgment can be understood only in the light of Christ's entire doctrine of the necessity for faith and for Baptism into His Church, in order to be saved.

But it seems that our Savior desired thereby to teach us that He calls all men to become members of His Body. For the most striking aspect of this whole scene is the astonishment of all those who discover that, in the person of the poor and the afflicted, it was Christ Himself Whom they were assisting. It follows, therefore, that they were not conscious of this when they came to the assistance of the needy, and had not the intention of doing such actions for Christ. Herein, indeed, we see the Catholicity of the Church! Her vocation is to gather together all men, and to teach them to see Christ in each of their fellows, as one of His members. Their acts of practical compassion on earth, will have won for them a favorable judgment from the Supreme Judge of all mankind.

3. The value of practical compassion in the Church of Christ

This page of the Gospel has a very special significance for our own times. We are surrounded by those who are hungry and thirsty; by those who are homeless, displaced, deported, expelled —victims of a political régime, hounded out of their own country and made to wander without any place or kindred to which they can belong; by those who are naked and sick; by those, who, in prisons and concentration camps, are being forced to drag out an existence in utterly brutalizing conditions; by all those, in short, who are in the particularly acute anguish and misery which mark our times. Christ teaches us that we must see Him in all of these. It is faith which performs this miracle, and thus gives a lightsome and divine meaning to all these human realities.

But what Christ demands from us is an *effective* act of mercy —an act of "compassion." The word *compassion* implies *suffering with* a person: weeping "with them that weep" (*Rom.*, XII, 15), and suffering with those whose grief may lie too deep for tears. To be compassionate towards others is to enter into the sufferings of others, so that those sufferings become our own; to put our shoulder to the crosses of others, that we may aid them and console them in bearing their sufferings. This demands from us the giving of our whole being: of a mind able to understand the sufferings of others; of a heart which is tinder to the fire of true pity; and of a will which is resolved to give practical assistance. How few merciful souls there are in a world corrupted by selfishness and the thirst for selfish pleasure!

O Jesus, our Supreme Judge, in what more striking way could You have taught us the place which human compassion holds in Your Divine Heart and in Your Church? He who does an act of sincere human compassion, can see You Yourself in every one of those whom he assists. Our whole human life is thereby illuminated and transformed; for at every moment and in every one of our fellow-men, we are called to assist You in the person of those who "labor and are heavily burdened" with their crosses and their sufferings.

67. BY SPIRITUAL MERCY

> *Put ye on therefore . . . the bowels of mercy . . .*
>
> (Col., III, 12)

Spiritual mercy is a very exalted form of charity towards our neighbor. It consists in an acute sense of the spiritual distress of humanity, plunged in sin; but this must be accompanied by a firm resolution to cooperate in the redemption of the world. It implies a communion of heart and of soul in the dispositions of the merciful Heart of the Redeemer, Who desires at all costs to deliver men from their sins and to lead them to salvation in His Church.

1. *Slaves—"the servants of sin"* (*Rom.*, VI, 20).

Men are slaves: slaves of the flesh and of the senses; slaves of ambition and the pursuit of honors; slaves of egoism and of pride, of passion and of ignorance; slaves of their temperament and their vacillating moods, of their habits and their instincts, of their cowardice and their weakness; slaves of money and of pleasures. The world is full of slaves.

To be merciful is to suffer—in intimate union with the merciful Heart of the Redeemer—on account of the anguish and stifling burden of this servitude of men under the yoke of sin . . . "Whoever committeth sin is the servant of sin," said Christ (*John,* VIII, 34). To be merciful is to acquire—in the contemplation of the pierced Heart of our Divine Savior—the sense of sin and of the evil of sin; and the conviction that sin is the only real evil, when we consider it in itself, in relation to God and to Christ, and also in its consequences and its ravages.

True mercy, in the image of Christ's mercy, is not a proudly condescending and pharisaic pity for poor sinners—an attitude in itself perhaps sinful. To be truly merciful is to understand and love sinners, because we know the extent and the depth of the evil within ourselves; because, like Saint Paul, we have experienced the warrings of the flesh and the spirit, and have discovered in ourselves the marks of original sin—our inclination towards evil and the weakness of our will. "For that which I work, I understand not. For I do not the good which I will; but the evil which I hate, that I do . . . For the good which I will, I do not; but the evil which I will not, that I do . . . I find, then, a law, that when I have a will to do good, evil is present with me . . . But I see another law in my members, fighting against the law of my mind and captivating me in the law of sin that is in my members. Unhappy man that I am, who shall deliver me from the body of this death?" (*Rom.,* VII, 15-24). We know that this "other law" of which Saint Paul speaks here, is in us, and that therefore we are of the race of sinners. Hence we love sinners as we love ourselves.

2. *Victims of sin*

Besides being slaves of their personal sins, men are the victims of the world's sins: victims of the social injustices of an economic system, and of the oppression and vengeance of political régimes; victims of public opinion and of the propaganda machine; victims of scientific techniques and progress, which have been deflected from their true purpose because society has willed to trample on the higher demands of the moral law; victims of that society, which has become the place of sin, the occasion of sin and the cause of sin. Society should

help men to fulfill their eternal destiny; instead, it ceaselessly
puts obstacles in the way of their attaining their supreme end
of loving and serving God. It has sought to set up its earthly
kingdom apart from God, without God, and even against God.
By its laws, its institutions, its manners, its immorality, it has
stifled the human person, corrupted youth, destroyed the family
and set man against man and nation against nation.

To be merciful is to feel, to the point of anguish, the sins of
the world, and to seek some understanding of all that is implied
in the sins accumulated by generations of men against the Divine
Law, against social justice and against charity; of all the evils
occasioned by the sins of every day, of every night, of every hour,
in drawing men into the miry depths where all resistance and all
liberty are smothered in their souls.

To know the richness of mercy is to share in the dispositions
of the Heart of our Redeemer by experiencing in ourselves something of the shuddering horror at the vision of the sins of the
world, which filled His Heart and made Him say: "I pray not
for the world" (*John*, XVII, 9). The Beloved Apostle, Saint John,
that echo of the Heart of the Master, wrote: "Love not the world,
nor the things which are in the world. If any man love the world,
the charity of the Father is not in him" (1 *John*, II, 15). Nay
more, he called us to fight against the sins of the world: "For
whatsoever is born of God overcometh the world" (*Ibid.*, V, 4).
Though this vision of the world's sins is abysmally sad, it leads
the Apostle to cry aloud the triumph of Christ and of our faith
in Christ: "And this is the victory which overcometh the world:
Our faith. Who is he that overcometh the world, but he that
believeth that Jesus is the Son of God?" (*Ibid.*, V, 4-5).

3. *The ignorance and blindness of men*

The worst element in all this, is the blindness and the ignorance of these unhappy people. They do not know what sin is,
or what is sinful. They have become incapable of seeing and
judging their own actions and those of the world, in relation to
a moral law and an ideal of life. They are no longer aware that
lying, theft, adultery, abortion and crime in all its forms are
sinful. They even pride themselves openly on committing them,
regarding such actions as proofs that they are broad-minded,
shrewd and alert people. The hierarchy of values is reversed.
They have decided to deny the Redemption or to ignore it; and
they do not realize that they are forging the weapons that will
turn on their own makers, and will destroy society. They have

claimed to establish a heaven on earth, and instead have turned the world into a hell.[1] They sought absolute independence of all higher authority, and they have thereby become slaves. They boast that they have secured happiness on earth, but know that they have created anguish. Their whole plan turns against them, and their alleged happiness is dryness and despair: yet they continue their fevered run after deceitful pleasures, and their indulgence in dishonest speculations and foolish ambitions.

O Jesus, from the height of the Cross, You saw the forces of human blindness and hatred massed against You, and You have given us an example of the most sublime spiritual mercy by asking Your Father to forgive Your executioners because they knew not what they were doing. Grant that, inspired by this example, we may be filled with immense and inexhaustible compassion for all those who are slaves of their own sins and who are the unconscious victims of the sins of the world.

IV

COMMUNION OF THE MEMBERS ONE WITH ANOTHER

68. IN FAITH

So we, being many, are one body in Christ; and every one members one of another.
(Rom., XII, 5)

The relationships of men with one another would be entirely transformed if they were raised to the plane of faith. The theological virtue of charity cannot exist without the theological virtue of faith. In order that men may be able to regard themselves as "members one of another," they must learn, through faith, to view all human relationships in the higher terms of the Mystical Body. In this way, faith becomes for men the source of reciprocal light and enrichment, and the principle of vital relationship among the members of the same Body.

---

1. (Compare Cardinal Newman's arresting definition: "Hell is the habitation of no human affections."—*Translator's note*).

1. *Faith is the source of reciprocal contacts*

Faith establishes a spiritual contact with the personal Christ, and—through Him and in Him—with the other members of His Body. By His Spirit, animating the faith of His members, Christ establishes a bond of union among His members, opening the heart of each in a warmth of charity for the others. He wills that, in Him, we should live a life of knowledge shared together; and that the same light of faith which makes us adhere to the Person of Christ, should also lead us to incorporate ourselves in the Whole Christ, and to see Christ in His members.

Egoism and faith produce opposite effects. Egoism makes us hug ourselves and draw a little tight circle about ourselves and our own interests: faith, on the contrary, makes us go out of ourselves to meet Christ in each of the other members of His Mystical Body.

Each person who bears the mark of the Divinity through Baptism, is a unique mystery through his incorporation in Christ; and it is to the threshold of this mystery that faith leads us. By faith, each of us enters into the mystery of the other person. Faith takes precedence even of love, for faith is the foundation of love. Thus, on a higher plane which is superior to all the oppositions of nature, faith is a principle of vision common to all the members of Christ. Through this principle, they discover that they are brothers in Christ, united with one another, sharing the same life, living by the same faith (*Ephes.*, IV, 5), and called to communicate to one another, by charity, the inexhaustible riches of Christ.

2. *Faith is the solid establishment and permanent foundation of reciprocal relationships*

In the first place, faith constructs the relationships of the members among themselves, and establishes their contacts with one another, on the principle of *reciprocal respect*. Christians who follow the logic and obey the demands of their Faith, treat one another with a cordial respect which, rising superior to all the conventions and nice social barriers of the world, favors and fosters genuine and sincere contacts among them, with nothing of the merely artificial, conventional, constrained or hypocritical. Faith is a school of respect, because each person is really regarded by the other, and is himself regarded in turn, as truly and really "sacred." It is a principle of vision; and therefore also a principle of judgment which invites each person to judge others, not according to appearances, but according to the profound and sacred realities which make them "other Christs."

Furthermore, faith fosters contacts among men, on the basis of *a reciprocal confidence.* What creates confidence and trust among men? Honesty; or again, personal merit, qualities, virtues; or yet again, a good reputation. But very soon, human limitations come to light, and confidence is destroyed. What maintains confidence and mutual trust among men, is a reality which lies beyond the limitations of the creature: it is the bond of union which each person has with Christ, and, in Christ, with his brethren. This is a bond which, by its very nature, is indestructible.

According to the extent to which this bond is slackened through the fault of men themselves, other causes of a human kind can enter in and can succeed in temporarily disrupting this confidence. But as soon as the bonds of unity in Christ are renewed by a recovery of faith, the climate of confidence and trust is restored.

3. *Faith effects mutual enrichment*

A person who, in faith, receives a benefit from his brother, derives from this a personal enrichment for this own soul. This is true of any benefit conferred by one person on another: it may take the form of a word spoken in season, a suggestion made, an example given, a service rendered. The person receiving this benefit, is aware that he owes it to the goodness of Christ, Whom, with the eyes of faith, he sees in the person of his generous brother. This has the effect of increasing his love for Our Lord, Who guides all these events in the life of His Body for the good of His members, with a constant and delicate solicitude for each member. His faith becomes more ardent and more firm. The example of the goodness of the other person will lead him to behave in the same manner towards his brethren in Christ.

On the other hand, he who gives, knows that he gives to Christ Himself. He gives for love of Christ, Whom, with the eyes of faith, he sees in his brother. He does not expect a recompense from men. He gives in faith, without seeing, perhaps, the result of his generosity; and in so giving, he receives an increase of grace, of new enlightenment and of charity.

O Jesus, our Head, grant that Your disciples may realize the full significance of that beautiful title: "the faithful," which they derive from their Faith. May they be ever more faithful to You, to Your Spirit, and to Your Church! But grant them also to under-

stand that, through their faith in You, it is You alone Who have the power to place them and to establish them in a condition of reciprocal fidelity one towards the other, so that the whole structure of their life may be founded on the unshakable basis of their human brotherhood in You, and not on fallible human qualities in one another.

69. IN HOPE

Looking for the blessed hope and coming of the glory of the great God and our Savior Jesus Christ .

(Titus, II, 13)

Hope is a virtue which too many Christians regard in an individualistic manner, as each person's certainty that he himself may be saved. But, in its object and in the means which it uses to achieve its object, hope is essentially a social, community virtue, and is bound up with collective issues.

1. *Its object*

The object of the virtue of hope is the confident awaiting of the Return of Christ. We Christians are certain that Our Lord will one day return, but this time in all His glory as the Supreme Judge, for the definitive establishment of the Kingdom and of His reign which will never end. This is affirmed by the Church's authentic *Credo,* the echo and interpreter of Scripture and of the most ancient Tradition. The first Christian communities are noted for having lived in expectation of this great event.

In what sense can it be said that each of us is personally involved today in a future historic event which seems to be so remote?

This is so, in the first place, because the perspective of the General Judgment, at which Christ will preside as Judge, has here and now a constant repercussion on the Christian's life. In the presence of the whole Body, each member will be judged by the Head on his behavior towards the Whole Christ during his entire life. No one can then plead that he is being taken by surprise, and that he has not been clearly warned. The teaching of Christ in this matter is clear and formal. He has announced this judgment and has described it in exact detail. He has declared that we shall be judged on our charity towards the members of His Body,

and that He will regard this charity as the proof of our love
for Him. We shall be judged on our charity, because charity
contains and animates all the other virtues; on our actions and
our omissions; on our most intimate thoughts and our most hidden
sentiments. All will be revealed before the whole world on that
great Day. This thought safeguards and protects us here on earth
in the hour of temptation, and stimulates us to a more ardent
generosity in discharging the duties of our state. It gives us the
joy and consolation of knowing that we shall contemplate, in
the souls of all the Saints, the splendors and the full blossoming
of the grace of our Head throughout all the centuries that are
now no more.

Furthermore, it is at that moment that our bodies will be
individually raised from the dead, to join our souls from which
they have been separated since our death. "The resurrection of
our bodies is delayed until the end of the world," says Saint
Thomas, "in order that all may be raised up together, and that
the joy of each soul may be increased by sharing in the joy of all."

Finally, it is in this hour that the collective work of the
Redemption of mankind will be consummated. This work has
been willed by the Holy Trinity in God's eternal plan, and it has
been and is being carried out on earth by Christ and by His
Church; but it will take on its full meaning only in the supreme
moment of our resurrection, when time shall be swallowed up
forever in eternity. Christians who are struggling to live a life
of faith, and who cooperate, throughout their earthly life, in
this work for the salvation of all mankind, should look forward
in hope to this Day; for then they will see the meaning of all the
sacrifices and the efforts they have made during their years on
earth.

2. *The means*

Hope bears not only on the End, but also on the means of
attaining that End: all the means offered to us by the Church;
all the treasures of the Communion of Saints.

Hope should also bear, in a secondary but a real manner, on
the reciprocal help which the members of the Body should give
to one another, not only by prayer and sacrifice, but in their
normal everyday encounters and relations. The fact that they are
drawn together by the same hope, disposes the members of the
same Body to assist one another. They are associated in the same
work; they rely on one another in their common task of building
the City of God. This shared hope already draws souls more

closely together, and attunes them to expect that supernatural help which they hope to obtain from one another.

It is then that Jesus, who keeps them united one with another, enables them to be "members one of another," in an active manner and in all their relationships. To one, He gives the grace to find in his brother a virtue which he had not hitherto remarked in him; while He makes another understand more clearly how much real holiness is involved in the struggle which his brother is making against a difficult disposition and against a particularly violent passion. Through the light and the action of Christ, each discovers some aspect in which his brother is for him a source of help and of cooperation.

The more souls throw themselves wide to the illuminating and transforming action of the Head, the more they will realize that this help and cooperation which they received from one another at any given moment, was precisely that of which they then stood most in need. They discover, with joy, that they complete one another. They learn that, in addition to the joy of giving to others, there is also the joy of receiving from others, and of being able continually to expect supernatural help from them. In the case both of him who gives and him who receives, it is Jesus Christ Who gives, receives, stimulates and draws unto Himself.

O Jesus, Your Christians have not yet understood all the riches You have placed in the virtue of hope. For many of them, to hope is to follow one of two courses: either to decide for something in which they blindly trust; or to hazard one choice simply because it appears to offer a better chance of success than its alternative. Grant to all Christians to realize that, when You announce an event, it is absolutely certain to occur; and that, when You make a promise, You fulfill it faithfully.

70. IN CHARITY

> *From whom the whole body, being compacted and fitly joined together, by what every joint supplieth, according to the operation in the measure of every part, maketh increase of the body, unto the edifying of itself in charity.*
>
> (Ephes., IV, 16)

Over and above the giving of benefits and/of services, and

even above the giving of ourselves, charity rises, in Christ, to the communion of persons: the communion of one with another. Every religious community must be characterized by this, if it is to fulfill its mission in the Church and in the eyes of the world. Even secular communities take on their full meaning only at that high level, when they are animated by the charity of Christ.

1. *The source*

"Charity is of God" (I *John*, IV, 7): the charity which unites two souls, has God for its origin. God is at work within them, to bring them closer together and to assist them in understanding each other. The source of love is the Blessed Trinity. The waters of infinite Love flow in the Heart of Jesus Christ. And it is He Who, as Head, sends His Holy Spirit into the hearts of His members, to spread in them that charity which is a participation in His own Charity, and, through His Charity, a participation in the infinite Love with which the Holy Trinity loves Itself and loves us in the Holy Ghost.

What, then is the mission of the Holy Ghost in the Mystical Body and in each of its members? It is a mission of unity, in the very image of His role as the Bond of Love and of Communication in the bosom of the Blessed Trinity! The Charity which comes from God and is communicated to us by the Holy Ghost, contains in itself, therefore, this tendency to unify souls, and the power to establish them in a reciprocal communion: the "Communion of Saints."

2. *The object*

What is the object of the charity which keeps two persons united one with the other, in Christ? It is not directly, for him who loves, the *human person* of the loved one. The theological virtue of charity raises souls to the level of the divine, and achieves a divine object. Is this object, then, directly and uniquely *God in the other person?* Does it mean that the one who loves should abstract in some way from the other person and contemplate God in His Transcendence, even to the point of becoming quite indifferent to the concerns of the other person on the human plane? By no means.

The object of this mutual communion is a mystery, a mystery living in each member—the mystery of his incorporation in Christ and his union with Christ. It is the mystery of his existence as a member of Christ, incorporated in the Christ-Head, participating in the life of the Blessed Trinity and of the whole Mystical Body: "that you also may have fellowship *with us*, and our fellowship may be *with the* Father and *with* his Son, Jesus Christ" (I *John*, I, 3). The object of their reciprocal communion is, therefore, their common bond with the charity of Christ, which makes them members one of another, members of the Whole Christ.

To be in communion with another person, in Christ, means more, therefore, than sympathetically understanding that person, and being united with him in his thoughts, his feelings, his trials or his joys: that is to say, it means more than the understanding and the realization of solidarity with him. All these dispositions are necessary if such communion between two persons is to exist: they are at once the condition and the effect of charity. To be in communion with another person, is to communicate in the mystery of the life of Christ in him, to communicate in the mystery of the Whole Christ. This implies that—by what is most interior, deepest, and at once most divine and most human, in us—we are linked through faith with the other person, and we seize upon what is most interior, deepest, and at once most divine and most human, in him, as a fellow-member of Christ. This is effected by a reciprocal communication of life and of love, which Jesus Christ Himself operates in both members, by His Holy Spirit, to such a degree that the good of the one becomes identified with the good of the other, and both now form but one in the same participation and the same communion in the same Mystery of the Whole Christ.

3. *The purpose*

What is the purpose of this mutual communion? Is the direct purpose, that he who loves may experience satisfaction or personal recompense, joy or peace, in this movement of charity? These are certainly the fruits of charity; but its purpose is here more detached, more generous, more universal.

Is the purpose, then, that the other person should find his consolation, his strength and his happiness, in this *élan* of charity of which he is the object? This also is an extremely beneficent *effect* of charity.

Mutual communion has for its essential purpose, the building of the Whole Christ. These human persons are raised to such heights of Divine Charity, in order that they may mutually assist the growth of Christ in each other, and at the same time in others. It is in order that, in the human community on earth which they create by their union of hearts, the supreme design of the Savior may be realized: "Father . . . that they may be one, as we also are one."

O Jesus, You have willed to establish in the very depths of the life of the Divine Persons, the foundation of that communion which exists between those who have become members of Your Body. When I am dealing with one of Your baptized, give me the grace, by Your Holy Spirit, to communicate in the mystery of His mystical identification with You; so that it may be indeed You Whom I love in him, and that I may permit him likewise to love You in the mystery of my mystical identification with You.

71. IN MEEKNESS

> *Blessed are the meek, for they shall possess the land.*
>
> (Matt., V, 5)

Meekness is one of the master-virtues of Christianity, and one of the most necessary in community life, while also being one of the most misunderstood virtues, and among those most threatened today by the cult of power. There is a strong tendency to look upon this virtue as a sign of weakness. The modern world admires the "tough," the violent, the strong, and contrasts them to their advantage with the "meek" of the Gospel. But this is a complete misunderstanding of the virtue; for meekness is strength, violence, conquest and domination.

1. *The nature of meekness*

Meekness is the respecting, in others, of their vocation and of their personality as members of Christ.

Each member has his personal place in the Mystical Body, as also his gifts of nature and of grace, and his own mission in relation to the good of the Whole Body. In the ordinary intercourse between man and man, respect for this plan of God is a rare thing indeed. The conventions of modern social life impose, of course, a certain tolerance of one another, an attitude of amiability, and the respecting of certain rules of politeness. But, in the depths of our souls, there is opposition. We are unwilling that others should differ from us, that they should think, feel and judge otherwise than we ourselves do. We grow testy and cool towards others, as soon as anything shows itself in them which threatens our own selfishness, our tastes, our opinions, our preferences and our rights. We may even become downright angry with what clearly contradicts our own selfish self-centeredness.

Meekness is a virtue which ensures self-mastery to the Christian, by helping him to curb his instinctive anger and his resentment.

Meekness is a participation in the meekness of the Christ-Head. It fits in perfectly with the plan of the Head, Who has willed that there should be a diversity of members, of functions and of gifts, in the unity of the Body and for the sake of that unity. He has willed this diversity, in order that all the members should be complementary, one of another; that they should all assist one another, collaborating in the same task; that no one should look upon himself as sufficient unto himself; that, in completing one another, the members of the Mystical Body should *together* tend towards the possession of a higher good.

Meekness, therefore, is not limited to the fact of our accepting that others are different from ourselves. This virtue has more than this negative aspect; it makes us positively wish, with sincere benevolence and good will, that each of the members should have his distinctive mark; and it causes us to rejoice in this diversity. For, by this virtue, we are made happy in this extraordinary and wonderful variety of members of the Mystical Body. But meekness carries us yet further and yet higher. It inspires us to communicate, or at least to strive earnestly to communicate, in the personal mystery of each soul, to throw ourselves open to each, and to welcome anything that may divulge that mystery, be it a word, a silence, a look, a confidence, a gesture, a hidden action.

2. *The conditions of meekness*

The virtue of meekness is a synthesis of two efforts which appear contradictory: on the one hand, submission; on the other, domination.

In the first place, it is *submission to reality*—reality in ourselves, in others, and in the events and circumstances of life. Every virtue is in itself a submission to reality, because, in the last analysis, *reality* for the Christian is the expression of the Divine Will. Patience, humility and self-oblation are submissions to reality, as meekness is a submission, but each has its own character. Thus, patience is a resigned acceptance of reality; humility is the logic of truth; and self-oblation is an offering of love. Meekness is characterized by a cheerful and radiant serenity. It does not permit itself to be dominated or crushed by reality:

it rises superior to, and dominates, every circumstance of life.

For, although it is a submission, meekness is also a domination —*a domination of the self* in order to put that self to the service of others, and to facilitate contacts and relationships. It is his aspect of *mastery*, which Christ, it would seem, desired to stress very particularly in the proclaiming of this Beatitude: "Blessed are the meek, for they *shall possess* the land." This is the symbol of the authority acquired by the meek, and of the enrichment brought by meekness. It does not mean simply that they, personally, shall always have perfect self-possession. They shall possess the land. In all circumstances, and wherever they may be, they will impose themselves on the situation and will dominate it. An angry person is a vanquished person. The meek conquer while being apparently vanquished.

But the metaphor of combat tends to falsify the perspectives of the virtue of meekness; for what meekness implies is the generous effort by which two people, instead of opposing each other, join in aiding each other to attain the same ideal, and to acquire a good which is superior to them both and which they possess together: truth, friendship, goodness, art.

Finally, if meekness is to be a supernatural virtue, it requires the grace of Christ, and must be raised to the plane of Christ. It would be a mistake to suppose that temperament is sufficient, though, of course, temperament must be taken into account, since it is a reality which cannot be neglected without serious consequences. But a temperament inclined to laziness, and devoid of spirit and of vigor, is not a solid foundation for the virtue of meekness. When faced with the necessity of exerting itself or of enduring what is burdensome, such a temperament quickly reveals its innate weakness. We look for the presence of the authentic virtue of meekness, in those who, being by nature inclined to anger, have succeeded in dominating their passions, by the grace and the virtue of Christ.

O Jesus, however meritorious and necessary our personal efforts may be to acquire the virtue of meekness, it is not by these efforts that we succeed in doing so. It is You, and You alone, Who enables us to acquire this virtue, by allowing us to participate in the meekness of Your Sacred Heart. Grant that we may enter more and more into this Heart, which burns with desire for the unity of all Your members in You. For it is through Your Sacred Heart that we must enter into relations with the other members. It is this Divine Heart Which will open to others our poor hearts, shut as they are in their own selfishness: it is

*this Heart Which will enable us to welcome others, to under-
stand them, to help them to be themselves and to fulfill their
mission as members of Your Mystical Body.*

72. WITH THE CHURCH SUFFERING

*For all those who sleep in the sleep of
peace.*

(Mass for the Dead)

The communion between us and the Holy Souls in Purgatory has not been severed. They belong to the Church, as really
as we do: they, to the Church Suffering; we, to the Church Militant. But it is the same Church in both cases, the same Mystical
Body of Christ. We can help them greatly by our prayers, our
offerings and our Masses. The Souls in Purgatory, moreover, have
a great mission to fulfill in the Church.

1. *Our mutual fraternal aid*

In her liturgy, the Church does not pray to the Souls in
Purgatory, or require us to pray to them; but, by her example and
her teaching, she instructs us to pray earnestly for them. They
stand in urgent need of our fraternal aid.

They need our help, *because they can no longer do anything
for themselves personally.* They are now powerless to merit for
themselves, and therefore can acquire no new merits. They look
for everything to the Whole Christ and to the Mercy of the
Father. Any person who does not realize that the Church comprises also this suffering part, which has been committed to him
as to the other members of the Church Militant, lacks a full
appreciation of the meaning of the Church, the meaning of the
whole Church. Prayer for the Souls in Purgatory is not a private
devotion. It is an act of the Church, an act of membership in the
Church, an act of solidarity in Christ. Let us remember in a
special way, all those who have no one to pray for them individually. The Church herself is mindful of them, in her collective
prayer: "pro omnibus defunctis."

Again, they need our help *because they are suffering.* Theirs
is a suffering of *expiation:* expiation of the temporal punishment
due to sins already pardoned. It is also a suffering of *purification:*
these souls have been subjected to the particular judgment. They
have seen themselves clearly and as they really are, they have

discovered the evil of sin, of their own sins and of those of the world; they are filled with remorse for not having understood, in time, the calls of Divine Love, for not having answered them, for having rejected them. This clear remembrance of their resistance is a torture in itself, because they now realize that God had a right to their love; and because they glimpse what could have been their degree of glory in eternal life, if they had been faithful. And now, they feel that they are poor and miserable indeed by comparison with what they might have been; and they regret the emptiness of their life and of their personal action while on earth. They know now the role that had been assigned to them in the Mystical Body. The vision of their selfishness during their earthly life, fills them with horror, when they see it against the mighty perspective of the Whole Christ.

Finally, this suffering is *a suffering of love,* and from this aspect it is the most searing of all. On the one hand, these souls love God ardently, with a love that is purer, more generous and more disinterested, by reason of the fact that it is more enlightened through their realization that God is indeed the Supreme Good and the One Thing Necessary. On the other hand, they are deprived of Him: not, of course, that they are rejected and cast aside, but they suffer because they are not yet able to enjoy the direct vision of God, the desire for which is now a devouring fire within them.[1]

---

1. (This idea has been magnificently expressed by Cardinal Newman in *The Dream of Gerontius.* The Angel tells the Soul that the

> sight of the Most Fair
> Will gladden thee, but it will pierce thee too;

and that the soul must

> Learn that the flame of the Everlasting Love
> Doth burn ere it transform.

Later in the poem come the splendid lines:

> Thou wilt be sick with love, and yearn for Him . . .
> There is a pleading in His pensive eyes
> Will pierce thee to the quick, and trouble thee.
> And thou wilt hate and loathe thyself; for, though
> Now sinless, thou wilt feel that thou hast sinn'd,
> As never thou didst feel; and wilt desire
> To slink away, and hide thee from His sight;
> And yet wilt have a longing aye to dwell
> Within the beauty of His countenance.
> And these two pains, so counter and so keen—
> The longing for Him, when thou seest Him not;
> The shame of self at thought of seeing Him—
> Will be thy veriest, sharpest purgatory.

This whole section of Newman's great poem is a fine commentary on the sufferings of Purgatory. (*Translator's note*).

2. *Their mission in the Church*

Though the Souls in Purgatory can do nothing for themselves, they can do much for us and for the Church.

They are, in the first place, the *witnesses of hope*. They are sure of their salvation, and they await, with entire certainty, the coming of the Savior. Unlike ours, their hope is not shadowed by the fear of personal failure, for they are no longer in a state in which they can endanger their salvation.

The Souls in Purgatory are also *apostles of charity*. They are fixed in the friendship of God, Who loves them and Whom they love. With what merciful love does not Jesus Christ encompass them! They are nearer than ever to Him: "In Christo quiescentibus"—they rest in Christ (*Canon of the Mass*). They are more perfectly attuned to His desires and to His great designs. Not only are they incapable of revolting against God because of their suffering, but they accept that suffering in a spirit of love. They adore the Justice of God, and communicate in all the infinite love which fills this justice in their regard. Moreover, they are concerned for the growth of the Mystical Body: they offer themselves for the increase of the Whole Christ, and perhaps they even collaborate actively in the advancement of the Kingdom. For how could God, in His Mercy, fail to be touched by their selflessness and their generosity?

Finally, the souls in Purgatory are, for us, *masters of purity and of holiness*. How beautiful they are in their state of grace and in their radiation of Christ! They compellingly remind us of the demands of holiness—of what intensive purification is necessary if we are to enter into the Glory of the Father. Their state is a silent appeal to us not to postpone our conversion to God from day to day, because the day quickly comes when it is already too late.

O Jesus, say unto all those who have just lost a loved one, that they must rely on Your Mercy; but also that they must not regard themselves as having fulfilled their duty towards their dear one by a few prayers said in the time of immediate mourning. If You have not deigned to reveal to us the actual state of those from whom we are parted for a time, is not this in order to provoke more constant relations of love between Your Church Militant and Your Church Suffering?

73. WITH THE CHURCH TRIUMPHANT

Communicantes.
(Canon of the Mass)

Each morning, in the Holy Mass, when the celebrant pro-
nounces these astounding words, his soul is caught up in a more
profound awareness of the dimensions of the Catholic Church.
Around this altar, where the Eucharistic Sacrifice is being offered,
the Saints of Heaven are present, and above all, the Blessed
Virgin Mary. By Christ and in Christ, we enter into relations
with them.

1. *The extraordinary greatness of this act*

"Communicants" . . . What an extraordinary act this is, by
which we, who are still pilgrims on earth and in time, rejoin in
eternity the Saints of Heaven! In Christ, the presence of the
Saints of Heaven becomes a reality for us, so that we are no
longer separated from them. They live in God by the life of
Christ— that same life which animates His Mystical Body and
keeps us united one with another.

Charity creates an unbroken link between them and us; for
charity, which accompanies grace, causes us to enter into eternal
life, even while we are on earth. By charity, we have "eternal
life abiding in us" (*John*, III, 15). Charity effects the passage
from death to life: "We know that we have passed from death
to life, because we love the brethren" (1 *John*, III, 14). Charity
lifts us to the level of eternity. It therefore transcends, in us, the
limits of space and time. The Saints are in the perfection of
eternal life; we are in the commencement of eternal life.

2. *Our community with the Saints*

For our part, we can communicate with the souls of the
Saints, with their person, with their virtues, with their merits,
with their prayer. Our prayers honor them, and contribute to
their glory by extending the radiance of their influence and by
manifesting their personal mission in the Mystical Body. But,
even when we are addressing ourselves to one Saint in particular,
we are communicating, in Christ, with all the Saints. We are
unceasingly supported by the prayers and by the merits of all
the Saints.

Their prayers for us are efficacious, urgent, and full of mercy. They are efficacious prayers, because they are the prayers of the elect, which are all-powerful with the Sacred Heart of Christ. They are urgent prayers, because the Saints love us with the same love with which they love God, and with which they earnestly desire the growth of the Whole Christ. They are merciful prayers, because the Saints know our needs and our struggles in our trials and tribulations on earth. They see us in the Light of the Word. In the Word, they are aware of everything on earth which it is necessary that they should know for the accomplishment of their mission in Heaven.

O Jesus, Our Head, it is indeed You Yourself Whom we contemplate and adore in the souls of Your Saints, with whom, through You, we enter into communion. Their example exercises, a powerful attraction over us, but this is not alone because it is, in itself, noble and elevating. Their example attracts us, above all, because it is Your Holiness which shines in them and is radiated by them; because it is Your virtues and Your grace which manifest their merits to us; and because it is Your Holy Spirit Who acts in them and in us, for the same mighty purpose —the building up of the Whole Christ.

CONCLUSION

74. A COMMUNITY OF CHARITY

> *And the multitude of the believers had but one heart and one soul. Neither did any one say that aught of the things which he possessed was his own: but all things were common unto them.*
>
> (Acts, IV, 32)

The primitive Church of Jerusalem, in its beginnings, is an excellent image of what the Church of Christ should be throughout the ages, on the spiritual plane, with the Communion of Saints: that is to say, it should be a community of persons having "but one heart and one soul," having a common purpose and destiny, and sharing goods and services.

1. A *community of persons*

In the Whole Christ, it is by their interior dispositions that the members communicate one with another. They are linked together by what is deepest in their souls, and that is why the Communion of Saints is possible beyond the limits of the body and of the visible world. This communication occurs through the same life of their divinized souls, through their life of charity and of grace; and still more profoundly through Christ, Who is the Life of their souls, the Principle of their supernatural life. It is in Him that they are His members, and are members one of another. It is He Who makes them communicate—*communicantes*—among themselves, being united with one another by what is deepest in their nature, to the extent that, in Him and with Him, they form "in a sense, only one (mystical) person"[1] —the Whole Christ.

The prayer of Jesus is accomplished: "that they all may be one in us." This interpenetration of souls, this communication in love, is the image of the circumincession of the Divine Persons, by which the three Divine Persons reciprocally exist Each in the Others, give themselves One to Another, and though distinct by their relations of origin, form all Three an absolute unity in the unity of the same Divine Nature which belongs whole and entire to Each of the Divine Persons.

2. A *community of goods and of services*

In Christ, all His Members are so united one with another, that everything done in charity by one member has its repercussions on all the others; and that, on the other hand, the good of all has its repercussion on each individual member. "He who lives in a state of charity, participates in all the good that is done in the whole world" (Saint Thomas: *Expos. in Symbol.*): he participates actively, by giving, and passively, by receiving. He participates passively, because the state of charity, through the void created in the soul by self-oblivion and by a throwing of itself wide to the whole life of the Mystical Body, puts the soul in a condition to receive; and he participates *actively* because the state of charity creates a condition in which he offers himself for the good of the whole Body.

Why does charity create this mysterious bond, and why does it exercise this universal action? In the first place, because the charity of the member participates in the charity of the Head, and therefore in its radiance throughout the entire Body and

---

1. Saint Thomas: "quasi una persona."

even through all mankind. An act of charity by a member cannot exist except by a participation in the charity of Christ. While it is the personal action of the member, its value comes from what there is of Christ in such action. As such, therefore, it shares in the universal fruitfulness of the Grace and Charity of Christ.

Furthermore, when it is perfect, charity—which is a participation in the Holy Spirit Who creates the unity of the Mystical Body—effects such a unity among the members of the Mystical Body, that each regards the good of the other member as his own good,[1] and rejoices in it. In Heaven, the joy of the elect will be to contemplate in the others the good accomplished in them by the Lord, and to associate themselves with that good, in order to give thanks as if they themselves had been the sole or the first beneficiaries.

3. *A community of destiny and of purpose*

One might excusably be led to imagine that, though united in the possession of the same goods, each member would pursue, on his own account, a personal destiny different from that of the others. But this is not so. The members are bound one to another in the pursuit of the same destiny and purpose: the formation of the Whole Christ for the glory of God and the Redemption of the world.

How can each member cooperate in the growth of the Whole Christ in mankind? The more Christ grows in the individual member, the more fruitful is that member's cooperation in the building of the Whole Christ. And, on the other hand, the more he cooperates in the great work, by the gift of his whole self, the more Christ grows in him. Christ gives Himself in greater measure to him, in proportion as he gives himself to the Whole Christ, by a charity which is selfless, universal, and faithful to the love of Him Who has "first loved us" (1 *John*, IV, 10).

O Lord, Who has chosen, for the conversion of the world—"that the world may believe" (John, XVII, 21)—the witness of a community of Your disciples united in Your charity, we thank You for having given us the Church. Grant that, by our way of life, we may never place an obstacle to the mission of charity and of unity which You have confided to Your Church in order that, animated by Your Divine Spirit, Your Church might gather to herself all mankind for the formation, in her, of Your Mystical Body.

---

1. Saint Thomas: "There is a sense in which what one possesses individually is the common possession of all the others; because perfect Charity makes each one regard the good of the other as his own good" (IV Sent., d. 49, q. 5).

PART THREE

THE MYSTERY
OF THE CATHOLIC CHURCH

*CHRIST'S ACTIVITY
IN THE CATHOLIC CHURCH
ANIMATED BY HIS SPIRIT*

FOREWORD

At this stage in his consideration of the Mystery of the Whole Christ, the disciple sometimes comes up against a difficulty. He has been attracted by the Head, directing and animating His Mystical Body. He has learned to admire this community of divine life and of charity, formed in Christ by the living members of this Body. But what, he asks, is the role of the Church, a visible society, in these relationships of souls with Christ?

The Christian realizes quite clearly, of course, at every stage, that he is in the Church and that he belongs to the Church. He is well aware that the Church gives him the Gospel, and explains it to him in order to transmit to him, in all fidelity, the true message of Christ. In the Doctrine and the Sacraments of the Church, he finds the light, the strength and the life which he requires to live like Christ and with Christ. And yet, he has still to discover the Mystery of the Church as a visible society in its relations with the Mystical Body.

Here he may be tempted to regard this matter in various ways:

a) He may envisage the Mystical Body simply as the invisible community of redeemed mankind, so that he thinks in terms of two Churches: one invisible, the other visible;

b) Or again, he may hold that this community of mankind in the Mystical Body contains only those who are in a state of grace, the presence of sinners being incompatible with this Body;

c) Finally, he may make a distinction between a Church which is a juridical society, and a Church which is a community of love.

All these are errors which must be cleared away if we are to understand the real nature of the Mystical Body.

How few there are, even among Christians sincerely regarding themselves as sons of the Church, who have sufficient spiritual enlightenment to give to the Church her due place in their relations with Christ!

For some, the Church is a troublesome intermediary between themselves and Christ. She distracts them in their personal relations with Jesus Christ. They prefer the little devotions of their own choosing, to the liturgy of the Church, to her High Mass and to her Sacraments. The doctrine of the Church, with her dogmas, seems to create constant obstacles to the spontaneous outpourings of their imagination and their sensibility. And what of the Church's magisterium? They will not obey fallible men: they have their own minds to guide them! So they sit in judgment on the heads of the Church, and find fault with the Encyclicals.

For others, the Church is something apart from their relations with Christ. They admit that they find help and light in the Church, when it suits them to have recourse to her. She is a useful addition, an exterior help, in certain cases. But what really counts with them is the possibility of establishing absolutely personal relations between themselves and the Humanity of Christ. They consider that the Church has no part in this intimate domain. This is demanded, according to them, by self-respect, and by respect for one's conscience and spiritual life.

For others again, the Church is indeed a necessary means of entering into relations with Jesus Christ in His Personal Humanity. But they do not see the Church as the Whole Christ. They take up an attitude of spiritual individualism, which satisfies them. They have not yet discovered the social and community aspect of the Mystical Body.

*   *   *

The Church is not an obstacle or a hindrance to the soul's relations with Christ. On the contrary, indeed, it is in the Church and through the Church that the soul knows Christ, enters into contact with Him, can communicate in His life, live by Him, continue Him, imitate Him and love Him.

The Church is the Sacrament of Christ.

The Church is the Mystery of the expansion and communication of Christ.

This is the aspect of the Mystery of Christ which the Christian is invited to contemplate in Part Three of this book. He will enter, by faith, into the Mystery of the Church: the mystery of her essential marks; the mystery of her hierarchy; the mystery of her Sacraments. He will come to understand that, today as throughout all the centuries, the Church reproduces and accomplishes in souls all that Christ, her Head, has lived. The Church herself is the great sacrament, because she is the visible sign

*of the divine grace, presence and action of Christ, and the chan-
nel through which the Divine Life of Christ is given to us. In
the voice of the Church, it is the teaching of Christ which we
hear, in its pristine purity. Through the Church, we are able to
re-live the mysteries of Christ. Through the Church, the actions
and gestures of Christ are continued and maintained, in all their
efficacious power. In the Church and through the Church, Jesus
Christ forms for Himself His Mystical Body, throughout the ages,
and draws all mankind into that Body, in order to build the
Whole Christ.*

*Such ideas, with their universal and community perspectives,
shatter the whole framework of a merely individualist spirituality.
From there, we pass on to isolate and consider the essential characteristics that distinguish this "new man"—the Christian in the
Whole Christ.*

CHAPTER ONE

Credo Ecclesiam

I BELIEVE IN THE CHURCH

THE MYSTERY OF THE CHURCH

75. THE MYSTERY OF A HUMAN-DIVINE SOCIETY

Christ also loved the Church.
(Ephes. V, 25)

"Christ, the Head and Model of the Church, is not whole and entire if we regard in Him only His visible Human Nature . . . or His invisible Divine Nature; for Christ is one *by* and *in* both these Natures. The same is true of His Mystical Body" (Pope Leo XIII: *Satis Cognitum*).

The tragedy of many unbelievers and even of numerous Christians is that they regard the Church as a purely human society. For some, the Church is a political or juridical society; for others, she is the guardian of the moral law or of an established social order; for the majority, her function is purely and simply administrative. All such people are blind to the *mystery* of the Church, and therefore fail to understand the meaning of her action and to open their minds to her message. On the other hand, even those who believe that the Church is divine, do not always acknowledge her human character in the ordinary conduct of their life. In what, then, does the mystery of the Church consist? It is so rich a concept that we must deal with this mystery by considering it in its different aspects.

1. *A human-divine society*

Primarily, the mystery of the Church is the co-existence, in unity, of her divine element and her human element, in such a way that the Church is one single reality. This reality is the Catholic Church, which is at the same time the Mystical Body of Christ, the Incarnate Word, Who unites the Divine Nature and human nature in the unity of His Divine Person. Like Christ,

therefore, the Church is at once divine and human in the unity
of one single reality. The essential reason why the Church is a
human-divine reality, is that she continues the Man-God, Jesus
Christ.

The human and exterior element of this visible society comprises the subjects who constitute it; the hierarchy who direct it;
the organization necessary to its full effectiveness in every depart-
ment of human nature; the growth of the Church in and through
the events of human history; and the liturgy and visible rites
of the Church, as well as her places of worship and her establishments.

The human element is the Mystical Body, with its Head, the
Man-God, Who animates it through His Divine Spirit. The divine
element is the Holy Trinity Who lives in the Church.

It is through the visible and human element of the Church
that the Christ-Head exercises His Priesthood and His Redemptive Action: through the living *magisterium* of the hierarchy;
through the Sacraments, the whole liturgy, and the preaching
of the Truth. The gestures and actions of the Church are those
of the Mystical Christ, Who is incarnated and Who lives in
the Church.

In this sense, the Church is an object of faith; for in the
Church, faith attains to the divine through, and in, what is
human. *Credo ecclesiam* . . . What we believe is that this visible
and hierarchical, Catholic and Roman Church, *is herself* the
Mystical Body of Christ in time. There is not, therefore, the visible
Church, on the one hand; and, on the other, the invisible Church
with a distinct and separate existence of her own. Nor can there
be any question of representing the exterior and visible Church
as the container, while regarding the Mystical Body as what is
contained; for the content can be distinct in its nature from the
container.

The Mystical Body itself is *incarnated* in this visible society
in which I see the Catholic Church, and which is the Catholic
Church. In living by the life of this visible society, I am living by
the life of the Mystical Body of Christ. Being in the Church, I
am in the Whole Christ. I believe this: *Credo Ecclesiam*.

2. *The Infinite Love of Christ in this mystery of the Church as
   a human-divine society*

The mystery of the Church is the mystery of the Whole
Christ: in other words, it is the mystery of that collective being
which Christ constitutes with those who have been redeemed

by Him and who are living by the life of His Spirit in His Mystical Body, the Church.

The Infinite Love which inundated the mysteries of the Incarnation and the Redemption, is the same love which has caused Jesus Christ to found His Church, in order to associate the Church with these two great mysteries, and thereby to constitute, with her, the Whole Christ.

In the *Incarnation*, the Word became man. He did not assume a nature *like* that of man, but man's *very* nature. He lived among men, as a *man*, and willed to submit to man's condition and to the laws of human nature. Both His love for mankind and His love for His Father led him to that unspeakably profound humiliation wherein "He emptied himself, taking the form of a servant."

Again, this same love caused Jesus Christ to will that His work should be accomplished in a manner compatible with human nature. His Church is a human society composed of men and subject to the psychological conditions of human life. Thus, the Incarnation is extended into time; for the Church continues the Mystery of the Incarnation. Through the Church and in the Church, Christ still lives among men, the Church being the sentient and visible contact between Christ and mankind.

In *the Redemption*, Christ did not will to save men without their own cooperation. Because He loved men, He willed to give them a share in His Redemptive Mission by allowing them to cooperate, as members of the Church, in the working out of their own salvation. They could not, of course, have any part in the acquisition of the merits of His Redemption, which He has communicated directly to His Church without the collaboration of men. It is in the *distribution* of those merits that Christ deigns to associate men with the work of Redemption.

"Dying on the Cross, Christ bestowed upon His Church the boundless treasure of the Redemption without any cooperation on her part; but in the distribution of that treasure He not only shares this work of sanctification with His spotless Bride, but wills it to arise in a certain manner out of her labor. This is truly a tremendous mystery, upon which we can never meditate enough: that the salvation of many souls depends on the prayers and voluntary mortifications offered for that intention by the members of the Mystical Body of Jesus Christ, and upon the cooperation which pastors and faithful, and especially parents, must afford to our divine Savior" (*Mystici Corporis Christi*. English translation: Canon Smith, C.T.S.).

O Jesus, our Redeemer, with what deep emotion do we not learn that, in Your measureless Love, You have deigned to confide the message of salvation to us poor creatures, to a human society caught up in the whole pattern of humanity; and to enable us to participate, as members of Your Church, in Your Redemptive Mission. The only way we can attempt to show our appreciation of this great mark of Your confidence, is to allow You to dispose of us and of our whole life, through Your Church in which we place all our confidence as we do in You Yourself.

76. THE CHURCH: ONE IN TIME AND IN ETERNITY

> *. . . that you may know that you have eternal life; you who believe in the name of the Son of God.*
>
> (1 John, V, 13)

There are not two Churches—one in time, the other in eternity. The visible Church, which is the Mystical Body of Christ, is at once in time and in eternity. We have here a great mystery. The Christian who does not enter by faith into this mystery, and who does not share in the profound life of the Church, is in constant danger of falling into one of two errors. He centers his thoughts exclusively on eternity, and despises the time of effort, of combat, and of constructive action in collaboration with his brethren on earth; or, on the contrary, he limits his attention to time, and is content to regard eternal life merely as a remote "Beyond" which can be of immediate concern to him only after his death.

1. *Even on earth, the Church initiates us into eternal life*

We have not simply been *promised* eternal life: we have been *given* eternal life.[1]

That life is not simply *to be expected* in the future: it has already *begun*.[2]

If we accept this gift of eternal life, a promise is indeed involved and there is something to which we look forward as not yet ours. What the future holds for us is the full blossoming,

---

1. 1 *John*, V, 11: ". . . that God *hath given* to us eternal life. And this life is in his Son." Cf. *John* X, 28: "And I *give* them life everlasting."
2. *John* V, 24: ". . . he who heareth . . . *hath* everlasting life." Cf. *John* III, 36.

in the beatific vision in Heaven, of this eternal life which we have already begun to enjoy on earth through Baptism and the Church.

Those who belong to Christ and to the Church do not live two distinct lives, one as it were superimposed on the other. Eternal life is one and indivisible. It is begun on earth and has a real existence even in the midst of the activities of time: it continues beyond death, as the same life in Christ, but with the fullness of the glory and consummation of Heaven.

It is in Christ that this eternal glory is given to us.[1] The eternal Word became man in time and took His place in the story of mankind, in order that men should have life—life in abundance, eternal life.

Through Baptism, we are incorporated in Jesus Christ Who, by His Resurrection and His Ascension, has entered, with His glorified Humanity, into the bosom of the eternal Father. As Head of the Mystical Body, He is now free from time, in His Glorified Body, and He rules over eternity. Through His Mystical Body, as yet growing to its full stature, Christ is still involved in time: He gives eternal value to the meritorious actions done by His members on earth with the help of grace and charity.

It is here on earth, amid the vicissitudes of time, that our personal being develops through charity; and at our death, it will pass beyond time, to be fixed eternally in the degree of charity it has attained on earth. Charity will not pass away: it will retain eternally the strength and perfection it has reached in us through every day of our earthly pilgrimage.

The Church is the mystery of eternal life communicated to mankind on earth and in time. At once both in time and in eternity, the Church establishes mysterious relationships between earth and heaven: direct and vital relationships between human persons here on earth and the Divine Persons of the eternal and immutable Trinity; exchanges of services between souls on earth and souls already entered into the glory of heaven.

2. *The Church enables us to live our eternal life through the various stages and events of our earthly life.*

Though eternal life has already begun in us, we have not been given it in its full splendor, but, as it were, in the form of a seed of eternal life which must grow and develop within us.

---

1. 1 *John*, V, 20: ". . . that we may know the true God and may be in his true Son. This *is* the true God and life eternal."

This development will take place in us through a progressive assimilation of the gift of eternal life given to us.

Eternal life is not given to us in the form of a celestial and glorious life, but in a form which befits our condition of "strangers and pilgrims": "knowing that while we are in the body we are absent from the Lord" (2 *Cor.*, V, 6).

Finally, we are not only creatures, but sinful creatures. Therefore this eternal life is given to us in a form which befits our conditions of sinful men who must fight and expiate and merit. Like the Divine Word, and faithful to the law of the Incarnation, the Church seeks out men where they really live and move: in their misery and their sin; in suffering and in the effort to make them live by that eternal life itself, through all the stages of their earthly existence, through the major and minor circumstances of their daily life, and in their various conditions, states of life and vocations.

The Church Militant belongs to this phase of exile, of preparation, of combat, of merit and of faith. By the Church Militant, we mean the whole visible Church, with her hierarchy, her Sacraments and Sacrifice: we mean, therefore, the Church in a form which is adapted to sentient, social and sinful human nature. In Heaven, there are no longer any Sacraments nor is there any hierarchy.

The hierarchy guides the members of Christ through the problems which life presents to the human conscience. The hierarchy leads them in their painful ascent towards the Heavenly City, by teaching them how to merit and how to begin their eternal life through the faithful discharge of the duties of their state and the demands of their everyday life.

The Sacraments graft the grace of Christ on all the important stages of their human life, in order to sanctify each of them and to give to the members of the Church the means of living their eternal life, in faith, hope and charity.

The Liturgical Sacrifice makes present to each generation in time, the Sacrifice of Calvary; and distributes to each the graces of Christ the Redeemer, now in the Glory of His Father.

O Jesus, our Savior, uphold us and lead us by Your Church, and be not wearied by our weakness and our cowardice, while we follow our course in the midst of perils which constantly threaten that treasure of eternal life we carry in earthen vessels. However wonderful our possession of eternal life here on earth, we indeed know that "it hath not yet appeared what we shall be" (1 John, III, 2), *and that we can have no conception here on earth of what it will mean to us to enter into the Light of Glory.*

77. THE FAMILY OF GOD

For by him we have access both in one
Spirit to the Father. Now therefore you
are no more strangers and foreigners; but
you are fellow citizens with the saints and
the domestics of God . . .

(Ephes., II, 18, 19)

By an act of infinite mercy, the Holy Trinity has deigned to call mankind to enter into intimate relationships with each of the Three Divine Persons. The Son has been sent into the world to gather all men together in Himself, and to introduce them into the family life of the Blessed Trinity. We can understand the full meaning of the Church only if we contemplate the Church in the Mystery of this Family of God which the Church constitutes even here on earth.

1. *The Church in her relations with the Blessed Trinity*

The Church receivès her birth and her life, in the bosom of the Blessed Trinity. It is the Divine Son Who founds and directs the Church, and it is the Holy Ghost Who unifies the Church.

It is into the bosom of the Holy Trinity that the Church must lead the members of the human family whom Christ has redeemed in order that, in Him, in the Divine Word, they may communicate eternally in the life of the Trinity. The final purpose of the Church is the building up of the Whole Christ for the glory of the Blessed Trinity.

The Church is, so to speak, the extension to mankind of the life of the Blessed Trinity. The mystery of the eternal Procession of the Blessed Trinity, and of the Divine Missions of the Three Persons, is extended to the Church and is continued in her. It is the visible missions of the Son and of the Holy Ghost which visibly constituted the Church, and these visible missions are continued in souls and in the Church by the invisible missions of the same two Divine Persons.

The return to the Father occurs in the Church through the missions of the Son and of the Holy Ghost. These two missions are inseparable one from the other, because they intercommunicate by the root of sanctifying grace to which they are attached, though they are, however, distinct in their effects, just as the two

Divine Persons are distinct from each other (*Saint Thomas*, 1, q. 49, a. 5, ad 3). The One, by the illumination of the mind, and the Other, by the kindling of the heart, sanctify souls through a process of interior assimilation, and thereby lead them to the Father in order that they may participate in the unity of God.

"Just as everything comes from the Father through the Son in the Holy Ghost, so too everything is returned to the Father by the Son in the Holy Ghost" (Saint Cyril of Alexandria—*In Joannem*, XI, 10). It is in the Church and through the Church that these movements of descent and of ascent are effected.

2. *"The Family of God"*

Would that Christians but knew how to taste the ineffable joys of their belonging to the Family of God! How they would love the Church for all this family life which they find in her and receive through her!

The infinite Love which the Father has for His Son in the eternal Trinity, is extended to His incarnate Son, reaching out to that Son in the Humanity He assumed by being "made flesh"; and, in Jesus Christ, Who incorporates in Himself redeemed mankind, that same Love embraces all the members of Christ's Mystical Body, made sons of God in God the Son. The Father loves them in His Son with the same love with which He loves the Son: He loves His Son as the Only Son Whom He engenders eternally as the Word; and He loves the members of His Son as His adopted sons, in the same Spirit of Love and because of His Son.

It is Jesus Christ Himself Who has revealed to us this prodigious truth, this astounding mystery: "That they all may be one, as thou, Father, in me, and I in thee; . . . that they may be one . . . and the world may know that thou . . . *hast loved them as thou hast also loved me . . . that the love wherewith thou hast loved me may be in them, and I in them*" (*John*, XVII, 21, 23, 26). But Jesus has linked this whole mystery with the effecting of the unity which men must form among themselves in the Church. Thus, the Church is introduced into the cycle of the Infinite Love of the Blessed Trinity, and is enveloped by the Love of the Father for the Son in the same Holy Spirit—"in societate cum Patre et Filio ejus Jesu Christo"—because the Church is but one with the Son, and because, in the Son, she has become the Family of God.

Furthermore, the Son associates the Church, His Mystical Body, with His Filiation, in order that, through His Spirit of Sonship, He may be able to draw the Church entirely into the love which He bears to the Father as His Son, and cause her to participate—through the Holy Spirit, the Soul of His Mystical Body —in His unity with the Father. The more we live this mystery of the Church, the more we share, in the Son, the life of the Blessed Trinity. The Divine Family has, in a sense, opened Its Society of Three-in-One, to allow entry, through the Mystical Body of Jesus Christ, to that redeemed humanity who are the members of the Family of God—that Family which is the Church.

"*We therefore humbly pray and beseech Thee, most merciful Father, through Jesus Christ, Thy Son, our Lord, that Thou wouldst vouchsafe to accept and bless these gifts . . . which in the first place we offer Thee for Thy Holy Catholic Church, to which vouchsafe to grant peace* (pacificare), *as also to preserve* (custodire), *unite* (adunare) *and govern* (regere) . . . *We therefore beseech Thee, O Lord, graciously to accept this oblation . . . of Thy whole family* (cunctae familiae tuae)" . . . (*Canon of the Mass:* English—Laverty Missal).

II.

THE MYSTERY OF THE HIERARCHY

78. THE SACRAMENT OF THE DIVINE PATERNITY

> *He that seeth me seeth the Father also . . .*
> *I am in the Father and the Father in me . . .*
> *Whosoever shall receive me receiveth not me but him that sent me.*
> (John, XIV, 9, 11; Mark, IX, 36)

By His whole teaching and by His entire life, Jesus Christ was the great Witness of the Father, the mighty Revealer of the Father, the incarnate Son in Whom dwelt the power and majesty of the Father. Seeing Christ, one saw the Father, full of goodness, of mercy, of paternal care for all men. To receive Christ was to accept the Father. This sublime mystery, which holds a central place in Christ's Revelation, is represented and continued by a visible institution in the bosom of the Church founded and guided by Jesus Christ. This representation and continuation is the mystery of the hierarchy, which is the Sacrament of the Divine Paternity, the visible sign which manifests and embodies the Paternity of God in relation to mankind.

*The distinctive characteristics of the doctrine of the Church
concerning the Paternity of God.*

As regards the Divine Paternity and our relations in the
supernatural order with the Heavenly Father, the Catholic Church
teaches a doctrine which is entirely her own and which distinguishes her from all other religions.

1) Unlike that of other religions, the doctrine of the Catholic
Church does not tend solely to provoke a filial sentiment of confidence in relation to the Heavenly Father. Her doctrine contains the message of Christ in which He revealed to the world
that henceforward there would exist, between God and men, *real
family relationships, based on paternity and filiation.* "He gave
them power to be made the sons of God" (*John*, I, 12). "And,
because you are sons, God hath sent the Spirit of His Son into
your hearts, crying: Abba, Father" (*Gal.*, IV, 4-6).

2) The Divine Paternity can be presented in a way which
ignores the essential role of Our Lord Jesus Christ, the Blessed
Trinity and the supernatural order. According to this conception,
these relations must be regarded in the following manner: in
Heaven, there is the Father Who exercises His Providence over
mankind; on earth, are men who yearn towards Him with a sentiment of filial confidence.

The doctrine of Saint Paul and of Saint John differs entirely
from this. Both Saints center the doctrine on the One Mediator,
Our Lord Jesus Christ, the Son of the Father, Who Himself has
said: "No man cometh to the Father, but by me" (*John*, XIV, 6).
It is Christ Who, associating the members of His Body with His
unique Filiation as "the Only Son," causes them to enter into
filial relations with the Father, by giving them His Spirit of
Sonship (*Rom.*, VIII, 14-17). *Their adoptive filiation must always
be referred to its connection with the Filiation of the Only Son.*
"For whom he foreknew, he also predestinated to be made comformable to the image of his Son; that he might be the first-born
among many brethren." (*Rom.*, VIII, 29). Having become sons
in the Son, we can therefore have real relationships of knowledge
and of love with the Father, in the Holy Spirit; we can have
family relationships with the Blessed Trinity, and special relationships with Each of the Three Divine Persons.

3) Our Lord was not content to reveal to men the existence
of family relationships with the Heavenly Father, or simply to
base our filiation on His own. *He came on earth to organize these
family relationships* in the society which is the Church.

The social, collective, community character of the Kingdom of God is indeed essential to Christianity. This family of the sons of God is designed to be a community so united in Christ that it forms but one body, the Mystical Body of Christ.

It is in the light of this fundamental revelation that we must contemplate the mystery of the hierarchy. The Pope is the visible Head of the human family on earth; and, for each particular diocese, there is a bishop whose mission is to represent for his subjects, in his own person, the Paternity of God, His fatherly goodness, His paternal providence—all directed to the salvation of souls—as also His paternal love for men.

Christ could have chosen to communicate His Spirit to each soul *directly*, in order to form in each the spirit of filial adoption which cries: Abba, Father. But in that case, the bonds of relationship and of filiation in a real family community, would not have been visible. The Paternity of God would not have been expressed in a sentient sign; nor would the brotherhood of men have had a visible foundation.

4) Finally, according to the doctrine of Saint John, the relationships of human brotherhood *should be established and organized, from the outset, on the union of the Father and the Son, and in dependence on this unity which is formed by the society of the Father and the Son* in the bond of love of the Holy Ghost. "That they all may be one, as thou, Father, in me, and I in thee . . . I in them, and they in me; that they may be made perfect in one" (*John*, XVII, 21, 23).

This is the whole central idea, emphatically repeated, of Christ's prayer of Priesthood to His Father. What a light it throws on the mystery of the hierarchy!

In his own diocese, the bishop holds the place of Jesus Christ. But, since in Jesus Christ is the Father Who sent Him, the bishop who holds the place of Christ is "the image of the Father."[1] He gives the Son and the life of the Son to his own diocese, in order that men may enter "into the society of the Father and of the Son."

O my God, since Your glory consists in the manifestations of Your Divine Perfections, we praise You for having revealed Your

---

1. Saint Ignatius of Antioch. In the beginning of the second century, this Saint superbly defined the mission of the Bishop: "It is the very power of God the Father that you should reverence fully in your Bishop" (Epistle to the Magnesians). "It is not to the Bishop in himself that your submission is made, but to the Father of Jesus Christ, to the Universal Bishop."

Paternity to us; and not only for having revealed that Paternity so dear to You, but for having rendered it visibly present to us in the institution of the hierarchy of Your Church. Thus, Your Church is not simply an extrinsic help to our human life; for in Your Church and by Your Church, the mystery of Your Divine Paternity is accomplished in the world.

79. THE SPIRITUAL PATERNITY OF THE BISHOP

> *For if you have ten thousand instructors in Christ, yet not many fathers. For in Christ Jesus, by the Gospel, I have begotten you.*
>
> (1 Cor., IV, 15)

We must think on the plane of faith, if we desire to grasp and to understand what is meant by the spiritual paternity of the Bishop. It is one of the fundamental realities on which Christ has willed to found His Church. The Apostle has told us what this reality meant to him in sorrow and in suffering: "My little children, of whom I am in labor again, until Christ be formed in you" (*Gal.*, IV, 19).

1. *Nature of the spiritual paternity of the bishop*

The bishop is a father to his flock because he gives them the true life—that of Jesus Christ. He must ceaselessly have in his mind and in his heart, that program of the Divine Master: "I have come that they may have *life . . .*"

Life, therefore, is the keynote to the bishop's mission, and not simply *administration*—or if administration, then *administration in the service of Life*. Neither is that mission merely one of *external works*, unless we read: *external works all directed towards the giving of life and animated by Life.*

The purpose of all the bishop's powers, and the very reason for their existence, is the engendering and nourishment of the life of grace and of the charity of Christ in souls. All his powers are directed to the formation of the Whole Christ.

By his magisterium of *teaching*, the bishop begets new sons of God in the Faith of Christ. The word is Saint Paul's, who told the Corinthians: "In Jesus Christ, by the Gospel, I have begotten you." Others may be "instructors," and even instructors in Christ; but they are not true fathers. For each diocese, there is only one father: the bishop.

By his ministry of *sanctification,* the bishop begets souls to the life of Jesus Christ. The bishop alone has the right and the power to administer all the Sacraments. In his diocese, he is the supreme priest of the divine worship, of which the Eucharistic Sacrifice is the center. It is he who gives the Holy Ghost to baptized persons in order to confirm them in the Faith. By his consecrated person, which forms part of the sacramental sign in the rite of Ordination, he gives a participation in his paternity to those of his sons whom he has called to be "cooperators of his Order"[1] in the pastoral magisterium, so that they, in their turn, may be fathers. But they cannot ordain other priests, for the bishop alone is the source of this paternity, having received it from Christ. It is through him that Jesus Christ ordinarily effects the work of sanctification in his particular diocese.

Finally, the bishop has the right of spiritual *government,* as head. He is head because he is the father of his flock, and in order that he may be its father. His government is an exercise of his paternity: it is a pastoral ministry of the spiritual education of souls, designed to enable them to live a Christian life in all the circumstances of life.

This government is necessary, also, in order that he may promote the common good of his own diocese. By his consecration, he is vowed to the service of his diocese. The episcopal state is constituted by the exercise of charity in that highest form which is the salvation of souls. In this is the perfection of his state. He is obliged to exercise pastoral charity towards his flock to the very end, and he must be ready to lay down his life for his sheep.

In this sense, he is a "perfecter"—one who perfects souls and leads them to perfection by all his powers as teacher, as sanctifier, and as head.

2. *The sources of the bishop's paternity*

a) The first source is *the fullness of priesthood* with which the bishop is clothed. He participates in the One Priesthood of Jesus Christ and in its fruitfulness, as profoundly as a merely human person on earth can do. In receiving its bishop, the diocese receives Jesus Christ, with all His saving and sanctifying Priesthood, and with all the means of Redemption and of Life.

b) Furthermore, the bishop's paternity originates in *his union with his diocese*—a complete and indissoluble union which makes that diocese his spouse, as is symbolized by the ring he

---

1. This expression is that of the Pontificale in the Rite of Ordination of Priests.

wears, with all the duties this mystical union implies, of solicitude, of fidelity, of total self-oblation.

The bishop alone has a personal right to be in charge of his people. The others, his cooperators in the diocese, receive that right as participated, partial and dependent on his (Saint Thomas, q. 186, II-II, a. 6). As successor of the Apostles, the bishop has the immediate responsibility of organizing the apostolate in his diocese. He is therefore responsible to God, to the Pope and to the Church, for all those who live in his diocese— faithful Christians, the indifferent, the unbelieving, the hostile, the pagan (*Canon* 1350). His is a missionary task.

It is a formidable task which obliges him constantly to ask himself: "Is the Church present in this diocese? Are all the treasures of the Redemption and all the means of salvation, available to those who live and who work here?"

c) But this union of a bishop with his diocese has such fecundity and carries such responsibility only because it is a *particular case of the general union of the Universal Church with Jesus Christ*. The Universal Church is not the sum total of all the particular dioceses: on the contrary, indeed, the dioceses derive from the Church. The Church has preceded them, and it is she who contains them and gives them significance. She has been entirely founded on the episcopate, which is *one* as the Church herself is one. How admirable, therefore, is the unity of the episcopate, which embodies the entire mystery of the unity of the Church.

It follows, therefore, that each bishop is not primarily the pastor of a single flock. He is primarily a pastor of the Universal Church, in union with the Pope and with the other bishops, under the authority of the Pope, the Supreme Head and the center of unity. By virtue of the Priesthood of Christ which the bishop possesses in plenitude, he is a source of spiritual fecundity spread throughout the entire Church. And the Mystery of Christ, which the Universal Church possesses, exists whole and entire in each particular diocese, because this mystery is contained whole and entire in the grace and the priesthood of its bishop.

This tremendous doctrine of the unity which exists between the Church and the episcopate, protects the individual dioceses against the dangers of particularism[1] and of selfish concern for their own interests alone.

---

1. (This term implies the danger that a diocese should come to regard itself as free to promote its own interests without concern for the good of the Church as a whole. —*Translator's note*).

O Jesus, Sovereign Priest, grant to Your bishops the grace to reflect the goodness of Your Father by the radiance of their paternal charity. Grant that, by the very exercise of their spiritual paternity, full of benignity, of solicitude and of self-oblation, they may be instrumental in raising up the souls of their priests, and of all those who approach them, to Your Father, with Whom You desire that all souls should be united.

80. THE POPE, THE HEAD OF THE CHURCH

Feed my lambs . . . Feed my sheep.
(John, XXI, 16, 17)

The Catholic mind is particularly shown in filial love for the Sovereign Pontiff. This ardent and profound love is characterized by veneration and devotion, by joyful submission and by delicate obedience, by attachment and by fidelity. But all these qualities are founded on faith in the mystery of the hierarchy as embodied in the august person of the Holy Father, the Vicar of Christ.

1. *The fact of the Papacy*

A two-fold certitude clearly and compellingly emerges from the principal texts concerning the institution of the Papacy by Our Lord.

In the first place, Jesus Christ announced, promised, and organized the government of His Church by giving full and supreme authority to a Head chosen by Himself.

Furthermore, the purpose and mission of this Head was to be the visible representation on earth of the Divine Master, when Christ should have withdrawn His visible Presence from His followers.

Christ willed that the authority of this Head should be plenary, and superior to all other authority. The Pope receives the power of the Keys which open and shut the doors of the house. The Keys are the symbols of his real power to bind and loose the consciences of men; the power to govern and to feed the flock. He is therefore the foundation of the edifice. His pronouncements and his verdicts are ratified in Heaven (*Matt.*, XVI, 17, 18).

On the other hand, while the Pope is the visible Supreme

Shepherd, the flock which he guides is not his, but Christ's.
"Feed *my* lambs . . . Feed *my* sheep . . ." Jesus Christ reserves
the flock to Himself. He remains *the* Head, the true Head, the
only Head of His Church.

2. *The doctrine*

The Pope is not the successor of Christ: he is the successor of
Peter. He is the Vicar of Jesus Christ—that is, he holds the place
of Jesus Christ, and acts in the name of Jesus Christ. He is the
depository of those powers of Christ which the Divine Master
Himself has confided to him, that he may exercise them in His
name.

The Pope is Jesus Christ visibly present among men. Through
him, Christ continues His Presence in His Church. In the sacramental order and in the order of sanctification, it is Christ Himself Who baptizes, pardons and consecrates, through the instru-
mentality of "dispensators"; and similarly, in the order of jurisdiction, and of government, it is Christ Himself Who continues
to govern His Church through a visible Head.

3. *The mystery*

The mystery of the Papacy is not to be sought in the fact
that, after the passage of two thousand years, the Pope is the
successor of Saint Peter; though we may indeed consider this
continuity of the Papacy through ages which have seen empires
rise and fall, as an astounding miracle manifesting Christ's all-
powerful and absolutely exceptional protection of His Church.

The mystery resides in the fact that it is Christ Who, as the
invisible Head of His Church, continues, in the person of a visible
Head, to lead the Church. "In virtue of the primacy, Peter is
none other than the Vicar of Christ, and therefore this Body has
only one principal Head, namely Christ, Who, continuing Himself
to govern the Church invisibly and directly, rules it visibly
through His personal representative on earth" (*Mystici Corporis
Christi*).

When the Pope teaches, faith makes us hear his words as
those of Christ Himself. We believe what the Pope speaks,
because faith assures us that it is not his own opinions that he
teaches, but the truth of Christ and the doctrine of Christ.

When the Pope governs his Church, our Faith teaches us
that it is Christ Who rules, through him, over the flock of the
One and Supreme Shepherd. There are not two heads, but One
Only Head. "Christ and His Vicar constitute only one Head"
(*Mystici Corporis Christi*). The Pope is the Head in the person

of Jesus Christ Whom he represents: with Christ, he constitutes only one Head.

Consider the manifestation of that love in the Mystery of the Incarnation, by which God became man, the Word was made flesh, the Eternal came into time. Consider, too, the Mystery of the Eucharist, wherein Christ gives His Flesh to be our food. In an analogous way, and according to the same sublime logic of His love, the mystery of infinite Love manifests itself, in another form and on another plane, in the mystery of the Church. "It is a well known fact that when Christ Our Lord . . . was about to leave this world and return to the Father, He entrusted to the Prince of the Apostles the visible government of the whole society which He had founded. *Such was His Wisdom that He could in no wise leave the social body of His Church without a visible head*" (*Mystici Corporis Christi*). Having become invisible through His Ascension and His entry into glory, Christ willed to make Himself visible to the eyes of our body, in a visible Head who would be His representative on earth.

The Father willed to manifest Himself in His Son, Whom He sent into the world. In Christ and by the Holy Ghost, He willed to be reconciled with regenerated mankind, in order to introduce this visible family, constituted by the Church, into family relationships with the Blessed Trinity. Similarly, it has pleased the Divine Father that the Pope, the Vicar of Christ on earth, should represent and embody the Divine Paternity to all mankind.

Whoever has come in contact with the Pope, has experienced as it were the revelation of the Divine Paternity. The Sovereign Pontiffs themselves have often expressed, in very moving words, their universal paternity over men—a paternity which it is their duty to manifest and to affirm, even in relation to those "who do not belong to the visible structure of the Catholic Church" (*Mystici Corporis Christi*).

This is not simply a touching sentiment, but a sublime reality. There is only one Father on earth, who incarnates the unity of the human family and the vocation of all men, to form one only family of sons of God in God's Son: in other words, to build up the Whole Christ.

"O God, the Pastor and Guide of all the faithful, look with clemency upon Your servant whom You have deigned to give to Your Church to be her pastor and Head. Grant that, by his words and his example, he may be able to draw all Your faithful into the paths of spiritual progress, so that he may attain unto eternal life with the flock that has been confided to his care."

(Liturgical prayer for the Pope)

III.

THE MYSTERY OF THE FUNDAMENTAL MARKS
OF THE CHURCH

81. THE MYSTERY OF THE APOSTOLIC CHURCH

> *Now therefore you are no more strangers
> and foreigners; but you are fellow citizens
> with the saints, and the domestics of God,
> built upon the foundation of the apostles
> and prophets, Jesus Christ himself being
> the chief cornerstone.*
>
> (Ephes., II, 19, 20)

The apostolicity of the Church is that property by which the hierarchy today can link itself, by an uninterrupted succession through the centuries, with the apostolic body of the Twelve, and with Our Lord Who instituted that body. The historical fact can be studied, in Apologetics, as one of the "marks" of the Church and as in itself an astounding miracle. But we have here also a great mystery, into which every loving son of the Church should enter by faith, that through it he may nourish his interior life and participate more intimately in the life and apostolic mission of the Church. Apostolicity corresponds to Catholicity. What Catholicity is to space, to the whole universe of space, apostolicity is to time, to time from its very origin . . . It represents an unbroken connection with a source.

1. The doctrine—"Credo Ecclesiam . . . apostolicam . . ."

What is the object of the mystery of the apostolicity of the Church?

In this visible organization which is the apostolic body of the hierarchy, and in its sacramental powers, there is a mysterious, divine, ever active force which keeps the Church in existence in accordance with her proper nature. This force is an all powerful virtue which goes out from the Blessed Trinity and is transmitted by the Sacred Humanity of Christ to the hierarchy. Thanks to this action made operant by the apostolic body, it is Christ Himself. By this mysterious influx, it is Christ Who continues to self Who forms and builds His Mystical Body through space and disseminate the life of His grace in souls and to teach the Truth to the world. By this action, it is Christ Himself Who communicates to the men of our age, as He has done to those of all previous ages, the same power of the Redemption.

Although its manifestations are visible for all successive generations, the apostolicity of the Church is truly a mystery in its principles, in its source. It is the mystery of the action of Christ making use of the jurisdictional organization of the hierarchy, and of the sacramental order, to form and to increase His Body which is the Church, and to preserve that Church as a permanent and living reality in the midst of human institutions which crumble and pass away. It is the mystery of the apostolic body, in as much as this body is the dispensator of divine grace and truth, in full dependence on Christ, the One Priest and Head.

It is this mystery which is the object of our faith in the apostolicity of the Church.

2. *Applications—How are we to communicate in the mystery of the apostolic Church?*

1) We are to do so by suffusing our lives with an ardent *faith* in this mystery, by believing in it *intensely*. This life of faith should animate all our relationships with the hierarchy. We must learn to see, with the eyes of faith, the action of Christ in the Sovereign Pontiff; in the bishops, successors of the Apostles; and in the entire Church which, today as in all past ages, pursues her apostolic mission. Faith must teach us to set aside those too natural viewpoints and too human judgments which, confining themselves to externals or to the weaknesses of God's human instruments, would fail to conform with Christ's design for His Apostles and their successors.

2) To communicate in the mystery of the Apostolic Church is to communicate also in *the dispositions which filled the souls of the Apostles in face of the mission which Christ was confiding to them.* Today as formerly, it is the same mission: "As the Father hath sent me, I also send you." That mission is unchanged: it consists of bringing to mankind the same message of salvation and the same life.

What one first remarks as characterizing the reaction of the Apostles when told of this mission, is a conquering, irresistible, indomitable *enthusiasm* in the midst of heaped-up opposition, blindness and threats.

Again, we notice their unwavering *conviction* that the message of Christ, in itself and without the least addition, contains the whole secret of the world's salvation: one only Master, one Savior, one Truth, one only Life—*His* Life.

Finally, the reaction of the Apostles to the announcement of their mission is characterized by a *respect* full of veneration and of loyalty, for this astonishing and sublime message which Jesus was commanding them to preach to the whole world, despite their ignorance and the poverty of the means at their disposal. They understood that this treasure of truth and of life did not belong as of right to themselves; that they must keep it unchanged and intact; and that their mission was to announce this message, whole and entire, to all nations.

O Jesus, our Head, grant unto all the members of Your Mystical Body an understanding of the apostolicity of the Church, so that they may firmly resolve to participate in her apostolic mission. Make them understand that it is You Who create the apostolicity of Your Church; and that, to those whom You have chosen, You make the promise which You gave to the first Apostles: "I will make you to be fishers of men." Your chosen ones tremble at the realization of their own personal powerlessness, but they courageously place all the supernatural confidence of their souls in this, Your tremendous promise. Grant, O Lord, that Your faithful may know the full meaning of all this.

82. THE MYSTERY OF THE ONE CHURCH

> *There are diversities of graces, but the same Spirit . . . the same God, who worketh all in all.*
>
> (1 Cor., XII, 4, 6)

There is, in the Church, a unity of order which can be clearly seen: there are the quite evident unity of goverment, unity of doctrine, and liturgical unity ("one Baptism"; one Eucharist). But this external unity, though very necessary in itself, is but the visible expression of a more profound, interior unity—the unity which derives from an internal principle of unity within the Church. This Principle is the Holy Ghost, Who animates the members and the Mystical Body as a whole. It is Christ Who creates, by His Spirit, the unity of His Body.

1. *The internal Principle of unity is the Holy Ghost, the Spirit of God, the Spirit of Christ*

The unity of the Mystical Body is not constituted by the members aiding and assisting one another. Such charity and mutual service are the *manifestation* of this unity, not its constitutive principle. The unity of the Church does not come from her members, but comes "down from above," from God Himself. It has existed in the Church since the Day of Pentecost. The Holy Ghost, sent by Christ as the fundamental Principle of the Church's unity, was given to the Church on that day, as the collective gift made to men in order to gather them together in unity.

The duty of the members of the Body is to respect the unity which exists in the Church since that day. They must enter into it and participate in it; they must communicate in the mystery of the unity of the Church, in order that, through this mystery, they may communicate in the mystery of the unity of the Father and the Son, the mystery of the Divine Unity Itself. "That they all may be one, as thou, Father, in me, and I in thee; that they also may be one in us" (*John*, XVII, 21).

We have here a lesson in humility, in dependence and in obedience.

Far from our hearts be the proud self-sufficiency of the heretics of every age, who have withdrawn from this unity in order to indulge their own ideas! And as for ourselves, poor sinners as we are, what have we done except to profane this gift of God by our sins and by our selfishness? This unity was an extraordinary gift given to the Church for the benefit of men: it was given to us by Christ, at the same time as he made us the ineffable Gift of His Holy Spirit. Every sin is a refusal and a scorning of this gift of infinite Love, because sin is a principle of division. It sets man against man; it divides a man even within himself; it rends the unity of all men in God.

2. *The Holy Ghost is the interior and immanent Principle of unity for each soul and operates in the soul*

The principle of unity in every human society is authority, the purpose of which is to make all individuals within the society work together for the common good of the society as a whole. Such authority seeks to fulfill its purpose by external means—by its laws, its directives, its commands; it cannot exercise any power, by interior means, over the minds, the consciences and the intentions of men.

In the visible and hierarchic Church, Christ has willed that there should be an authority, to fulfill this mission of unity. But the goverment of the Pope, of the bishops, and of those who exercise authority in their name, is designed to serve the work of unity accomplished in souls by the same Holy Spirit Who inspires the spiritual leaders of the Church.

For this Divine Spirit who animates the Church, fills also the souls of the just: He lives within them, leads them, acts in them, and animates them interiorly in order to make active within them the life of the theological virtues of faith, hope and charity. Now, these virtues have as their effect, to gather souls together in unity. The same faith turns them towards Him Who is the same Source of supernatural life and the same Truth for each and all; they are raised up, by the same hope, towards Him Who is their Supreme End and the sole Source of their beatitude —God, the Blessed Trinity; the same charity makes them participate in the life of the Blessed Trinity, through their incorporation in One and the Same Jesus Christ.

Thus, the Holy Ghost, by His immanence and by His efficacious and interior activity, ensures and develops the unity of the Church.

3. *The Holy Ghost is the Principle of unity, above all because He is numerically One, Unique, and the Same in all the members and in the Church as a Body.*

Any attempt to analize the unity of the Church, in all its depth and significance, must lead necessarily and ultimately to this truth.

Grace, that sublime created gift, has not the power, of itself, to effect this perfect unity. It makes the members like unto one another, and draws them more clearly together by making them more "conformable to the image" of the Divine Model (*Rom.*, VIII, 29). But, of itself, it does not bind souls together in a numerical unity, because, though it is a single quality, it adapts itself to the particular personality of each. In becoming the spiritual life of each soul, grace individualizes itself in each, and multiplies the various expressions of itself with the number of those who receive it.

The Holy Ghost *alone* is numerically the same in Christ and in the members of His Body; numerically the same in each member of the Church and in the Church herself. It is the Holy Ghost Who effects the unity of the Church, because He gathers all the members together in His own unity.

In this truth, we discover an aspect of the mystery of unity which is extremely rich and fruitful for the interior life.

"Since even the least action conducive to salvation cannot be produced without the Holy Spirit, how can numberless multitudes of every nation and every race conspire with one intent to the glory of the Triune God, save by the power of Him Who is breathed by the Father and the Son with one eternal love?" (*Mystici Corporis Christi*).

Over and above the acts which visibly manifest the unity of the Church, we must ceaselessly tend towards that higher unity whose source is the indwelling and interior power of the Holy Ghost in souls, the unifying presence "of the Divine Spirit, Who, in the words of the Angelic Doctor, 'numerically one and the same, fills and unifies the whole Church'" (*Mystici Corporis Christi*).

There is always, however, a danger that we will possess even this principle of unity in an individualistic manner; and therefore we must tend towards a yet higher degree of unity. This higher degree consists in the collective possession of this Divine Spirit which should commence here on earth in the Church as the first plan of the Heavenly City. These are indeed most powerful motives urging us to a life which is more and more selfless, more and more purified from all voluntary attachment to sin, and ever more obedient to the Spirit of Christ.

O Jesus, our Divine Savior, we know indeed that the unity of the Church will be complete only in heaven, when "God shall be all in all." But we know also that it is Your divine plan to effect the unity of mankind, now, in Your Church, even though this work of manifestation can be pursued on earth only through a ceaseless warfare against sin and in the midst of much weakness and failure.

83. THE MYSTERY OF THE CATHOLIC CHURCH

"Credo Ecclesiam Catholicam."
(Nicean Creed)

The Catholicity of the Church is her universal expansion throughout the whole world. Underlying this exterior and visible fact, we must discover a mystery whose contemplation can have immense significance for our interior life. To be a Catholic is to communicate in the mystery of the Catholicity of the Church, and, through that mystery, to communicate in some of the most sublime aspects of the mystery of Christ as continued in His Church.

1. *Catholicity is, first of all, the capacity and the power which the Church possesses, in herself, to reach out to all men and to receive and save them*

In herself and in the life she possesses, the Church has the means of redeeming all men and of leading them to salvation. This is what is principally meant by the "Catholicity" of the Church.

When Christ commanded His Apostles to go forth and teach all nations, He made a public announcement concerning the Church and the power of adaptability in the very nature of the Church. For the Church *is* the Church only if she is universal, that is, Catholic.

This is demanded by *the very principle of life which animates her.* Jesus Christ is the unique and universal Principle of salvation for all men. It is He Who must gather all men together in Himself: it is He Who creates the Catholicity of the Church.

Furthermore, the Catholicity of the Church is demanded by *the very movement of His Heart,* of His Spirit, of his charity— the movement which He inspires in His Church. Now, this movement of infinite love reaches out to all men, seeks to save all men and to bring them into the Church.

Finally, this mark of the Church is demanded by *that very life of charity* whose nature is to spread itself abroad without accepting any limit to its extension. To limit charity is to stifle it, for charity can subsist only by continual expansion. Charity is authentic, only on condition that it excludes no one and gives itself to all.

To be Catholic, to participate in the Catholicity of the Church, is first of all, therefore, to have a sense of the universal which expresses itself in concern for the needs of all souls and in preoccupation with the welfare of the whole Church. For Catholicity is the very opposite of everything that savours of the little sect, of race, of exclusiveness and of the self-centered.

2. *The Catholicity of the Church is also her aptitude for giving a religious significance and an eternal value to all the values of mankind*

By "the values of mankind," we mean the qualities of their civilizations, their cultures, their various national customs, their techniques, their sciences, their arts, their modes of thought—in a word, the values which pertain in all human conditions and ways of life.

The Church is certainly independent of all these and is bound up with none of them. But the Church respects them all *for what they are in themselves*—a participation in the creative action of God. Moreover, she loves them as *the raw material* which she is called upon by God to inform, to purify and to transfigure.

The Church respects the diversities and individual characteristics of every race and of every civilization. This unlimited variety is even necessary to her, because through such diversity she can radiantly manifest, in its harmonious unity, the riches of the gift of God which is able to assimilate all, to gather all together in Christ, and to offer to the Creator His whole human work in glorious homage to His Divine Majesty.

To be Catholic is, therefore, to be sympathetic towards all human values; to have an understanding attitude towards all that is human; to respect all the diversities of mankind; and to be watchful for what is of spiritual value in human realities, so as to make such value the point of insertion for that apostolic effort which will raise all these things to God.

3. *Finally, the Catholicity of the Church is that interior dynamism which urges her to embrace all mankind in the unity of the Mystical Body*

The Church is a living organism which is still growing and has not yet attained to full stature. She will attain to that stature only when she has become the Whole Christ, by gathering all men to herself. She is the grain of mustard seed which becomes a universal tree. She is the germ of supernatural life which Jesus one day placed in the world to energize the mass of mankind.

It is absolutely miraculous that the astounding growth and spread of the Church through time and space has not injured her unity, which, humanly speaking, was constantly threatened. Indeed, this growth and expansion served but to manifest her unity in a yet more splendid fashion, and to strengthen it yet more.

Finally, therefore, to be Catholic is to be acutely and constantly aware of the misery of those great sections of mankind who have not yet received, heard or understood the message of salvation. In a more concrete manner, it is to cooperate actively in all the missionary works and in all the generous endeavors of those apostles who go into remote lands to implant the visible

Church in Christ-starved lands. Everywhere and at all times, to be Catholic is to communicate in that interior movement which kindles in the Church an ardent will to extend herself to the uttermost parts of the earth and to all men, that all may be drawn into the Mystical Body of Christ. In a word, to be Catholic is to communicate in the mystery of the Catholicity of the Church.

O Jesus, Redeemer of the world, You did not come into the world to found a religion among all the other religions of the earth, but You brought to mankind religion itself, as something designed to unite all men with the Father, in You, the Universal Man, the Man-God; to make them the sons of God; and "to renew the face of the earth" by Your Divine Spirit.

84.   THE MYSTERY OF THE HOLINESS OF THE CHURCH

> *Christ loved the church and delivered himself up for it, that he might sanctify it . . . that he might present it to himself a glorious church, not having spot or wrinkle . . . but holy and without blemish.*
>
> (Ephes., V, 25-28)

The holiness of the Church is shown in her doctrine, in her liturgy, in all her enterprises everywhere and at all times, in the multitude of Saints she has brought forth in every milieu, in every walk of life, in every stage of life. But, as with the other "marks" of the Church, we must contemplate this "mark" in its most interior aspect, as the *mystery* of the holiness of the Church.

1.   *The holiness of the Church derives from the holiness of Christ*

The Church is holy in herself, *in her essence, because she is the Body of Christ.* The mystery of her holiness is that this holiness derives from, and is composed of, the holiness of the Man-God. As God, Jesus is infinite holiness and this holiness is of His very essence. As Man, Jesus is holy by reason of His hypostatic union, and because of the sanctifying grace which, with all other gifts, He possesses in fullness. "Without me, you can do nothing" (*John*, XV, 5). "Christ is the author, and efficient cause of holiness" (*Mystici Corporis Christi*)—of all holiness, and therefore of the holiness of the Church.

The Church is holy in herself, *because she is animated by the*

Holy Spirit, the Spirit of holiness Whom Jesus Christ gives to His Church to abide with her forever. The Church knows that she possesses this gift of the Holy Spirit. He is her Divine Guest, her soul. Through Him, she enters into constant relationship with the Blessed Trinity, and she introduces all the members of the Mystical Body into that same relationship.

The Church is holy in herself, *because she is the Whole Christ.* The Whole Christ is Our Lord Jesus Christ, the Man-God, incorporating regenerated humanity in Himself, throughout space (Catholicity) and time (apostolicity), in order to form one single Body (unity), His Church, which He animates by His Holy Spirit: "that he might sanctify it . . . that he might present it to himself . . . holy and without blemish." The final purpose of all this, is, therefore, the holiness of the Church. All her other properties tend to this central property which itself contains them and is demanded for their full significance.

Finally, the Church is *holy in her purpose, in her mission,* which is the mission itself of Jesus Christ. Christ came to save souls by delivering them from sin and by giving them life—His Divine Life: that is, He came to save them by sanctifying them. For holiness comprises two elements: a negative element, which is purification from sin; and a positive element, which is union with God. This, too, is the mission of the Church: she has been created by Christ in order that she may foster Saints.

2. *The holiness of the Church is a redemptive holiness*[1]

Those who, like the Pharisees, are amazed and scandalized to find sinners in the Church, have completely failed to understand her mission of sanctification. Nevertheless, Jesus had indeed prepared the mind of men to understand this mission. He had not come to call the just, but to call sinners (*Matt.,* IX, 13), "to seek and to save that which was lost" (*Luke,* XIX, 10), "not to judge the world, but to save the world" (*John,* XII, 47).

The same is true of the Church. The mystery of her holiness is that she produces Saints from sinners; that Christ the Redeemer continues, in her and by her, the Redemption of the world by working on the sinful stuff of humanity in its full reality; that Christ makes use of the sins of men and the consequences of their sins, in order to transform men into Saints; that Christ never wearies at the spectacle of men constantly putting obstacles in

---

1. The phrase is from Mersch: *Théologie du Corps Mystique,* II, p. 231. Cf. de Montcheuil: *Aspects de l'Eglise,* p. 72: "The Church is the Redemption in application . . . the Redemption in action."

the way of His work of sanctification, and that He continues to love them and to desire their sanctification, whatever may be the depth of their misery and the multitude of their sins.

Jesus associates His Church with His Redemptive Mission. He accomplishes that mission in and through the Church. Holiness is given to us in the Church, but that holiness is not ours without an effort. Man is born, not a Saint, but a sinner. Even after Baptism, his human nature is still wounded and retains a strong inclination to evil. Holiness, therefore, can be acquired only by a constant effort, by a warfare waged today and every day, and by a conversion ceaselessly renewed under the efficient action of the grace of Christ, calling us to participate in His Holiness by participating in the Holiness of His Church.

O Church of Our Redeemer, most holy Mother, we love you for all the compassionate tenderness with which you strive to free us from our sins. We love you for the solicitude with which you pursue the true good of our souls, blind and weak as they are: that solicitude which is persevering, untiring, demanding, and when necessary even severe. We love you for the divinely human love which causes you to ally yourself with our sinful human nature, to descend into our human clay and to accept our nature as it is, with all its sin, in order to raise it up and sanctify it.

IV.

PARTICIPATION IN THE MYSTERIES OF CHRIST THROUGH THE SACRAMENTS

85. PARTICIPATION IN THE MYSTERY OF THE DEAD AND RISEN CHRIST

> *Know you not that all we who are baptized in Jesus Christ are baptized in his death? For we are buried together with him by baptism into death; that, as Christ is risen from the dead by the glory of the Father, so we also may walk in newness of life.*
> (Rom., VI, 3, 4)

We have already considered the sacramental character given by Baptism, and the fact that this Sacrament makes us sons of God and incorporates us in the Whole Christ. But why does it produce these effects? Does it do so of itself? The rite of Baptism emphasizes the idea of a true participation in the Death and in the Resurrection of Jesus Christ. The primitive rite enjoined immersion in the water, and the rising of the baptized person out of the water. In the rite as we know it, the ablution, the exorcism and renunciations of Satan, the light and the white veil, are still retained. They recall to mind the profound significance of the baptismal liturgy.

1. *Participation in the mystery of the Passion and Death of Christ*

In Baptism, we participate, first of all, in the mystery of the Cross and in its transforming and sanctifying virtue: freedom from sin, freedom from the Mosaic Law, freedom from "the old man" and from all that would be an obstacle to the inflowing of the new life, that of Christ, into our souls; in a word, a radical purification.

But we must consider this more closely. These effects can be explained only because Baptism causes us to participate *in the very mystery* of the Passion and Death of Christ, in as much as this mystery constitutes, with that of the Resurrection, the mystery of our Redemption, the cause and the act itself of our salvation. We are saved only by the Cross of Christ, by His Death. It is necessary, therefore, that the soul should be brought into contact with this mystery of the redemptive immolation of the Savior. This contact is sacramental: it is Baptism. Baptism plunges us in the Death of Christ as in a spiritual cleansing from which we emerge entirely purified. How is this so? Because Baptism makes us die to sin, in Christ Who died and Who buried with Himself all human infirmities, the consequences of sin, in order that He might conquer sin. The contact effected in Baptism is certainly not of our soul with a corpse, but it is a spiritual contact with the sufferings which Christ has endured in His Passion "even unto death," for love of us and to save us. "The sufferings of the Passion of Christ are *communicated* to the person baptized, so that—since he becomes a member of Christ—it is as though he himself had endured these sufferings; and consequently all his sins are forgiven through the sufferings and the Passion of Christ."[1]

Let us delve to the limit of this matter. We have seen that

---

1. Saint Thomas, III, q. 69, a. 2, ad I. Compare: "To every baptized person, the Passion of Christ is communicated in order to heal him, as if the baptized person had himself suffered that Passion and had died." Idem, in the *corpus* of the Article.

the mystery of the Passion and Death of Christ is thus applied to the baptized soul in order that this soul may enter into it, may be plunged in it. This again is in order that such a soul, being henceforth associated and united with Christ so as now to form but one with Him "in the likeness of His death" (*Rom.*, VI, 5), may be called, by the very fact of his baptismal vocation, *to a share in the intimate mystery of the soul of the Savior, offering up His life for the salvation of the world.* Herein is the full meaning of the Christian life; and it is his Baptism which contains this full meaning for the Christian and reveals it to him. Again, this is the full meaning of the Eucharist and the Sacrifice of the Mass. Now, Baptism is completely orientated towards the Eucharist, the source of life, the continuation of the Sacrifice of the Cross, the center of the sacramental order.[1] The desire for the Eucharist is placed in the soul of the baptized person, and he receives the grace of the Sacrament of the Eucharist.

2. Participation in the mystery of the Resurrection of Christ

To participate, through the Sacrament of Baptism, in the mystery of the Resurrection of Christ, is to participate in *the effects* of this mystery. These effects can be summed up in a single one: the application. The mystery of the Redemption, in its full scope, comprises the Passion and Death of Christ, and His glorious Resurrection and Ascension into Heaven.

Through Baptism, we are redeemed persons who are saved in hope. The Redemption by Jesus Christ is extended to us. Saint Paul assures us that we are already raised up in Christ, our Head. This is indeed an astonishing and illuminating thought!

The Apostle clearly means that we are raised up in hope, and that, since our Head is now the Conqueror of death, His Resurrection is the pledge and the cause of the resurrection of our body. The principle of our resurrection is already within us, and we have the right to the heritage of eternal benefits.

Furthermore, to participate sacramentally in the Resurrection of Christ, means that our soul participates *in the very life* of the Risen Christ.

By His Resurrection, our Head has entered into the glory of Heaven, His Sacred Humanity being glorified, spiritualized, entirely divinized, and penetrated with the Holy Spirit. The Risen

---

1. Saint Thomas: "By Baptism, man is disposed to the reception of the Eucharistic. Hence, by the mere fact that children have received Baptism, they are destined, by the will of the Church, to receive the Eucharist" (III, q. 73, a. 3).

Christ communicates to us, in Baptism, the life which He possesses in His glorified soul.

This life, in the first place, is the divine life, the life of the Blessed Trinity. Baptism gives us this life. "I baptize you in the name of the Father, and of the Son, and of the Holy Ghost." The soul becomes the temple of the Blessed Trinity.

But we do not live this divine life in the same way as God lives it: there is no question of that life having sprung up in our souls at Baptism as it does in the bosom of the Blessed Trinity. We are not God. What Baptism effects is to enable us to live *by* this divine life of the Holy Spirit, in which *we participate* through a life that is divine.

This participation, this divinized life which is communicated to us, is a participation in the very life of the Holy Ghost, which Christ dispenses by His Resurrection, in order to bring us under the transforming action of His Divine Spirit. It is the mighty gift of the Holy Ghost Himself, Whom Christ had promised that He would send to mankind. Before Christ's Resurrection, He had not yet given this Divine Spirit: "for as yet the Spirit was not given, because Jesus was not yet glorified" (*John*, VII, 39).

This divinized life is the complete regeneration, "the laver of regeneration and renovation" (*Titus*, III, 5), of him who has "put on Christ." It is given in dependence on Christ, Who becomes, by His Holy Spirit, the Principle of the supernatural activity of the members of His Body.

Finally, to participate sacramentally in the Resurrection of Christ is to communicate in the mystery *of the soul* of the Risen Christ. The Risen Christ becomes the center to Whom all souls are drawn who desire to be saved; for in Him they find life, peace and joy, and they adhere to Him for Whom they have been created.

Thus, His divinized and glorified Humanity assimilates all men to Itself, by the Holy Spirit, in order to form the Whole Christ. To communicate in His Soul, is to share His will and His desire to draw all men to Himself and to introduce them, in union with Him, into the Divine Family, in eternal life.

"O God, Who illuminates this most holy night with the glory of the Resurrection of the Lord, preserve in the new children of Your family the spirit of adoption which You have given to them (through Baptism); so that, renewed both in body and in soul, they may serve You in cleanness of heart." (Deus, qui hanc sacratissimam noctem: Liturgy of Holy Saturday).

". . . for those also whom You have deigned to regenerate by

*water and the Holy Ghost, giving them remission of all their sins,
we beseech You, O Lord, to accept this oblation of our service . . ."*
(*Hanc igitur*, in the Mass of Holy Saturday).

86. PARTICIPATION IN THE MYSTERY OF THE PARDON GIVEN BY CHRIST OFFERING HIMSELF IN EXPIATION FOR THE SINS OF TH EWORLD

> *"May Our Lord Jesus Christ Himself absolve you . . ."*
>
> (Words spoken by the priest before giving Absolution)

Penance is certainly the Sacrament which is most liable to be
considered and to be received in a purely individualist manner.
In this Sacrament, everything takes place in the silence of the
soul itself and of its personal relations with God. And yet, this
Sacrament takes on its full meaning only when it is considered
in the light of the Mystical Body.[1]

1. *Person and community*

The nearer a person approaches to God; the more he becomes
aware of his own misery, and the more also does he feel the need
for truth in his relations with God and with his brethren. In the
eyes of God, he knows that he is guilty, sinful and nothing in
himself; but he knows, too, that this is not the reality he presents
to his fellow-men. He suffers at the thought of this mask of
hypocrisy which hides his real self, and he desires to drop this
mask, so that others may see him as he knows himself to be in
the sight of God.

But a twofold obstacle opposes this desire. First, there is the
law of charity, which rules over all. A member of the Mystical
Body must not be a stumbling block, a cause of scandal, for the
others: he must "edify" the Whole Christ. Furthermore, no human
person or society has the right to violate the sacred domain of

---

1. Here we are not considering this matter on the juridical and canonical plane.
We do not deal with the necessary and sufficient conditions for the validity of the Sacrament. We are addressing ourselves to Christians who have resolved to live their life
of membership of Christ with ever increasing intensity.

conscience. In Confession, Jesus Christ, our Head, has found the means of harmoniously reconciling the rights of truth and the right of charity, the rights of the person and the rights of the community.

On the one hand, each sinner can confess his faults and can lay aside the burden of his sins, so as to recover peace of conscience, by sincerely acknowledging, in the presence of a qualified representative of the Church, what he is in the sight of God: misery, sin and nothingness.

On the other hand, by reason of the fact that a minister of the Church intervenes here in the name of God, the community is present, in a sense, at this act of purification and of reparation. It is not only to God, but to the whole Mystical Body, to the Church in Heaven and on earth[2] that the sinner confesses his trangressions, because no sin is purely individual, every sin having its repercussions on the life of the Mystical Body.

All the formulae used by the priest express this *social* character of Confession. He must first deliver the sinful soul from the bonds "of excommunication and of interdict," those disciplinary penalties which cut off the guilty person from the society of the Church: in other words, he must restore to the penitent the right to social communion in the Mystical Body. Then, he absolves the penitent from his sins, in the name of the Blessed Trinity and through the divine virtue interiorly exercised in the sacramental sign.

2. *Participation in the mystery of Christ*

In the Sacrament of Penance, as in all the others, there is a connection with Christ and with His Passion, a participation in the mystery of Christ, an action of the Christ-Head.

The proper grace of this Sacrament, its greatness and its beauty, is that it makes us participate in the reparatory, painful and expiatory love of Jesus Christ, offering to His Father the infinite merits and satisfactions of His agonizing Heart, for the sins of the world.

Baptism has already introduced us into this mystery of the Passion of Christ, and, because of the faith of the Church, the regenerative virtue of this Sacrament has been applied to our

---

2. "I confess to Almighty God, to Blessed Mary ever Virgin, to blessed Michael the Archangel, to blessed John the Baptist, to the holy Apostles Peter and Paul, and to all the saints . . ." (to which the bishop or priest, in the Confiteor of the Mass, adds: *"and to you, brethren"*) ". . . that I have sinned . . ."

souls. In the Sacrament of Penance, which revives in us the grace of our Baptism, our personal contribution is very important. It is the acts of the penitent—confession, contrition and firm purpose of amendment—which constitute the *matter* of the Sacrament. It is through them that we can participate *in the mystery of the expiatory and reparatory satisfaction made by Christ,* with all the reparatory love which we can express in each of these acts, for the redemption of our own sins and those of the world.

We must prove that love by a sincere, generous and humble *accusation* of our sins, confessing what costs us an effort to admit —those sins, intentions and motives of which we are ashamed and over which we would draw a veil.

We must do so, as well, by a deep *repentance* for having offended Him Who has loved us so much, and Whose merciful love still waits to pardon us.

Finally, we must make a strong and unwavering *resolution* to be more faithful to Christ, so that in future we may compensate for our ingratitude by a more obedient love.

But all this is possible only because Jesus Christ acts in this Sacrament. He is present *in the grace of humility* which invites the soul to realize clearly and poignantly its own misery, to admit this misery sincerely in Confession, and to accept it generously. He is present *in the part played by the theological virtues:* faith in the efficacy of the Redemptive Sacrifice; hope and confidence in the mercy of the Father; and charity, which, at first imperfect, increases more and more, through the constant and earnest reception of the Sacrament itself, until it grows to the height of perfect charity—the love of God for Himself, for His holiness and for His infinite goodness.

Again, Christ is present *in the grace of Absolution:* "May Our Lord Jesus Christ Himself absolve you." The repentant sinner is absolved in Confession by Christ Himself—by Him Who said to the sinful woman crouched in repentance at His Feet: "Go, thy sins are forgiven thee."

But to what extent does Jesus pardon us? The measure of His pardon is the measure of our participation in the mystery of His sufferings for the sins of the world (Saint Thomas, III, 9, 72). Christ Himself must introduce us into the mystery of His painful oblation and of His infinite satisfaction. For "in Him we live, in Him we merit, in Him we make satisfaction by producing fruits worthy of repentance. It is from Him that they derive all their value. It is by Him that they are offered up to the Father. It is for His sake that the Father accepts them" (Council of Trent,

Sess. XIV, ch. VIII). By Baptism, we have become sons in the Son; and, in the Sacrament of Penance, we live the painful part of the mystery of His filial life—His offering of Himself to the Father in reparation for the sins of men. We participate in his "reverence" (*Heb.*, V, 7) towards the Father, and in His adoration; but also in His merits and in His satisfactions. Therefore, we need no longer consider our own powerlessness, for what is of power is the mystery of Christ, which repairs all, compensates for all, and re-establishes the order disrupted by sin. What is demanded of us is that we should enter into this mystery, communicate in it, and form but one with the Man-God, our Head, Who calls upon His whole Mystical Body to cooperate in His Redemptive Mission of taking away the sins of the world. Our own sins are part of that mass of ignominy which has crucified our Divine Savior.

O Jesus, our Redeemer, we thank You for having given us peace, through this Sacrament of Your love. But grant that we may not degrade this peace into something selfish or pharisaical. We make no claim to be better than the rest of our brethren, for indeed we are all sinners. But at least we promise that we shall endeavor, in each succeeding Confession, to enter more intimately into the infinite satisfactions of Your Sacred Heart, in order that, in You and with You, we may participate in the redemption of our own sins and of those of our brethren.

87. PARTICIPATION IN THE MYSTERY OF PENTECOST

> *But when the Paraclete cometh, whom I will send you from the Father, the Spirit of Truth, who proceedeth from the Father, he shall give testimony of me.*
>
> (John, XV, 26)
>
> *And they were all filled with the Holy Ghost.*
>
> (Acts, II, 4)

Virility, so far from being an exceptional virtue among Catholics, is indeed one of the distinctive characteristics of authentic Catholicism. The Church has a Sacrament which communicates Christian virility to the members of the Mystical Body, with a view to promoting the common good of the Church, and in order to give to each member the resolution and fortitude which he requires if he is to fulfill his mission in the Body, and thereby share in the apostolic mission of the Church.

1. *A mission*

It is the bishop who—as successor of the Apostles, as chief priest and head of the apostolate in his diocese—confides, through the Sacrament of Confirmation, an official, public and social mission to those who receive it. This Sacrament marks the Christian's coming of age in the spiritual life. Until then, he had been, as it were, a child in the domain of religion. By Baptism, he was *born* into the Christian life; though, of course, Baptism already laid upon him the duty of showing consideration for others, of helping them, of "giving" to the other members, since he himself is indebted to the whole Body and there is reciprocal communication of life within that Body.[1]

However, though the baptized person had already a duty of apostolate, he had not yet received, from the ecclesiastical authority, a *mandate* conferring on him a personal *mission* in the service of the Mystical Body. This precisely is the distinctive role of the Sacrament of Confirmation, which is to confer on each recipient the personal mission of defending the Mystical Body; of bearing witness to Christ at all times by the example of his life, especially in circumstances where the honor of God is threatened and the eternal salvation of the neighbor is imperilled—circumstances which call for vigorous and courageous affirmation of the truth.

Thus, the apostolic value of this witness becomes greater when the confirmed person bears it in a *public* capacity as an official representative of the community of the Mystical Body. It is in this sense that Confirmation is the Sacrament of Christian virility and of growth to the age of spiritual manhood. By the fact of having received this Sacrament, a person is called upon, and is qualified, to undertake responsibilities in the domain of the apostolate, not as a head, but as a member. How few Christians there are who realize that they have been called, through the Sacrament of Confirmation, to regard themselves as responsible

---

1. "Baptism imposes the duty of the apostolate, since it is through Baptism that we become members of the Church, that is, of the Mystical Body of Christ. There should be, among the members of this Body, a solidarity of interests and reciprocal communication of life. The members should assist one another; no member can remain inactive; each receives, and therefore each should give in return." (Letter of Pope Pius XI to the Cardinal Patriarch of Lisbon: 10-11-1933).

for the whole Mystical Body, and as belonging to the Church by right of their being adults in the Faith!

2. A power

The spiritual power which will help the Christian to fulfill this difficult mission in an atmosphere heavy with paganism and materialism, is a grace of *"Confirmation"* in the Faith. This is identified as the grace of fortitude; but the description is accurate only in the perspective of the full plenitude of this grace of "Confirmation." This is not to be read as though the Sacrament bestowed the virtue of fortitude and the gift of fortitude alone, to the exclusion of other virtues and other gifts. For it is the ensemble of virtues and of gifts which here produces a condition of Christian virility characterized by courage, energy and fearlessness in bearing witness to the Faith. It is a grace of profound convictions, and of an enthusiasm arising from a holy pride in belonging to the Church and in fulfilling a mission in her service. It is a grace which will show itself visibly in active zeal, and in apostolic and missionary charity.

3. Participation in the mystery of Pentecost

This grace of "Confirmation" possesses such efficacy because it is itself a participation in the mighty outpouring of the Holy Ghost which occurred in the Cenacle at the first Pentecost, and in which the apostolic life of the Church commenced. This event transformed the soul of the Apostles. Only a few hours earlier, they had been little men, full of cowardly and shrinking fear; now, possessed by the Holy Ghost, they were the stuff of heroes and of martyrs. They set out to conquer the world, and there was no obstacle that could make them turn aside. It was this grace which really transformed them into Apostles: it is this same grace which is communicated by the Sacrament of Confirmation, in order that "the same Spirit" may animate the personal life of the Christian, and make it an apostolic life in the service of the Whole Christ.

"O Lord, Who has given the Holy Ghost to Your Apostles and Who has willed that, through them and their successors, this Holy Spirit should be transmitted to the rest of the faithful, look with clemency upon our humble ministry, and grant that the *same Spirit may come into the hearts of those whose foreheads we have marked with Holy Chrism and with the Sign of the*

Cross. Grant that this same Spirit *may dwell in their hearts, and* make them the temple of Your glory . . ."
(Prayer recited by the bishop at the end of the ceremony of Confirmation).

88. PARTICIPATION IN THE MYSTERY OF CHRIST'S BUILDING OF HIS BODY IN UNITY AND IN CHARITY

THE SACRAMENT OF THE UNITY OF THE WHOLE CHRIST

That they may be one, as we also are one;
I in them . . .

(John, XVII, 22)

The Blessed Eucharist is the Sacrament which makes the unity of the Mystical Body. But we must not imagine this Mystical Body as something already complete and perfected: it is always in process of growth, like a living organism. What was required in order that this great unifying design of Our Savior should be accomplished, through the instituting of this Sacrament? In the first place, it was necessary that the obstacle to unity should be cast aside. Then, that this Sacrament should contain in itself a unifying power. But this Sacrament is fully communicated to us, only through a participation in the great mystery of Christ.

1. *The fight against sin, the obstacle to unity*

The precise and immediate aim of the Blessed Eucharist is not purification from sin, since Our Lord has given us another Sacrament for this specific purpose; though we must add that venial sins are forgiven by the increase of charity procured by the reception of the Blessed Eucharist.

But what the Blessed Eucharist affirms is the *incompatibility* which exists between itself and the sins which destroy the unity of the Mystical Body; mortal sins, deliberate and serious sin against charity. "If therefore thou . . . remember that thy brother hath anything against thee . . . go first to be reconciled to thy brother" (*Matt.*, V, 23, 24). It would be a sacrilege to receive the Blessed Eucharist with a deliberate feeling of hatred in one's heart for another; because such a sentiment is a flagrant contradiction of what is signified by this Sacrament of unity.

He Whom we receive in the Blessed Eucharist, is Christ immolated for the Redemption of the sins of the world. The Eucharistic Christ comes, therefore, to make us participate in the great battle by which He has vanquished sin. He desires to continue to wage this warfare against sin, with His Church, with us, and in us. Of course, this can be said of the whole Christian life; but it has a special application to the Blessed Eucharist. In this Sacrament, the immolated and glorified Christ is really present in the very action of His Redemptive Sacrifice, in order to engage us personally in the warfare which He ceaselessly directs against sin, regarded as the obstacle to unity, and therefore especially against those sins whose roots in us are selfishness and egoism.

2. The proper effect of the Sacrament

The Blessed Eucharist is specifically directed towards the unity of the Mystical Body, and hence it is that this Sacrament gives us an increase of charity.

Let us examine this more closely, however, because individualism can insinuate itself even here. Not everyone who receives Holy Communion, does so in order to extend to others the benefit of his charity, and thus contribute to the establishment of the Mystical Body, in love.

What is of paramount importance in the Blessed Eucharist, is unity in the Mystical Body, in the Church. Charity is produced in this Sacrament as an effect. Through this Sacrament, the Christ-Head builds His Body in unity. The Blessed Eucharist does not merely *cooperate* in producing this unity, by the fact that it brings people closer together through charity. The Blessed Eucharist *creates* the unity of the Mystical Body, since this Sacrament really and substantially contains Him in Whom the whole Church is united and forms but one: Jesus Christ Himself. For, in His Church, Christ is the center of unity, by His Sacred Humanity, by His Body, by His Soul, by His Redemptive Sacrifice through which He has reconciled men with God and reconciled them with one another. They each receive one and the same physical Body of Christ, and eat one and the same Bread of Life—"unus panis, unum corpus"; and this has the effect of knitting each one more closely with Christ, the member with Him Who is the Head, this in turn having the effect of uniting each member more closely with all the other members of Christ's Mystical Body. In short, what is effected in communion in the Mystical Body.

3. Participation in the mystery

But how does this communion in Christ produce such a unity? The explanation is that the Blessed Eucharist, through this phe-

nomenon of spiritual nourishment, effects a vital assimilation of
our souls to Christ in Holy Communion, and a transformation of
our souls in Christ, through love. It fuses us, so to speak, with
Christ and with the intimate dispositions of Christ. In a more
particular manner proper to this Sacrament, it makes us participate in the great mystery of love through which Jesus offered
Himself entirely to the Father, in order that men, liberated from
sin and nourished with His life, should all be one in Him as He
is one with the Father. The Eucharist gives Christ to us in this
very act of His return to His Father, in order that we may enter
into that return with the dispositions demanded by unity; or
rather—since we cannot repeat sufficiently that it is Christ Himself Who acts in the Eucharist—it is Christ Who introduces us
into the mystery of His passover to His Father through His
Redemptive Sacrifice, in order that, where He is in unity with
the Father, we also may even now be united with Him, through
the Blessed Eucharist . . . "That they may be one, as thou,
Father, in me, and I in thee . . . Father, I will that where I am,
they also whom Thou hast given me may be with me . . ." (John,
XVII, 21, 24).

"Sanctify, O Lord, these gifts which are offered to You for
the unity of the Christian people. Through them, grant unto us,
in Your Church, the benefits of unity and of peace."

"Though we are many, we form but one (mystical) body and
are nourished with one food, for we all share the same Bread and
the same Chalice."

"The Communion which we have just received, O Lord, is
the sign of the union, in You, of all those who are faithful to You.
Grant, we beseech You, that it may also effect unity in Your
Church."

(Secret, Communion and Postcommunion of the Votive Mass for the Unity of the Church)

89. PARTICIPATION IN THE MYSTERY OF CHRIST'S CONSECRATING AND SANCTIFYING HIS CHURCH BY HIS PRIESTHOOD

> For every high priest taken from among
> men is ordained for men in the things that
> appertain to God . . .
>
> (Heb., V, 1)

The Sacrament of Holy Orders is pre-eminently the Sacrament whose very essence is a participation in a mystery of Christ:

the mystery of His Priesthood. The priesthood of the priest on earth, is not distinct from, nor is it added to, the Priesthood of Jesus Christ. There is only one Priesthood: that of the Sovereign Priest, of the Only and Eternal Priest. It is He Who, by the ministry of His Church and of His priests, continues to fulfill His Redemptive Mission among men, and to foster the growth of His Mystical Body for the glory of His Father. Therefore, if we are to understand in what the sense the priest is, as it were, "another Christ," we must contemplate his priesthood in the light of the Priesthood of the Supreme Priest. We must consider the essence, the acts and the subjective elements of Christ's Priesthood; because the priesthood in the Church is simply the continuation and extension into time of the Priesthood of Christ.

1. *In its very essence*

Jesus Christ is Priest from the Incarnation and by reason of His hypostatic union. His mission is a priestly mission, just as His vocation is a priestly vocation. The essential quality of the priest lies in his being a mediator between God and His people. Now, Christ is the Mediator *par excellence*, because the Incarnate Word came on earth to re-unite mankind with God, and it is in Him that God unites Himself with mankind: in a personal union with the human nature which He has assumed in His Son; and in a mystical union with all men redeemed in His Body which is the Church.

The priest is as another Christ, "because he is marked with the indelible character which makes him a living image of the Savior" (Pope Pius XII: *Menti Nostrae*). This character makes the priest a consecrated person and a mediator, like Christ Himself.

How glorious and exalted is this vocation of the priest as a *consecrated* man! By his consecration, the priest is dedicated to the things that appertain to God. He moves among men as, by his very definition, the witness to things divine and eternal.

This character which distinguishes the priest from all other men, also decides the entire orientation of his life.

It rules *his relations with God,* to Whom alone his whole activity must be directed. Like Christ, to Whom he belongs with every fiber of his consecrated being, he must be "about the Father's business" (*Luke,* II, 49); he must be constantly "solicitous for the things that belong to the Lord," and never "solicitous for the things of this world" (1 *Cor.,* VII, 32-33).

He must give the first preference in his life to prayer, to con-

templation, to the Divine Office, to the liturgy, and to the love
of God as manifested in his apostolate.

This character must also rule *his relations with the world*. As
a consecrated man, he has been separated from "the world and
the things that are in the world": like the Church herself, he is
in the world but no longer of the world. For, again like the
Church, he is *in* the world only in order that he may save
the world.

The effect of his consecration is not to make him shun the
world and all that is human. It binds him and dedicates him to
the Mystery of the Incarnation. In dependence on the Incarnate
Word, this consecration is that of a *mediator*—of one who, far
from shunning the world, stands between God and men in order
that he may unite men with God, and God with men. He offers
to God the prayers and the sacrifices of men; he restores the
world and the creation to God. Moreover, he communicates to
men the life and the mercy of God, and the truth and the grace
of Jesus Christ.

The Incarnation took place for the sake of the Redemption:
the Son of God came into the world in order to redeem mankind.
We can find an analogy here with the life of the priest. He, too,
lives in the world and moves among men, not in order that he
may live according to the values and passions of this world, but
so that he may gain a more sympathetic understanding of men's
infirmities, and save mankind through his participation in the
mystery of the Redemptive Sacrifice of Christ.

2. *The Priesthood of Christ contemplated in its actions*

Consider, first of all, the *Sacrifice of the Mass*, which is the
efficacious rite of mediation. The consecration of the priest is for
the Eucharistic Consecration. It is this Eucharistic Sacrifice which
defines his priesthood.

The Sacrifice of the Mass, the center of Christian worship, is
also the center of the life of the priest. It is above all in the Mass
that he is "another Christ," that he takes the place of Christ. "This
is *my* Body . . . This is *my* Blood."

Moreover, his priesthood continues the Priesthood of Christ
in *all the acts* by which Jesus put souls in relationship with God
and accomplished His Redemptive Mission. In the name of Christ
and in the person of Christ, the priest has received, through his
consecration, the power to produce all the sacramental rites destined for the salvation of the faithful. It is he who has the mission
to pray and to act in the name of the Christian community and as

head of this community. Because he is marked with the character of the priesthood, all the actions which he performs as "minister and dispenser of the mysteries of God" (1 *Cor.*, IV, 1), are as the actions of Christ, the Sovereign Priest. Each of his priestly acts acquires, by virtue of his consecration, a real and authentic value which makes it pleasing to God, and which draws down upon men the grace and mercy of God.

Finally, we must remember that it was not by prayer and sacrifice only that Christ accomplished His priestly mission of Redemption. He did so by His whole life and teaching, and *by all His acts of charity as the Good Shepherd* who brought to men the treasures of the Redemption. Again, there is an analogy with the priest. "As the Father hath sent me, I also send you" (*John*, XX, 21). Everything in the priest's life and mission should be directed to the service of the Mystical Body, to the service of the Redemption and the formation of the Whole Christ. "Until Christ be formed in you" (*Gal.*, IV, 19). Herein is the whole purpose of his ministry: that he should teach the truth; that he should carry out faithfully all the functions of his pastoral ministry; that he should organize and animate the most varied forms of the apostolate; and that, always and everywhere, he should be "another Christ," so that he may be able to continue Christ and to form Christ in the souls of men.

3. *In its subjective elements*

Finally, the priest should contemplate and imitate the Priesthood of Christ *in its subjective elements*—that is to say, *in the interior religion of the Sovereign Priest.* The whole life of the priest should be an imitation of Christ, an interior conformity with Christ, a cultivation of Christ's virtues: His humility, His meekness, His obedience to His Father, His detachment and His purity; but, above all else, the priest must make his own that spirit of sacrifice and that charity with which Christ offered Himself to His Father for the Redemption of the world.

He must be "another Christ" by the laying aside of all that is tainted with the self. He must be "another Christ" by the complete oblation of himself to Christ, so that the Sovereign Priest, by His Holy Spirit, may lead him, fashion him, transform him and make him think as He does, will what He wills and love like Him.

All this work of assimilation to Christ is possible because the Sacrament of Holy Orders not only confers the character of the priesthood, but also gives the grace of the priesthood. The sacerdotal character causes the priest to participate in the *powers* of Christ's Priesthood. The grace received in the Sacrament, causes him to participate in the *holiness* of Christ, the Sovereign Priest. This grace consists in an increase of sanctifying grace and, with it, an increase of charity, of the infused virtues, and of the gifts of the Holy Ghost. Moreover, this grace gives the priest the right to certain special assistance and actual graces which guide, enlighten and sustain him in the discharge of any particular or difficult duty of his calling.

O Jesus, Sovereign Priest, grant that all Your priests may understand that, when they teach, it is not their own ideas or their own truth that they should preach, but Your Truth, Your Words, Your Commandments; and that, in the exercise of their apostolate, it is not their own action which counts for the formation of the Whole Christ, but Your action and that of Your grace. Grant to them an intense belief in the power of their priestly grace, so that Your faithful may find You and You alone in Your priests.

90.   PARTICIPATION IN THE MYSTERY OF THE UNION OF CHRIST AND HIS CHURCH

> *Husbands, love your wives, as Christ also loved the Church and delivered himself up for it; that he might sanctify it . . . that he might present it to himself, a glorious church, not having spot or wrinkle . . . holy and without blemish.*
>
> (Ephes., V, 25-27)

In the Old Testament, the metaphor of marriage is often used to describe the relations of God with His chosen people. Saint Paul shows that the union of Christ and His Church is the model of the Sacrament of Matrimony. This, however, is no mere symbol or metaphor, but a reality. It is a reality which is a sublime ideal to be contemplated, but also one in which Christian marriages should participate as in their source. For Christian marriage takes on its full significance only if it is implanted in the relations of Christ with His Church, and is united with this mystery. This is true of it, both in its purpose and in its very essence.

1. *The purpose*

The true purpose of the Sacrament of Matrimony is the extension of the Mystical Body of Christ.

In what sense is this so? Were not the couple already called, before their marriage and by the very fact of their Baptism, to cooperate as members of Christ in extending the Mystical Body? This is certainly true; but the Sacrament of Matrimony constitutes a new and particularly efficacious form of this social mission. This is especially clear from three points of view.

a) Christian marriage has the same purpose as that of Christ's union with His Church: the formation of the Mystical Body. It gives Christ new members of His Mystical Body, and provides new children of God for the Church. It is collaboration in creation, for the purpose of the Redemption.

b) Through the Sacrament they have received, the husband and wife should cooperate in the Redemption, by their union itself. *As Christian spouses, that is, as two members of Christ forming now but one,* a new bond attaches them to the Church: their family becomes a living cell of the Church. Through their shared life, participating in that which Christ lives in union with His Church, they should increase in holiness and thus cooperate *in the Redemption.*[1] Together, they participate in the divine life, in the mystery of the union of Christ with His Church, of the love of Christ for His Church, and of His total giving of Himself to His Church. It is thus especially that their mutual sanctification is effected, and the supernatural fruitfulness of their union is assured. It is not sufficient that they should contemplate this mystery from afar, as if it were something whose transcendence lifted it to a world other than theirs. They are called to enter into this mystery, so that they may shape their lives in accordance with it. This mystery must be communicated to them in order that it may manifest itself in them.

c) Finally, if this mystery lives in them and if they live by it, their home itself will be made apostolic with a radiating and

---

1. "This is truly a tremendous mystery, upon which we cannot meditate enough; that the salvation of many souls depends upon the prayers and voluntary mortifications offered for that intention by the members of the Mystical Body of Jesus Christ, and upon the cooperation which pastors and the faithful, *and especially parents,* must afford to our divine Savior" (*Mystici Corporis Christi*).

conquering charity. Thus constantly purified, strengthened and sanctified, their union will bear public witness, of a special kind which only Christian marriages can give, to the wonderful transformation which, through His Church, Christ effects in human love, and in that most human act which ensures the transmission of human life. For when this union is established in Christ, the whole of conjugal and family life is transformed, and the world is given the witness of the fully human and divine happiness of a home wherein husband and wife impart to each other a mutual participation in the life of Christ in the Church. Through such a home, the unbelieving world is shown the evidence of the love of Christ and of the Church for husband and wife, for the family, for mankind.

Thus, Christian married couples are witnesses to, and collaborators in, the Mystery of *the Incarnation,* continued in the Church of Christ.

2. *In its very essence*

It is the human love itself of the couple, one for the other, which becomes, through the Sacrament, the source of grace. The sign of the Sacrament is the gift of self made by husband to wife and by wife to husband, which is the expression of their love. But, like the Blessed Eucharist, this Sacrament is not a transient act; it is permanent, and is exercised during the whole life of the married couple every time this mutual giving is renewed in the myriad acts of married life, thereby continuing to express the mystery of Christ.

For Christ enters into Christian marriage in a direct, active and efficacious manner. He is present as a bond which, by the sacramental grace and by His charity, preserves the union of husband and wife and makes that union participate *in the fundamental mysteries of His own union with His Church.*

In the mystery of His unity: Christ is so intimately united with His Church, that He and the Church become one mystical Person—the Whole Christ. It is thus, too, with Christian couples married in Christ. The sacramental grace places in their souls a principle of unity which unifies them daily more and more, if they are faithful.

In the mystery of His indissolubility: Christ is united with His Church forever. The Whole Christ will one day be in eternity, when Jesus Christ the Conqueror has merged His whole Church on earth in His Church Triumphant. The supernatural love of husband and wife is not of time, but of eternity. It is made for eternity and has an eternal value.

In the mystery of His Holiness and His Purity. In Christian marriage, Christ is always active to purify the heart from the earthly egoism which divides and the egoism of the pride which opposes, true marital union; and from every type of egoism which centers the individual on self, and prevents husband and wife from understanding each other, pardoning each other's short-comings, and accepting in each other what is different and complementary. Christ is ever active in each partner so that he or she may discover the fine human qualities, and the riches and beauty of divine grace in the other; and that each may be conscious of his or her responsibility before God for the soul of the other, for its purity, its holiness, its salvation, so that each may present the other to Christ without "spot or wrinkle . . . holy and wihout blemish."

In the mystery of His generosity even unto sacrifice: "as Christ also loved the Church and delivered himself up for it." There is no love without giving; and there is no complete love without complete giving—and therefore, without sacrifice. Such love is a grace merited by the Passion of the Savior, and communicated to the Christian husband and wife: it is a love which bears the mark of the Cross. To enter into this mystery is, therefore, to accept the demands of this love, marked with the sign of the Redemption, in the inevitable trials of human life and of the life lived together in Holy Matrimony.

Finally, Christ is present to Christian married couples through their participation *in the mystery of His fecundity.* Christ gives to His Church His whole life and all His gifts. He does so in order that His Church may be the Mother of souls, through that maternity by which she gathers the children to herself in order to bring them forth in a new birth to the life of the Son, and to make them the children of God—"sons of God." This maternity of the Church is extended to all mankind. The union of Christian marriage also gives children to the Church—children whose parents should form them in the image of Christ by giving them a good Christian upbringing. For Christian parents should not regard their children as merely their own, to be brought up in whatever way they please: these sons and daughters are also the children of God, belonging to the family of God, and the fruit of the union of Christ with His Church.

O Jesus, grant that many homes may realize the splendor of

*the mission which is theirs in Your Church. May husbands and
wives understand that their love for one another is, in You, a
participation in the infinite Love with which God loves Himself,
and with which He loves them in uniting You with Your Church.*

91. PARTICIPATION IN THE MYSTERY OF CHRIST IN FACE OF SICKNESS AND DEATH

I was sick . . . and you visited Me.
(Matt. XXV, 35, 36)

Christ did not stand by and tolerate disease as something
good in itself, but He "healed such as had any sickness." He
Himself experienced suffering; but He conquered it and made
it an instrument of Redemption. Like that of Christ, the Church's
attitude towards those who are sick is one of maternal care and
concern. She has a Sacrament of the sick. She consecrates their
condition, because they have a fruitful mission in the Mystical
Body. When disease becomes a threat to the person's life, she
redoubles her compassionate vigilance and her mercy. In all
circumstances, she endeavors to imitate Christ and to bring souls
into conformity with the Divine Model, in order to assist them
to endure their suffering and thus give it a redemptive value.

1. *In the face of sickness*

The Sacrament of the sick has been instituted as a divine
remedy, not only for the soul, but also for the body.

The Church does not despise the body: she respects it, and
desires and seeks its cure. She imitates her Head, Who healed the
sick. She prays God to give them perfect spiritual and bodily
health.[1]

However, while the Church certainly seeks both the health

---

1. "By the grace of the Holy Spirit, heal, we beseech You, O Lord, all the
weakness of this poor sufferer. Release him from all his infirmities; grant him pardon
of all his sins; remove from him all the sufferings of soul and body. Restore him
to perfect spiritual and corporal strength, so that he may be able to resume the discharge of his duties" (*Liturgical prayer of the Sacrament of Extreme Unction*).

of the body and of the soul, she respects the hierarchy of values. She prays God to restore the health of the body, if He wills to do so, but for the good of the soul and in order that the soul may be able to accomplish its duties more perfectly.

The Church seeks, above all, to ensure the mastery of the soul over the body. She dreads the reverse of this, which is the disorder and the consequence of sin. When the body is weakened, exhausted and overwhelmed by sickness, the soul is crushed, powerless to exert itself in thought or to rise above its suffering by an effort of will and of love.

The Sacrament of Extreme Unction has been instituted to combat all the *weakness,* produced by sickness, in the body and in the soul—the soul's weakness being due to that of the body, and also to all the consequences of sin. This Sacrament gives the patient the strength to dominate his suffering, by making him participate in the sovereign domination of Christ over disease and sin.

From a merely human point of view, a sick room presents a picture of powerlessness and utter defeat. The Church enters there, and all is changed. She brings an atmosphere of victory and of hope, of purification and of liberation, of salvation and of life. She repeats the words of Saint James (*James,* V, 15):

"And the prayer of faith *shall save* the sick man . . ." This is the grace of confidence and of hope.

"And the Lord shall *raise him up* . . ." This is the grace of comfort and of strength.

"And if he be in sin, the sin shall be *forgiven him* . . ." This is the grace of complete purification from sins and from the consequences of a life of sin.

In that hour, the Church proclaims the right and the mastery of Jesus Christ over the body and the soul, and over each of the senses which she purifies by anointing with holy oil, the symbol of alleviation and of strength.

2. *In the face of death*

The discipline of the Church reserves this Sacrament to patients who are in danger of death. With a delicate and maternal compassion, the Church desires that they should be ready to face the supreme combat. The whole life of the Christian is "a warfare" (*Job,* VII, 1). His Baptism already signified the struggle between Christ and Satan, in which, from that hour, the Christian is personally involved.

But with death, the hour of supreme combat and of utterly

final decision has come. All the will to live, fundamentally implanted in human nature, rears up in one last effort. It is not in man's nature to accept death, since death is not part of his nature, but is the consequence of Original Sin. Jesus Himself deigned to experience, in His human nature, man's instinctive repugnance at the thought of death, in order to teach us not to be surprised at experiencing, in our turn, the same repugnance, but to conquer it, to rise above it, to offer it as an expiation and reparation for sin and to transform it into a victory over sin for the Redemption of the world.

By the Sacrament of Extreme Unction, the Church assists the dying person to face the final combat with serenity and fortitude, in peace and in abandonment to Christ, Who, if such be His adorable Will, can restore him again to health. What is important, in that moment, is this state of security in the hands of an omnipotent all-loving Christ. It is He Who is acting on the soul, in this Sacrament. It is He Who now aids the soul to make the great journey through the gateway of death.

By the holy "Viaticum" of the Eucharist, which the Church administers to the dying person, Jesus Christ accompanies him, with His strength and His life, on this final journey. The Blessed Eucharist is the Sacrament of the passage of Jesus to His Father; and each time the now dying person received this Sacrament during his life, his whole being was put in the proper disposition for the passage and the return to the Father. But now, it is no longer that passage in its spirit, but in all its reality. Jesus draws and assimilates to Himself the member of His Body; He gives to the dying person a participation in the dispositions with which, when dying on the Cross, He offered His life and His death for the Redemption of men. "Father . . . into thy hands I commend my spirit."

The Church desires that the disciple of Christ, in conformity with His Divine Master, should make a complete sacrifice of his life and of his death, to God, for the Redemption of the world. This sacrifice can become a veritable feast for him who believes intensely in the Resurrection. But in order that it may be a true sacrifice, it must comprise, on the one hand, abnegation, the harrowing of the soul and all that the reparation and expiation of sin demands; while, on the other hand, it must be the expression of a generous offering, consecration and love, and of faith and hope in the resurrection of the body and in the perfection of Eternal Life in the Whole Christ, entered into the glory of the Father.

"*Depart, Christian soul, out of this world, in the name of God, the Almighty Father, Who created you . . . in the name of Jesus Christ, Son of the living God, Who suffered for you . . . in the name of the Holy Ghost, Who has filled you with His gifts . . . in the name of the angels and of the archangels . . . in the name of all the Saints in Heaven . . . that today you may enter into the place of peace and into the holy City of Heaven . . . Amen.*"

(From the Prayers for the Dying)

CHAPTER TWO

Credo in Spiritum Sanctum Vivicantem

I BELIEVE IN THE HOLY GHOST, THE SPIRIT OF LIFE

PRINCIPAL TRAITS OF THE CHRISTIAN LIFE
IN THE WHOLE CHRIST

92. THE LIFE OF A NEW CREATURE

> *If, then, any be in Christ a new creature,*
> *the old things are passed away . . . all*
> *things are made new.*
>
> (II Cor., V, 17)

Do we realize how we are radically changed, in our very being and in our outlook on people and on things, by our insertion in Christ? Do we understand that this change does not consist solely in a moral effort, however important in itself this effort may be, or in obligations of worship: that it consists essentially in a transformation of *our being itself*, through our participation in the life of Christ?

1. A *fundamental renunciation through participation in the Mystery of the Death of the Savior*

We are quite aware, of course, that the Christian is bound to accomplish acts of renunciation, of penance and of mortification. But here there is question of something quite different, namely, of belonging to Christ so as to live no longer for themselves, but for Christ: "And Christ died for all; that they also who live may not now live to themselves, but unto him who died for them and rose again" (II *Cor.*, V, 15). This demands a renunciation of our natural tendencies; an immolation of our sinful human nature; a crucifying of that proud and egoistic nature which claims that it is sufficient unto itself and that it can lead itself in complete independence.

Our *thoughts* should not be ours alone, marked with inevitable poverty and narrowness; they should be those *of Christ.* Now, by the mouth of the Psalmist, God says to us: "My thoughts are not your thoughts" (*Isaias*, LV, 8). Therefore we must lay aside completely our own points of view, and allow the Holy Spirit to communicate to us the thoughts of Christ, our Head. This complete renunciation of our own ways of thinking is all the more imperative because we have no means of seeing clearly the designs of Christ for us, but must grope our way in the twilight of faith.

Our *feelings* ought to be no longer those of a selfish heart, or of a nature given over to its passions: they should be the feelings of Christ. "For let this mind be in you, which was also in Christ Jesus" (*Philip.*, II, 5). This, too, involves a total reformation. We must feel and love like Christ and with Christ, so that we may enter into the sentiments of His Sacred Heart, which His Holy Spirit communicates to us: the feelings and desires of our Head, Who wishes to accomplish the Redemption of all mankind, to conquer sin, to make love triumph, to glorify His Father, to build up the Whole Christ. How mean, miserable, and paltry, therefore, do not our feelings and desires appear, by contrast with this call! What a reformation is needed if we are to detach our hearts from their egoism, their prejudices and their passions, in order that we may communicate in the desires and feelings of the Heart of Christ!

Our *wills* ought to be no longer our own: "not my will," Jesus Himself has said. Our purposes should be those of God, those of Jesus our Head, always in full conformity with the Will of His Father. How difficult indeed it is, to renounce our own wills, to submit to the Divine Will, and to obey those who show that Divine Will to us! We want to be the captains of our own souls. Jesus explicitly demanded this renunciation, when he said to Peter: "Another shall gird thee and lead thee whither thou wouldst not" (*John*, XXI, 18).

In order to enter into the mystery of the Whole Christ, we must begin by stripping ourselves of ourselves, so that we may be ready *to receive all from Him,* from Jesus Christ. This is the first requisite for being a new creature.

2. *A new life by participation in the Mystery of the Resurrection of Christ*

Such a gift, given to us by the grace of the Eucharist, leads to a total change in our very conception of life: "all has been made new . . ." "Now, therefore, you are no more strangers and foreigners; but you are fellow citizens with the saints" (*Ephes.*, II, 19).

This gift implies in us, first of all, *a sense of the eternal*—a sense of the place which the thought of eternal things must henceforward take in our existence and our manner of life, in our judgments and our plans. "Therefore, if you be risen with Christ, seek the things that are above, where Christ is sitting at the right hand of God" (*Col.*, III, 1).

Furthermore, this gift awakens in our soul *the taste and the love for things eternal*—"mind the things that are above, not the things that are upon the earth" (*Col.*, III, 2). This goes hand in hand with an acute appreciation and a profound conviction of the shortness of human life, the hollowness of earthly things, and the vanity of all that is merely of this world and that does not bear the seal of eternity.

This taste and love in us for the eternal, also takes the form of an ardent thirst for a life which does not pass away, for a love which continues forever—the love of "Jesus Christ, yesterday and today, and the same forever" (*Heb.*, XIII, 8).

The gift thus given to us, kindles within us *a constant preoccupation with the eternal* and *the will to follow eternal values* in all our earthly enterprises, in our mundane activities and our ordinary social relationships. What a transformation it is in the life of a Christian, to be able henceforward, by the grace of faith and of hope, to enter into eternal life; to be able, by charity, to inform our actions with eternal values and to heap up for ourselves "treasure in Heaven," by sealing our works of love with the seal of eternity, by steeping our every human action in the stream of eternal love, and by seeing all things from the viewpoint of eternity—"sub specie aeternitatis." We belong to the Church, which is of itself a heavenly institution, reaching into eternity even while she exists and lives on earth. "But our conversation is in heaven" (*Philip.*, III, 20).

O Jesus, to be in You a new creature, is to live by Your Divine Life, so as no longer to live except for You and in You. It is to enter with You, here and now, into the eternal life of God, and allow ourselves to be transformed in Your life—in the very Life of God Himself. Grant that, thus transfigured in the sight of all our brethren whom we desire to win over to Your love, our life may become our manner of affirming the Transcendence of the Eternal.

93. AN INTERIOR LIFE

> *That he would grant you, according to the*
> *riches of his glory, to be strengthened by*
> *his Spirit with might unto the inward man,*
> *that Christ may dwell by Faith in your*
> *hearts.*

(Ephes., III, 16)

The interior life is not a process of introspection in which we pursue our analysis of our mental states, and tenderly cultivate our ego for the selfish purpose of, as it were, taking the pulse of our soul. Neither is the interior life an evasion of activity, a kind of refuge from action regarded as the enemy of interior peace. It is not solely a life whose actions are all of an interior nature, such as to meditate and ponder the things of God, and to offer ourselves in union with God in our prayer. There are other ways of uniting ourselves with God; and exterior action should be inspired by the interior life.

1. *The nature of the interior life*

The interior life is a life whose *principle* is interior. The animating center of the whole interior life is within the soul: for the members of Christ, this Center is the Holy Ghost, the Spirit of Jesus. The Holy Ghost, Who constantly inspired and directed the Sacred Humanity of the Savior on earth, is the Same Who wills to inspire and direct the whole interior life and the exterior activity of the members of Christ. He enlightens; He attracts; He kindles in the soul, according to the particular circumstances and needs of each member, the "divine discontent" which stimulates, and the peace which reassures. He raises in the soul that cry of filial love: "Abba, Father." He leads it to practice the virtues, in order to assimilate it to the Divine Model. He causes it to adhere to the Will of the Father. He fashions the soul by His gifts, and keeps it quietly in the possession of those gifts. The presence of the Holy Ghost within us, is the presence of an ardent, luminous, energizing Life, by which infinite Love is ceaselessly occupied in moving us, moulding us, and folding itself like a garment about us.

To lead an interior life, therefore, means to be attentive to this Presence and to this action of the Divine Guest dwelling within us. It is to be ever alert for the calls of His love; it is to become aware—by faith, hope and charity, but also by the fruits of the gifts of the Holy Ghost—of those invisible and mysterious realities which inhabit the interior world of our soul. Finally, it is to keep our soul in dependence on the Holy Spirit within us, for the organization of all the activities of our life.

2. *The interior life is the inspiration of exterior activity and of the apostolate*

The interior life is fidelity to the Spirit of Jesus, Who desires to lead and direct us, both in our external actions and in our prayer.

Action, therefore, is not to be regarded as incompatible with and *opposed to* the interior life. Indeed, action which is *not* animated by the interior life, is simply bustling, dangerous and sterile agitation.

Neither are the life of prayer and the life of action to be regarded as *distinct* one from the other. Action should also be prayer, an elevation of the soul to God through the accomplishment, by right and fitting means, of the Divine Will as expressed in the duty of our state now demanding our attention.

A logical distinction can be made between the religious *exercise* of private devotion and of liturgical worship, on the one hand, and the *exercise* of exterior activity of a purely human and profane kind, on the other. But, even there, we must not seek the solution of the problem in compromises or concessions between one type of exercise and the other; nor, moreover, must we seek it in an artificial and unreal balance of the interior and the exterior within the soul, as though the soul preserved its equilibrium by spending its time in a wise use of two clearly defined "compartments."

The solution must be sought *in the unity of the interior life, this unity deriving from the unity of the Interior Principle Who animates it.* It is the same Holy Spirit Who, by grace, urges the soul at one time to exercises of the virtue of religion—exercises animated, be it noted, by love; and Who urges that same soul at another time to exercises of the virtue of charity towards the neighbor, in social life. It is the same interior Principle Who guides such a soul in its prayer and in its action. It is the same Spirit of Jesus Who, both in prayer and in action, inspires in the soul the theological virtues, and also the particular moral virtues suited to the conditions of action and of prayer. It is the same Spirit Who, taking in each circumstance the direction of the soul, actuates His gifts within it: at one time, His gifts of understanding, of knowledge and of wisdom, which are more especially designed for the contemplative life; at another time, His gifts of fortitude, of piety, of counsel and of the fear of the Lord, which are more especially apposite to the active life—though, of course, the predominantly contemplative gifts are also decidedly necessary in the exercise of the active life, and the gifts predominantly those of the active life have their role in the life of prayer.

Finally, when we are no longer dealing with a purely profane and temporal action, but with one properly pertaining to the apostolate, there is *no longer any distinction* to be made between the interior life and the apostolate. The interior life is essentially apostolic. The interior Principle Who animates the soul, is this Holy Spirit Who constantly awakens, sustains and develops a concern for the building of the Whole Christ, in the interior life of the members of the Mystical Body.

O Church of Our Savior, how then can certain people hold you in suspicion as a hindrance and a stumbling block to their interior life, because they see in you an exterior society! It is in you and through you that we receive the Holy Ghost. And is not the proper office of your maternity to place at the service of the Spirit of Life dwelling in our souls, your hierarchy, your doctrine, your Sacraments, your liturgy, and the whole life of the Mystical Body itself?

94. A LIFE OF COMBAT

I came not to send peace, but the sword.

(Matt., X, 34)

Christianity is not, as its detractors maintain, a religion of comfort, of ease, of calm assurance for this life and for a life beyond the grave. It is not a religion of sentimentality and weakness. It is a religion of virility, of strength, of courage; and, at the same time, a religion of meekness, of mercy and of compassion. These two categories of virtue are complementary, one of the other; and both are equally necessary in the life of combat which the Christian must lead, more especially when the field of that combat is his own nature.

1. *This truth is affirmed by Holy Scripture*

The Gospel is the story of the combat which Jesus Christ has inaugurated and has waged against the prince of this world: "Now shall the prince of this world be cast out" (*John*, XII, 31). The establishment of the Kingdom of God can be accomplished only by a bitter and relentless struggle which wrests from Satan the world over which he holds sway. "Again the devil took him up into a very high mountain" (*Matt.*, IV, 8). The temptation in the desert is only one episode of the combat which still continues between Jesus Christ and him who is the embodiment of evil. Christ is now and forever the Victor: He has "overcome the world" and Satan (*John*, XVI, 33). He reigns; but His Kingdom is not yet completed. Christ, the Head, is now in the glory of His Father, and His members must enter the struggle He commenced and continues, in a world still dominated by sin.

Saint Paul has described this combat between the flesh and the spirit. For Saint John, it is the warfare between "the darkness" and "the light," between the world and Christ. In the Sequence for the Mass of Easter Sunday, we say: "Death and life were locked together in that awesome struggle: the Prince of Life died, and behold He reigns, deathless."

2. *Against whom is this combat directed?*

The combat presents a double aspect: a social aspect, and an aspect personal to each member. But these two aspects are inseparable.

The social aspect.—The member of Christ can fight against no other enemies than those against whom His Head ceaselessly fights. He is engaged in a vast and powerful campaign of liberation and of conquest. Now, this campaign fundamentally implies warfare against the world, against sin, against the Devil.

By "the world," in the sense Christ gave to the term, is meant the creation in so far as it is under the domination of sin. It is not the creation as it issued from the hand of God, for that creation is good, and, as Genesis tells us, "God saw that it was good" (*Gen.*, I). It is precisely these good elements contained in the creation, which must be delivered from the thraldom of sin.

Neither does the term, "the world," refer to human nature such as it was created by God. On the contrary, indeed; for it also is good. The activities of man which are in conformity with his true nature as a rational being, are good.

"The world" is sinful human nature—that is, human nature which, stained and wounded by Original Sin, has revolted against God, refuses to submit itself to Him, regards itself as self-sufficient, and finds its pleasure in itself without reference to God. It is this nature which we receive at birth. There dwells Original Sin: a sin of nature in its origin.

"The world" is human society in so far as it favors, develops and cultivates this disrupted and disordered human nature diverted from the supernatural purpose for which we were created by God.

The personal aspect.—At the same time, each member of Christ must wage this warfare within himself, to the extent to which "the world" holds sway over him or he remains a slave to sin and to the evil tendencies of human nature. This takes the form of a warfare against the flesh. We must not read this as meaning warfare against the body as such, for the body is also a work of God's creation, and therefore good: our warfare is against body and soul, in so far as they are under the domination of "the world" and of Satan. Warfare then, against the egoistic self which is completely centered on its own interests, and shuts out love.

For the member of Christ, as for the Church herself, this warfare consists in being *in* the world, but not *of* the world.

3. What are the weapons of this combat?

The most effective weapon we have, is the Cross of Jesus crucified and risen from the dead.

How can this be, for is not the cross the symbol of defeat, of destruction, of death? How then could it be a weapon? Is not the cross "a stumbling block?" (*Gal.*, V, 11). Is it not "foolishness?" (1 *Cor.*, I, 18).

The cross was certainly all this in the eyes of Christ's enemies and of all those who had desired to stifle His work by condemning its Author to the ignominious death of the cross. This was, indeed, in their judgment, the significance of the Cross; and the witnesses of the Cross saw it as symbolizing the utter defeat and annihilation of Christ. And it is this same error of judging by appearances, which cripples all those who look only at the externals of the cross in their life. We do not know how to regard the cross as it is in the plan of God; in other words, to see its inner reality.

Three days after Christ's Crucifixion, what remained of these human judgments? *The Cross had become the instrument of the victory of Jesus Christ* over Satan and the world, over sin and death. It is by the Cross that Redemption was assured to mankind. Henceforward and forever, it stood as the symbol of God's love for men; of the most generous and most heroic love, which was expressed by Christ's laying down of His life in order that men might have eternal happiness; of a love most magnanimous because this total oblation was made for sinful men, who would be ungrateful for, and indifferent towards, this decisive proof of God's love. The Cross became, for all time, the means which mankind must use to be raised up to the true life—the divine life in the glorified Christ.

O Jesus, we are following Your example, in our warfare against sin in ourselves and in the world, by using Your Cross. Grant that we may ever have an acute awareness of the misery of the world plunged in the abyss of sin; but that we may also have an ardently optimistic and unshakably confident faith in the all-triumphant power of Your liberating Cross.

95.   A LIFE MADE FRUITFUL BY SACRIFICE

> *Whosoever shall lose his life for my sake and the gospel, shall save it.*
>
> (Mark, VIII, 25)

The mystery of the Cross is at the heart of Christianity. It dominates and illumines Christianity, as it dominates and illumines the life of every Christian. By his Baptism, the disciple of Christ has been incorporated in his Master, in order that he may participate in the mystery of the Passion and the Resurrection of the Savior. He will bear that mystery with him throughout his entire life, by submitting to the law of sacrifice. But what is the nature of this law? Is it mutilation, slavery, suffocation? Many believe that it is all of these, but they are deceived. For it is a law of purification, of service, of personal development and perfection: it prepares the way for, and gives assurance of, the Resurrection.

1.   *A law of purification*

One of the most dangerous errors of our time is to regard

the supernatural as being merely the completion of the natural, the simple crowning of human nature such as it now is, with its lusts, its passions, the consequences of Original Sin which remain even after the Redemption accomplished by Christ. On the contrary, the mystery of the Cross must be applied to us, and we must ourselves re-live it, if we wish to participate in the mystery of Christ, and to live, in Him, by the life of God. There must be a purification of the self, by sacrifice.

The soul must be purified of that spirit of *self-sufficiency* by which a man feels no need of God, of God's help, of supernatural desires or of hope. It must be purified of the spirit of *independence* by which a man withdraws himself from the law of God and from the Will of the Master. Finally, it must be purified from the spirit of *pleasure* by which the sensual self finds its supreme good and its purpose in creatures.

A person would delude himself were he to suppose that he is safe from this triple spirit, simply because he has been preserved from mortal sin or has been restored to grace. It constantly appears in varying degrees and in different forms. Can even a person who is leading a full spiritual life, claim that he is never guilty of *self-sufficiency* by relying on his own merits, or, when engaged in some mundane work, by relying on his natural aptitudes and his own lights?

Who, then, would dare to assert that he constantly adheres to God's entire plan for him, and submits himself always to the action of grace? A person who achieved such holiness, would be absolutely without sin. But Saint John teaches us that he who says he is without sin "is a liar and the truth is not in him."

Finally, although it is true that those who truly desire to belong to Christ, easily succeed in turning away from gross pleasures, who among them would be so bold as to maintain that he never becomes *attached to* this life, to a calling, to some possession and even to his monastic cell?

Sacrifice is demanded at every stage of the spiritual combat, if we are to purify ourselves of that self which opposes the life of Christ within us.

2. *A law of service*

Sacrifice is not an end, but a means to the exercise of charity. Sacrifice is never demanded by God, simply in order that a man may *renounce* himself, but in order that he may *give* himself. What scope should sacrifice have in our lives? It should be directed against everything in us which can be an obstacle or a hindrance to charity, to the very life of Christ in our souls.

Jesus did not merely say of His disciple: "let him take up his cross": He immediately added: "and follow me." To follow Christ is to walk in His footprints, so that we may be led in whatever direction He chooses for us. To follow Jesus, is to accompany Him in His apostolic Ministry, to cooperate with Him in His Redemptive Mission. The primary purpose of our "taking up" our cross, is that we may join in this great work of charity. Without this intention and without the driving force of charity, the sacrifice would be in vain. Saint Paul, envisaging even the greatest form sacrifice can take, went the length of saying: "And if I should deliver my body to be burned, and have not charity, it profiteth me nothing" (I *Cor.*, XIII, 3).

3. *A law of development unto perfection*

The purpose of sacrifice, in the religion of Christ, is not to quench the light of human intelligence, to cripple the energies of the will, or to stifle the generous aspirations of the heart, the legitimate powers of love and the delicacy of human feeling. Neither is its purpose to suppress the passions proper to the human soul. They are useful and good, because they help the soul to attach itself to good. In order that the passions may exercise their beneficent role, they must be regulated, disciplined, purified; and this is the precise function of sacrifice. Through sacrifice, we must develop all that is good in human nature, and we must liberate this gift of God from the slavery of sin which shackles it, and from the meanness of egoism which stifles it.

Sacrifice should result in the growth of our true personality as sons of God. It is not the aim of Christian sacrifice to crush the human personality; what must be cut are the bonds which keep that personality captive to selfish, proud and sensual passions, and thereby diminish it or hinder its proper growth. The aim of Christian sacrifice is to ensure self-mastery, under the all powerful action of grace.

O Father, You have not created mean and miserable slaves, that they might glorify You by their abjectness. One Alone, Your Son, Your Word, can give glory to You; and He has not despised human nature, but has exalted it. He came on earth to conquer sin and to enter into Your glory, in order that, by impregnating our sinful life with the liberating power of His sacrifice, He might be able to make of each life a free homage of love and of restitution to Your adorable Paternity, so that, in Him, we may live here and now by the life of Your Divine Family.

96. A LIFE OF FELLOWSHIP WITH THE
BLESSED TRINITY

*I am come that they may have life and
may have it more abundantly.*

(John, X, 10)

We must clearly distinguish two sublime realities in our souls as members of Christ. In the first place, there is the life of God Himself, the interior life which the Blessed Trinity lives within Itself; this life is within us through the indwelling of the Blessed Trinity. On the other hand, there is the divinized life of our souls, deified by sanctifying grace. The abundant life announced by Jesus, is constituted in us by mysterious exchanges which occur between these two lives. But we receive all this life, only by our incorporation in the Mystical Body through the Church and the Sacraments.

1. *A life of fellowship with the living Persons of the Blessed Trinity*

This life has been described by Saint John (1 *John,* I). In its origin, it is eternally in the bosom of the Father; in its *manifestation,* it has been made known by the Incarnate Word, and the Apostles have met it in the Person of Christ. Saint John's words are very vivid: "That which was from the beginning . . . which we have looked upon and our hands have handled." He declares: "we have seen and do bear witness and declare unto you the life eternal." And he goes on to underline the purpose of this witness and declaration: "that you also may have fellowship with us, and our fellowship may be with the Father and with his Son Jesus Christ."

Such, then, is the Christian message: no less than a call to a life in common with the Divine Persons of the Blessed Trinity! According to the divine plan, this message should lead souls to the exalted height of Him Whom the Offertory of the Mass calls "the living and true God" (*Deo vivo et vero*). If it is not presented in this full plenitude, it is a truncated message, and the result of this will be spiritual anaemia among souls. For they will know nothing of the enthusiastic eagerness of love, or of the splendors of their religion.

But it must be carefully noted that the Apostle, before revealing this life in common with the Divine Persons, says first of all: "that you also may have fellowship *with us* . . ." with us, the Apostles; with us, the first Christian communities; with us, the Church. Here, then, there is no place for isolation and individualism. It is *together* that we participate in the family life of the Blessed Trinity, through a life of charity as members of the same community in the Mystical Body of Christ. It is *in* the Church and *through* the Church that Christians can enter into relations with the Divine Family.

Saint John does not say that this splendid ideal of life is something reserved to a privileged *élite* whom he is addressing; on the contrary, he holds out this ideal to *all* Christians. All will not succeed in realizing this ideal, because of the evil use they make of their liberty by making it a liberty to sin. But, as far as God is concerned, no reservations have been entered.

2. *This truth conveyed in metaphorical language*

How are we in communion with the Father and the Son? Through the Holy Ghost, the Spirit of the Father and the Son, the Spirit of Love, the Spirit of Life.

The divine life in us is something *springing up*. In the depths of our soul, the Blessed Trinity lives Its mystery. Within us, the Father begets His Son, and from their love proceeds the Holy Ghost as their Gift One to the Other. By a constant movement of love, the Holy Ghost lifts up our soul, divinizes it, causes it to enter into relations with the Divine Family, through grace.

The Holy Ghost ceaselessly causes a whole life of grace and of virtues—of faith, of hope, of charity, of the spirit of sacrifice, of humility, of fortitude, of generosity—to spring from this deified soul. Ordinary natural energy is completely powerless here: it is necessary that the Spirit of Life should be present.

Again, this life in us is *circulation* and *reciprocity*. The Three Divine Persons dwell within us, in order to receive our adoration; but while this is indeed so, we must avoid any metaphor which would suggest a *static* condition of any kind whatever. There is no room here for the exercise of imagination. We are dealing with a mystery of the most vital *dynamism:* our entry into the current of the Divine Life. This mystery is the communication from the Blessed Trinity to us, who are incorporated in Christ and in the Church, of the Divine Life, of graces, of all divine gifts. From us, through the Church and in Christ, there rise up to the Blessed Trinity, our prayers, our transports of love, our oblations, and all the expressions of the ardent life of our soul transfigured by the supernatural life.

The life of a soul is a life of *knowledge* and of *love*. It is in this communion with the Spirit of Life, the Soul of the Mystical Body, and in His light and under the impulsion of His love, that our souls receive new knowledge and fresh enlightenment. They are kept in readiness for the gifts of love which the Holy Ghost inspires in them.

Similarly, it is this communion in one and the same Spirit of Life which causes a springing up of generosity, of kindness, of compassion, among souls, *among the members of the Body;* a mysterious circulation and exchange of thoughts, of feelings, of services; an unceasing communication of prayers, of good offices, of mutual aid, of gifts and of pardon—in short, of a life in which the members know one another intimately, understand one another, and love one another.

3. *What is meant by our communication, in Christ, in the life of the Blessed Trinity?*

To communicate in the life of the Blessed Trinity is to be introduced—by Christ, in Christ and with Christ—into the Divine Family, so that we may enjoy the intimacy of the Three Divine Persons, may communicate in Their life of light and of love, and in the full happiness of the Infinite Love with which They love One Another in the bosom of the unity of their Divine Nature. It is to be happy with the Happiness of God, and to be happy in the knowledge that nothing can be added to this happiness.

Again, to communicate in the life of the Blessed Trinity, is to communicate, through a living Faith, in the infinite Love by which the Father has so loved the world as to send His Beloved Son on earth that He might redeem us all by the Holy Spirit in His Church.

To communicate in the life of the Blessed Trinity, is to keep our souls in a state of readiness, so that, in their silent depths, we may communicate in the Holy Will of an infinitely merciful Providence, Who guides the smallest details of our life towards that one purpose He has assigned to it: our participation in the life of the Divine Family, as sons in His Son.

To communicate in the life of the Blessed Trinity, is to communicate in the whole plan of love which seeks to gather all men together in the unity of the charity of Christ, so that they may be all united in one, in the image of the Blessed Trinity, and that God may be "all in all."

To communicate in the life of the Blessed Trinity, is to communicate in the transcendence of its mystery. The further the soul penetrates into the mystery of the Triune life of God, the more it realizes that the depths of this mystery become more and more unfathomable. This does not mean that the mystery becomes more foreign, more exterior, more remote for the soul. On the contrary, the soul is introduced into it, so that this mystery lives in the very depths of the soul. Indeed, the more the soul humbly opens itself to this mystery and remains dependent upon it, the more it comes to realize that it was created for the contemplation of this very mystery. In Christ, therefore, this mystery is not inaccessible to us. We cannot, of course, understand it; but yet its riches are inexhaustible and ineffable for us. To communicate in this transcendence is, therefore, to preserve our joy in it, to will that this mystery should indeed be so, and to be happy that it cannot be otherwise; rather than to be filled wih a certain bitterness and chagrin at our powerlessness to gaze into the depths of the Light and the Love that are contained in this mystery. Finally, it is to be convinced that our entry into this mystery, however real such entry may be on earth, is but a beginning; and that there is an immense abyss between this possession in faith, and the beatific vision of the Blessed Trinity that awaits us in heaven.

O Jesus, we praise and thank You for not having willed to leave our souls thirsty and faint in the desert, and subject only to one law, however beautiful that law may have been. Your Revelation is more than a message of Truth: it is the communication of a life. Your redemptive message calls us to communicate in mysteries which are nothing less than the expression of the true life of the One and Eternal God. The moral life of Your Church consists simply of the demands made on us by the life we must live in You, in Your Mystical Body.

97. A LIFE OF LIGHT

For God, who commanded the light to shine out of darkness, has shined in our hearts, to give the light of the knowledge of the glory of God, in the face of Christ Jesus.
(II Cor., IV, 6)

For every son of the Church, the words in which God "commanded the light to shine out of the darkness" in the creation of the world, reverberate still in the Church, in the midst of the darkness of the modern world. How many there are who walk in the night, having no lamps in their hands. They are without ideals and are at the mercy of every blind event; life and the world have become absurd to them, and there is nothing left in which they put any faith; they are a prey to spiritual chaos and a sterile pessimism such as the world has seldom known, and whose ultimate and logical end is impotent despair. But the Christian knows that he can derive from the doctrine of the Church, the light which enlightens all his human life, and that he bears in his own soul a life of light.

1.　A light illumining his human life

The Christian's faith enlightens him concerning *his human destiny*: a personal destiny as a son of God, because each person must render an account to the Supreme Judge, of the efforts he has made to become assimilated with the only Son; a community destiny also, because no one will save his own soul by acting alone, especially since his egoism vitiates even his seeking of salvation, but each will save his soul in union with his brethren, through charity, in the Mystical Body which is the Church, in the Communion of Saints, and for the sake of the Whole Christ. Furthermore, the Christian destiny is of a community nature, because the God towards Whom hope ceaselessly carries us, with the conviction that He will be our eternal happiness, is the God Whom we can possess through charity alone. And when hope has fulfilled its purpose and has ceased, charity will still remain. This God Whom we shall then contemplate in the beatific vision, is the Blessed Trinity, and the Blessed Trinity is now, and shall always be, the Common Good of all . . . "That God may be all in all" (1 *Cor.*, XV, 28).

The Christian's faith enlightens him concerning *the real meaning of our human personality*: the mystery of the grandeur and misery which is each one of us in our personal being, created by God, wounded by Original Sin, redeemed by Christ, transfigured in Christ, called to become "another Christ" by the gift of all that we are, for the extension of His Mystical Body in the midst of all the events of life, and despite all the obstacles arising from ourselves and from others.

We thus obtain light on the meaning of our earthly life, and accept this life as a warfare to free ourselves from all that could hinder or prevent the accomplishment of the Mystery of Christ within us.

We learn the meaning of our efforts, of our daily work, of our inner conflicts and contradictions, of our weakness and our failures, of our generous renewal of effort, of the conquest of ourselves and the acquiring of virtue. We obtain light on the meaning of sin, of suffering, and of the Redemption; on the meaning of love—of all legitimate love in its nobility and fruitfulness; on all our relations with our fellow men, our brethren in Christ.

Lastly, we are enlightened by faith, *concerning the place which man holds in the world*. While, as a creature, he is subject to God and ceaselessly dependent on the grace of Christ for everything by which he can gain eternal merit, man is the master of creation, which he must develop by his work and put to the service and betterment of a world made more worthy of him; while, at the same time, he succeeds, by the power of the Divine Spirit, in dominating human events themselves, so as to make them serve his spiritual progress and his growth in charity.

2. *A life in the divine light of the Holy Ghost, the Soul of the Church*

In the heart of the public and complete Revelation, there is a personal and progressive revelation for the individual Christian. It is not something added to that complete Revelation; but it applies the public and complete Revelation to each soul, so that, from being a doctrine, it is transformed into a *life* in each soul.

The Revelation becomes a life of light, because He Who is the Light ("lumen de lumine") lives in us; because He "enlighteneth every man that cometh into this world" (*John*, I, 9); because through faith, He infuses a light into our mind, a true participation in His Light as the Word of God.

It is a life of light, because, in the Light of the Holy Ghost, the truths revealed by the redemptive message nourish the soul, and become its food in prayer and in its moments of holy silence and of inner recollection. The soul assimilates these truths . . . and lives them. Jesus Himself has declared: "But the Paraclete, the Holy Ghost, whom the Father will send in my name, he will teach you all things and bring all things to your mind, whatsoever I shall have said to you" (*John*, XIV, 26).

Again, it is a life of light, because, apart from those moments of special and vivid enlightenment, the soul which remains in dependence on the Holy Spirit and responsive to His grace, has a steady conviction of where it is going and of how it should act, guided by the light of faith, of prudence, of wisdom, and of obedience to the Church. And even when some case of conscience arises for such a soul, and the soul is hesitating on the brink of a decision, it knows that, when it has invoked the Light of the Holy Ghost, it will not go astray. By seeking only the glory of God and His Will in the duty of its state, the soul is sure of remaining in the light.

Finally, it is a life of light, because the soul which is illumined with the life of Christ, casts its light on all those whom it meets. By seeing the living evidence of this life, others come to realize that a higher, divine light dwells in such a soul, and they are led to wish that they also may possess this same light.

O Lord Jesus Christ, You have defined Yourself as "the Light of the world," You have said that Your life is "the light of men," and You have promised that he who follows You will not walk in darkness but will have "the light of life." Help us, we beseech You, to walk in Your light. Grant that every Christian may realize the sublime and exacting responsibility of the mission of light You have confided to him, demanding of him that, like You and in Your Church, he too should be "the light of the world" (Matt., V, 14).

98.   A LIFE OF WISDOM

> *Howbeit we speak wisdom among the perfect; yet not the wisdom of this world . . . but we speak the wisdom of God in a mystery, a wisdom which is hidden . . .*
>
> (I Cor., II, 6-7)

This life of wisdom is a synthesis of three kinds of wisdom: that of human reason; that of faith; and that of a gift of the Holy Ghost. It gives to the life of the members of Christ, as it were a complete personal countenance, which distinguishes it quite clearly from the human wisdom of the philosophers.

1.   *The wisdom of human reason*

The Church places an astonishing trust in the human reason, both in the intellectual order and in the moral order. Indeed, it is the Church which today protects the human reason and upholds its great eminence.

All healthy spirituality should tend to the formation of balanced minds and characters. Such balance must exist, above all, in the integration of souls in Christ; but, at the same time, they must be humanly balanced—that is to say, they must be rational beings. By this, however, we do not mean that they should be purely speculative or cerebral beings, or beings devoid of imagination and sensibility; for, by the term *rational beings*, we mean those who, through calm and firm self-discipline, have made themselves masters of the blind powers, the irrational tendencies and the lower appetites which exist in each one of us, and have so subjected them to the rule of reason that the human reason is able to submit the whole being to the action of divine grace.

Holiness is the work of grace and of charity. Viewed from the standpoint of man's own effort, it is a masterpiece of the human reason. For the Saints alone are perfectly rational, because they alone are logical to the utmost limits of the rational. Sanctity reveals itself in human life, by a wisdom, a serenity, a harmonious balance, which are the reflection and the sign of interior order existing within the soul.

2. *The wisdom of faith*

Because faith is light, it is also wisdom. The wisdom of the Christian is characterized by a *sense of reality*, which enables the Christian to see things as they really are. It does not deny the things of the world and their beauty, but it enables the Christian to look upon all things with a clear and penetrating glance, so as to see in human things what there is of God, and what there is of sin.

Christian wisdom brings the same realism to bear on man and on human nature. There is a type of realism which is desiccating and pessimistic; and there is a realism which liberates, because its point of view takes in a complete perspective—that of the whole order, the entire nature, of man, which Christ has come to save, and which He wills to offer up to His Father. Our temperament, our character, our passions, our physical qualities and our health, and all that is human in us, should become a means of sanctification, in the plan of Redemption. Therefore, instead of regarding such matters as so many obstacles thwarting us and shutting us within the gloomy prison of ourselves, we must regard all that is human in us as the means we must use in order to live, in Christ, a life of sonship, offered with greater ardor to the Father.

Christian wisdom knows how to strike *the golden mean*. It avoids two contrary extremes which are error or evil—the one

by defect, and the other by excess. It seeks just proportion and
measure, while at the same time it has a horror of mediocrity.
It gives to each thing its value and significance in relation to Him
Who is the measure of all things. It does not demand from human
things, more than they can give.

Christian wisdom has *a sense of order.* It assigns each person
and each thing to the proper place. It respects the hierarchy of
values established by God, and does not confuse what is higher
and what is lower in man and in the world. And, because Christian wisdom rests on the tranquillity of order, it enjoys peace
and spreads peace around it.

Christian wisdom has *a sense of the Cross,* for it is the
Cross which determines the specific nature of this wisdom. While
the world—meaning those who are possessed by the spirit of
the world—does not understand the Cross even in the slightest
degree, Christian wisdom admires the beauty and the fruitfulness of the Cross. For Christian wisdom finds peace in filial
abandonment to the crucifying wishes of the Heavenly Father:
perfect joy in generously accepted deprivations; true liberty in
self-oblivion and abnegation; fruitfulness of life in exercises of
constant self-oblation; and the conditions of Resurrection and
of the Life of Glory, in death offered up, as Christ offered His
Death, in a spirit of redemption for all mankind.

3. *The gift of wisdom*

The gift of wisdom, which the Church infuses into the soul
of the baptized person, produces in that soul, under the illuminating action of the Holy Ghost, a sweet and penetrating knowledge
of the Transcendence of God, of His Wisdom, of His adorable
Perfection.

But this knowledge has the particular character of being
obtained by experience of love. What the soul discovers, through
the action of the gift of wisdom, is indeed the very Object of
faith: God, uncreated Truth, infinite Goodness, Holy Trinity;
and, in this sense, it still remains within the domain of faith.

There are, however, profound depths in this Object of faith
—depths to which the soul attains by the illuminating intuition of
love, and, as it were, under the touch of the divine. By a kind of
intimate experience, souls "taste and see that the Lord is sweet"
(*Psalm* 33). They obtain lightning-glimpses of the infinite abysses
of love in God, far beyond what faith expresses to them . . . "For
the Spirit searcheth all things, yea, the deep things of God" (1
Cor., II, 19). By the effects of this divine action within it, the
soul tastes the happiness of finding its delight in the wisdom of

the eternal Decrees, filled as they are with Love. It is happy in the thought that it will never succeed in reaching the utmost limits of these depths of infinite Love: that, the more it penetrates these depths, the more clearly will it appear that they stretch out endlessly, and infinitely surpass the powers of the soul to sound them fully.

In order to rise to these heights of knowledge, the *Gift* of God, the gift of the Holy Ghost, is necessary; but it is also necessary that the soul should be in a condition *to receive*, should be passive under the divine touch, and should participate more intimately in the Sonship of the Incarnate Word. For it is the property of the Son to receive all from the Father, His whole life of light and of love.

The gift of wisdom is an invisible mission of the Word which impresses on the soul a resemblance to the proper relation of the Word, the Thought of the Father, the Splendor of the Father's Glory—but, says Saint Thomas, of "the Word in as much as He breathes love." May we not regard the invisible mission of the Son, in the gift of wisdom, as that *of inducing a state of receptivity in our soul*, so that, in the Son, in His image and through His mysterious contact, we may receive from Him, by the Holy Spirit, a participation in the life which He receives from the Father. Is not this the very summit of our participation in the Triune life of God, in Christ? Is it not supreme wisdom, therefore, to keep our soul in a condition wherein we look to God for all things, to receive all from Him, and to live by the very life of God.

O Christ, our Savior, we are quite willing to be regarded by men as "fools," because we have resolved to prefer Your Gospel and the doctrines of Your Church, to the maxims of the world; to choose, lovingly, the folly of the Cross; to adore the wisdom of Your loving designs in all the events of our life; and no longer to live except by the life of God.

99. A LIFE OF LOVE

You shall abide in love.
(John, XV, 10)

The duty of loving God and our neighbor, is "the whole law" (*Matt.*, XXII, 10); yet, how many Christians there still are who regard this duty as merely a legal obligation. They do not realize that it was a life of love which Jesus brought to us, and that it was His intention that we should live this life of love in the community of love which is His Church. In the Church, everything is organized with a view to the reign of charity.

1. A permanent condition of charity

The Divine Master asks us to remain in His love. He is not content with occasional acts of charity, performed at random and according to a passing whim. It is a permanent state of charity which He expects from His disciples—that is to say, a permanent disposition of the soul towards supernatural love. Herein, precisely, is the virtue of charity; for the idea of the stability, of a fundamental orientation, is of the very essence of this virtue. Such active orientation is not incompatible with semi-deliberate failings which are due to the frailty of our poor human nature, and which do not essentially injure the Christian's relations with his brethren, or with Christ and the Blessed Trinity.

On the other hand, the deliberate and persistent disposition of the movement contrary to charity, rejects this state. In our relations with others, such a disposition takes the form of jealousy, spite and bitterness, consistently fostered in the soul; while, in our relations with God, it shows itself in a rebellious, recalcitrant and deceitful will.

Again, this permanent state of charity positively demands a habitual tendency of the soul to good, to kindness, to all that leads it towards its brethren. But, above all else, it involves a complete willingness to give; a state of oblation to the Divine Master for the Redemption of the world; a constant readiness of the soul to answer every call of divine love, and to meet every demand of fraternal service.

But the word "state" can carry the suggestion of "static," and it is important to rule out any such suggestion here. We are in the full dynamism of life. In faithful souls, this dynamism is a habitual energy of charity. A soul in a state of self-oblation for the Redemption of the world, is constantly alert, active and radiant: it grows in love in proportion to the measure of its giving. There is no question of an increase through repeated exercise, as is the case with an acquired virtue. Charity is a theological virtue, not only by reason of its object—God in Himself or in one's neighbor—but by reason of its principle, and therefore, in its very source. It is God Himself Who increases charity in a soul. Saint Paul teaches us that it is the Holy Spirit, the Spirit of Love, Who is poured forth in our hearts.

2. A life of love under the action of the Spirit of Love

The Holy Ghost is the mutual love of the Father and of the Son, in the bosom of the Holy Trinity. He is the fruit of their love; but, for us, He is also the pledge of their love. It is He Who keeps us united to the Father and to the Son, in love. It is through Him that the Father and the Son are united with us, in order to make us communicate, through Him, in Their life of love.

Thus, the Holy Ghost is the Gift in Person: The Gift Whom the Father and the Son give to each other; and also the Gift made to our souls by the Father and the Son. It is in giving us this Holy Spirit, that the Father and the Son give themselves to us. We possess Him as Their Supreme Gift, the Gift Who is the pledge and guarantee of all the other gifts of Their love—and, in pride of place, the gift of charity.

This gift is made in every mission of the Holy Ghost; but the mission is not solely this gift.

The invisible mission of the Divine Persons evokes, at once, the idea of a *resemblance* to the Person sent—a resemblance to the personal quality which that Person possesses as of Himself. This resemblance is effected in our souls by a gift which is, as it were, the imprint of this Divine Person.

Now, the Holy Ghost is the Gift of God and the Love of God; and the gift which He bestows on us and which makes us like unto Him, *in as much as He is the Gift and the Love of God,* is the charity which He pours forth in our hearts. This makes us realize, with a rush of joy and gratitude, what the nature of this life of love is and must be, to which we are now called, and which increases in us with the growth of charity, marking each one of the invisible missions of the Holy Ghost. It is a *state of oblation* which the Holy Ghost comes to impress on us. He comes to awaken our souls, in order to purify them from all selfishness, and to fix within them a *permanent tendency to give.* And if Christians are responsive to this influence, they will also come to know what an extraordinary power of unification and of communion there is in the Church, to enable souls to give themselves one to another, through the Holy Ghost.

O Divine Spirit, Who fills the Church of Jesus Christ with the fire of Your Love, create within us, more and more profoundly in Your image, a permanent condition of giving; in order that, in dependence on You, we may realize our whole life of love by participation in the infinite Love of the Father and of the Son— in that very Love Who is You Yourself in the bosom of the Divine Family.

100. A LIFE OF POWER

Gladly, therefore, will I glory in my infirmi-
ties, that the power of Christ may dwell in
me . . . For when I am weak, then am
I powerful . . .

(II Cor., XII, 9-10)

It is not by the virtue or the gift of fortitude alone, that the Christian is armed for the spiritual warfare of human life. His condition of virility and power is created by a whole complexus of theological and moral virtues. But his whole life will become a life of power, only in the measure in which, renouncing the weaknesses proper to his own egoism, he lives as a member of the Mystical Body.

1. *"That the power of Christ may dwell in me."*

In Jesus Christ, the Christian, as a member of His Body, possesses all the goods and participates in all the riches of the Head which are capable of being communicated to the human soul. The more the Christian has decided to count no longer on himself, the more also does the power of Christ live in him: the power of His grace, of His virtues, of His Spirit.

Furthermore, as a member of the Mystical Body, the Christian participates in that power which Christ, his Head, exercises over the world. Herein is a source of inexhaustible energy, because nothing can limit or detract from the sovereign dominion of Jesus Christ. It is through a participation in the power of Christ that the Christian is able to fight victoriously against Satan, against sin, and against all the forces of evil. It is through this participation, that the Chrisian gradually succeeds in mastering temptations and the excitement of the instincts and of the motions of nature which arise within him. In this participation, also, he finds the strength to master, by his work, the elements of the creation, and to make them serve the higher ends of his destiny. It is through an ardent faith in the power of his Head Who dwells within him, that the Christian surmounts everything that would at first sight appear to be an obstacle, in order to transform it into a means of promoting the charity with which he desires to enrich the whole Mystical Body.

2. *"Members one of another"* (Rom., XII, 5)

Isolation means weakness: for man is made in order to communicate in the life of his fellow men. This is true on the human plane. It is in social life that man finds the satisfaction of his needs: it is his own very needs which demand that he should enter into relations with the others. This is also demanded for the perfecting of his own personality itself; for the more this personality is thrown wide to the enriching influence of knowledge and of love, the more it is developed and made perfect.

The natural plane is never more than an image of the supernatural plane. It is destined, in the designs of God, to make us grasp more fully the mysterious realities of the invisible world. Consecrated souls of a missionary family, which extends its action to the four quarters of the world, derive great strength from the certainty of belonging to a great Body, and of receiving from that Body a constant access of power.

But it is above all in the Mystical Body that the social energies of the Christian are deployed. The Christian feels that he is immersed in a life of power which nothing can weaken, when he participates in the Divine Sacrifice of the Mass; when he realizes, through faith, what the *"Communion of Saints"* can mean for him—communion in the life of the Church Triumphant, when he enters into spiritual contact with the Blessed Virgin, the Apostles, the Martyrs, the Doctors of the Faith, the Saints of Heaven and of the earth (Cf. the *Communicantes* of the Mass); and when he unites himself effectively with all the members of the Mystical Body. He knows that this life of power in which he is immersed, is unchangeable, because it exists beyond the reach of time and of all that passes, of all that is extinguished and that dies. In living by the life of the Church, he participates in her strength; for the Church has received the words of eternal life, and the gates of Hell shall not prevail against her.

3. The certainties of Love

"But in all these things we overcome, because of him that hath loved us; for I am sure that neither death, nor life, nor angels, nor principalities, nor powers, nor things present, nor things to come, nor might, nor height, nor depth, nor any other creature, shall be able to separate us from the love of God which is in Christ Jesus our Lord" (*Rom.*, VIII, 37-39).

Here we have the strong cry of victory, in which the Apostle expresses his enthusiastic realization that he is loved by God, by the Father, by infinite Love itself. He possesses the proof of that love in the very existence of Christ, in the gift of the Son and of the Holy Ghost. A soul has not yet entered into this life of enthusiasm, of strength and courage, or into this certainty of being victorious which sweeps through the soul of Saint Paul, until it has understood that it too is personally loved by this same infinite Love; and has heard, in its depths, this word of love spoken within it and to it by the Divine Word, through the Spirit of Love. When once the soul has heard this word, obstacles, contradictions and trials no longer count for it. "I am sure . . ."

Two persons who have discovered that they love each other, protest that nothing can henceforward stand in the way of that love. They feel that they are ready to conquer all the difficulties that life can offer. Their love is their strength.

So, too, it is in the love of Christ that the Christian finds his true strength.

O Jesus, Our Lord, it is not in one solitary day of happiness that You have revealed Your love for us; it is at every moment that Your Spirit of Love desires to kindle and lift up our souls, in order that, supported by Your power dwelling in each of the members of Your Mystical Body, we may receive from You the power to extend Your kingdom on earth, by our collective effort and by the irresistible power of Your charity.

101. A LIFE OF HOLINESS

As he chose us in him before the foundation of the world, that we should be holy . . .

(Ephes., I, 4)

In proposing for our imitation men like ourselves, whose authentic holiness she guarantees, the Church proves herself to be a wonderful teacher of mankind. Of course, the Saints are not always capable of being imitated by us in precise detail; and, moreover, we are so far removed from them. Nevertheless, we are all called, by an eternal vocation, to become Saints. How, then, is holiness accessible and possible to us?

1. *The elements of true holiness*

The first element, which rules all the others, is *the grace of Jesus Christ.* It is not we who sanctify ourselves. It is Christ Who sanctifies us.

Our holiness is not the crowning of a series of energetic efforts of the will, by which our nature succeeds in gaining the mastery over its defects and in attaining to a human perfection.

There is only one holiness—the Holiness of Christ. *Tu solus Sanctus:* Christ alone is holy. We can become holy, only by a participation in His Holiness.

In what does this participation consist? We must avoid two pitfalls: on the one hand, a kind of *quietism;* and, on the other, a regression to merely natural *activism.* The first is a supine attitude of complete passiveness, which would exclude all effort on our part; and the second obtains when, having agreed in principle that Christ sanctifies us, we go on to behave in practice as though the whole issue were finally dependent on the efforts of our own will.

This leads us to the second element: *an adherence, in fully loving and active faith, to the sanctifying action which Christ exercises within us, as His members, through His Holy Spirit and through His Church.* Every action which we accomplish with this disposition, is holy in the eyes of God.

However, in order that it may be marked with the seal of true holiness, there must be a third element: *an entry into the mystery of the Cross.* There is real holiness when this adherence, through faith, hope and charity, is willingly given to a wish of Christ in some matter towards which, at first, we felt a natural repugnance and a shrinking from the painful effort it demanded of us.

Holiness implies at once *a separation* and *a union.* A *separation* from the idols and the obstacles which stand in a way of our sanctification by Christ: in short, the conversion of a rebellious will, born of selfishness, into a will obedient to the Divine Will. A *union with God,* Who alone is Absolute Holiness, by our entry into the mystery of Christ and by His life taking entire possession of our soul. "I live, now not I, but Christ liveth in me . . ."

2.   *The relativity of all human holiness*

Without belittling the personal contribution, we can say that the holiness of every person is necessarily relative.

In relation to Christ, human holiness takes the form of a tending towards Him, an effort at conformity with Him, and a desire to draw nearer to Him. The whole meaning of our life on earth is contained in this gradual ascension towards the ideal of holiness which is incarnated in the Sacred Humanity of Christ.

Furthermore, the holiness of each member is relative *in its connection with the whole Mystical Body.* True holiness is the holiness *of a member of Christ.* Nothing at all would remain to us, were we to attempt, by a purely arbitrary effort of imagination, to single out our own exclusively personal part from the rest of the Body, from the Communion of Saints, from the whole collective life of grace in which we are plunged, from the whole life of the Church; and our protest that, in doing so, we were merely attempting to analyze our own part more closely, would be in vain. For, if a member has attained a degree of holiness by a true divinization effected within him, it is because he has participated in the holiness of the entire Mystical Body; in other words, it is because Christ has sanctified him through His Church and through the instruments of sanctification of which the Church disposes in His name. In the first rank of these instruments, is the Redemptive Sacrifice perpetuated in the Eucharistic Sacrifice, by which graces come to us at every moment.

Finally, a man's holiness is relative *in its relation to his very condition as a sinful creature.* He is holy in the measure in which the grace of Redemption saves him from his sin and from his sinful self. But human nature remains, with its inclinations to evil. As long as we are on earth, there is no absolute liberation from the danger of sin.

This also explains why it is so difficult to judge the holiness of others. A person who appears, in certain moments of weakness, to be the victim of his own temperament, is perhaps at that very moment, holy in the sight of God, because he is making a struggle against that temperament in order to submit to the grace of Christ. On the other hand, the apparent absence of passions and of defects is not, in itself, a sign of holiness. The holiness of a man is not the holiness of an angel: it is that of a sinner who is constantly redeemed by the grace of Christ the Redeemer.

"O Almighty Father, give to Your servants the dignity of the priesthood. Grant that the spirit of holiness may reach to the very depths of their hearts."[1] *May the ideal of holiness never become dimmed in the souls of Your sons and daughters, who one day have glimpsed its beauty. Sustain us by Your grace, so that the desire for holiness may never become weakened within us by our experience of our own weakness, by our knowledge of men, or by the sad spectacle of those dried and disillusioned souls who, through weariness or cowardice, have abandoned this life-giving ideal.*

---

1. Words pronounced by the bishop during the Ordination of a priest.

102. A LIFE OF LIBERTY

*For you, brethren, have been called unto
liberty. Only make not liberty an occasion
to the flesh; but by charity of the spirit
serve one another.*

(Gal., V, 13)

Liberty is a magnificent gift of the Creator. Christ has come
to give us the liberty of Redemption and the means of being free.
But true liberty is not given to us, whole and complete; it is a
conquest of every day, an effort of every moment. It supposes
three essential things: a breaking with the slavery which shackles
man; the exercise of self-government and self-control; and a free
giving of ourselves to Jesus Christ.

1. *A breaking with the slavery which shackles man*

By the life which He brings to us, Jesus Christ is constantly
engaged in freeing us from all the different types of slavery which
weigh upon us.

He liberates us from our slavery to ignorance, to error and
to doubt, by His life and by His Truth which makes us free
(*John*, VIII, 32); from our slavery to selfishness and to evil
habits, by His life of love; from our slavery to our whims and
our waywardness, by His life of wisdom; from the slavery of
the flesh and of the senses, by the life of His Spirit; from our
slavery to our weaknesses and our cowardice, by His life of
strength; from our slavery to our pride and our self-sufficiency,
by a life founded on self-sacrifice; from the slavery of unrest
and of anguish, by His life of peace.

Thus, Christ is our Liberator from all the slavery of sin. He
is also our Liberator from base human respect and from slavery
to the world, to public opinion, to the demands of social *milieux*.
He attaches us to Himself, as to the One Thing Necessary (*Luke*,
X, 42).

2. *Self-government and self-control*

God has placed in the hands of each person, the responsibility for his own personal destiny and the conduct of his life.
But, being a member of Christ, each person does not pursue his
destiny in isolation: he does so with Christ, His head and with
the Mystical Body of Christ.

Here, too, while Christ breaks a man from his natural slavery and purifies him, He is also at work through an *educative* action which, by the grace of the Holy Ghost in conjunction with the exercise of human liberty, should lead a man to the acquiring of self-mastery and self-control.

This educative action is directed to *the intelligence,* through the virtue of faith and through graces of light, which teach a man to know his final purpose in life, the means by which he must fulfill that purpose, and the obstacles he must overcome in doing so. Through the action of the Holy Spirit sent by the Head, he must acquire a sound judgment and an enlightened mind, in the conduct of his life.

Again, this action is an education of the *will* and of the *character.* The Christ-Head, by His grace and by His Spirit, helps the member of His Body to acquire, through spiritual warfare, a mastery of the spirit over the flesh and the passions; to resist temptations; and to develop a vigorous personality which reveals itself in the choices he makes, the decisions he reaches and the projects which he carries out effectively.

The action of Christ does not aim at suppressing a man's efforts, but aims at sustaining him, and at freeing him by enabling him to acquire effective control of his own interior liberty.

The action of Christ does not alter a man's temperament; for the grace of Christ acts upon a man's temperament, taking that temperament as its starting point, building upon that temperament, in order to sanctify him. The grace of Christ helps each person to make good use of his temperament, to discipline it and to make himself master of it.

The action of Christ is not directed towards completely eliminating all exterior obstacles: its purpose is to give to each person, by the help of grace, the strength to triumph over them. Thus, it does not aim at removing from a person's life, the mystery of the Cross: on the contrary, it seeks to make every member enter freely into that mystery.

Furthermore, this educative action is *an education of the heart.* We do not give sufficient thought to this constant action of Christ's charity within us, poured forth by His Holy Spirit in order to form our heart on the Heart of our Lord and our Exemplar. This charity is ceaselessly operative within us, to help us in acquiring the mastery over our heart by detaching it from its selfishness. It purifies the heart from its passions; it inspires us with higher motives for loving; it substitutes the power of devotedness, of warmth and generosity, together with the joy of giving, in place of the dryness and coldness of the selfish heart.

3. A gift of the self to Jesus Christ

What an astonishing and wonderful thing is the infinite respect and the extreme delicacy with which Our Lord treats our human liberty!

He is the Master of all His gifts. But he has not willed to make us robots, even though as robots we should be endowed with those gifts. Rather has He preferred to expose Himself to the risk of our sin, in order to leave us free. Why has He done so? Because He willed that we should go to Him as free persons, responsible for our choice, masters of our actions, and capable of a contract to which we commit ourselves entirely. He desired the gift of our love—of the love which enables us to act with full liberty.

It is the Holy Ghost, the Soul of the Church, Who inspires this love in us, and gives us this love. The more we are responsive and committed to this love, the more will our personality be delivered from the influences which enslave it; the more also will it discover its true reality, capable of thinking, judging, willing and of freely loving God and the neighbor according to the proper law and hte noble aspirations of its nature divinized by grace.

Hence is it that, when Saint Paul had taught the doctrine of the call to liberty and the means of acquiring liberty, he could logically conclude: "By charity of the spirit, serve one another" (*Gal.*, V, 13).

O Jesus, I now understand how the personality of each person, while being a member of the Mystical Body, is not sacrificed to the whole or rendered anonymous in the community. I realize that it is fully safeguarded in its most essential liberty; and still more, that it blossoms in the giving of itself to Christ and to the other members—that it perfects and realizes itself in its complete abandonment to the Holy Ghost for the triumph of love.

103.   A LIFE OF PEACE

*Peace I leave with you; my peace I give
unto you; not as the world giveth do I
give unto you.*

(John, XIV, 27)

The peace of Christ is not the peace which the world gives.
Our Lord distinguishes the two types of peace, and opposes them
one to the other. It is of the highest importance that the Christian
should not confuse the two, in his soul and in his life. Otherwise,
he will find that he is the victim of an illusion and a deceit. The
peace of Christ is not incompatible with interior warfare, or even
with great tempests within the soul. Its place is in the very depths
of the soul. It is the fruit of unity in Christ, in the Whole Christ.

1.   *Unity in the Whole Christ*

The peace of Christ is a gift of Christ. It is not the effect of
sense-perception, or of imagination or of temperament. Saint Paul
tells us that it is the fruit of the Holy Spirit, the fruit of the
Spirit of Jesus.

Our Lord does not give us this peace fully and once for all.
It is He Who, by His Spirit, constantly creates this gift in the
members of His Body; or, more exactly, He renews it ceaselessly
within them, when it has so often been agitated by the passions,
or temporarily overthrown by the events of life into which confusion has been brought by sin.

Christ renews His peace, by re-establishing in us and in the
world, the unity of God's design. "My peace I give unto you . . ."
The peace which He gives us is *His* peace, not only in the sense
that it comes from Him, but because it is a *participation* in His
peace, in the peace which fills His own soul, in the peace that
comes from His grace, His charity, His Spirit, and His unity.

The Redemption has transformed the relations of men with
God, and thereby also transformed those of men among themselves. It has re-established, and indeed "in a yet more wonderful
manner," the unity willed by God in His plan of love, which sin
had disrupted by its work of division, of opposition, of hatred
and of destruction.

It is Christ Who re-establishes this unity, in Himself. By
reconciling humanity with God, *Christ has reconciled humanity
with itself.* By establishing family relations between men and
their Heavenly Father, making them all sons in Him, the Only
Son, Christ has made them brothers one of another in the unity

of the Whole Christ. He has established the unity of men among themselves, by making them participate, in Him, in the unity of the same life—His life, the life of His Spirit.

Christ has also re-established *unity in the interior of man himself*. In Christ, each man recovers something of that original unity of his being, which once existed in his nature through the submission of the senses and of the human reason to God.

Peace is the tranquillity of order. The peace of Christ is the tranquillity of the order which Christ re-establishes in man and among men, by His Divine Spirit, in order to re-establish in His Mystical Body, a unity like to the unity of the Father and of the Son in the Holy Ghost; or rather, to re-establish a unity by which men can share, in Him, the unity of the life of God.

2. Types of false peace

The peace of Christ is not a kind of comfortable security which enables the Christian to settle down with a quiet mind to the enjoyment of the permitted good things of the world, having put himself in favor with God by the discharge of a few external duties of religion or the giving of some alms.

Christ does not wish us to settle down among the things of this world, as though we had here a lasting city. On the contrary, he has come to place in the mind and in the soul of man, a principle of tension which obliges him to a ceaseless quest for greater perfection: greater self-perfection, and wider horizons for his plans and for his too natural viewpoints. This principle is faith, a principle of unity; a stimulating, elevating principle, yet a principle which does not agitate the soul, because it is a higher and unifying light which seeks the One Thing Necessary. So far, therefore, from being in conflict with the true peace of Christ, it is one of the essential elements of this peace.

Furthermore, the peace of Christ is not *that kind of tranquil assurance* which certain practicing Christians seek to establish against the risks of the after-life, by a wholly exterior submission to the prescriptions of the Law of Christ. It is not Christ's wish that any such assurance should be found in Him, for He roundly condemned the self-complacency of the Pharisees, satisfied with themselves and with their works. Thus, He has placed in the heart of man, a second principle of tension which obliges him not to count on his own effort, or even on his own merits. This principle is hope. It turns the thoughts of men towards the after-life, but only in order that they may look, for confidence of their salvation, to the Goodness and Mercy of God. It is the principle which detaches from the world, the soul which would seek to rely on its own reserves; but only in order to cast that soul into the Heart of Christ, and make it draw, with absolute confidence, upon the inexhaustible merits of its Divine Redeemer and Head. It is a unifying principle, also, because it makes the soul look to Christ alone for all things, and because it frees the soul from the multiplicity of vain desires and from the chaos of its own contradictory tendencies. Its measure of such freedom, will be the degree in which it will taste peace.

Finally, the peace of Christ is not *a selfish enjoyment* of the benefits bestowed on the believers by the Redemption; nor is it *an indifference* to the sufferings of those who have not yet received these benefits, coupled with a smug conviction that one's own personal salvation is assured. For the peace of Christ is found only in the charity of Christ, in self-oblation for others, and in the will to cooperate in the Redemption of the world. Jesus Christ has implanted in the heart of the members of His Mystical Body, a third principle of tension, which can occasion an implacable hand-to-hand warfare between the tyrannical demands of natural selfishness, and the imperious calls of love. This principle is charity, which, at every moment and towards every person, creates disquiet in the soul. Here again, this painful effort of giving oneself to others, awakens the soul from a stolid and slothful torpor, but only to communicate to it the peace of Christ in the satisfaction and the unity of a love, of one and the same love, which desires to know neither rest nor repose.

"O Lord Jesus Christ Who has said to Your Apostles: Peace I leave with you, my peace I give unto you, *look not upon my sins, but upon the Faith of Your Church": that profound, ardent, invincible faith which was manifested in the life and the sacrifice of the Apostles and the Martyrs, in the teaching of the Council and the Doctors, in the courageous battles of the Pontiffs and of the Confessors, for the defense of the Truth: that faith which animates Your whole Church, in her liturgy, her hierarchy, her doctrine: the faith of all the Saints throughout all the centuries. It is by participating in the unity of this faith of Your Church, and in living by the faith of Your Church and entrusting myself to her guidance, that I shall enjoy the true sweetness of Your peace.*

104. A LIFE OF JOY

These things I have spoken to you, that my joy be in you, and your joy may be filled.

(John, XV, 11)

Is it not a cruel mockery to talk about joy in a world heaped high with suffering and anguish? And yet, the message of Christ and of the Church is a message of joy. For *joy* is precisely what the message of Christ imports: "perfect joy" brought to a world which is a prey to sufferings or is the victim of its own deceitful pleasures and false joys. Joy is an effect of charity, a fruit of the Holy Ghost, the atmosphere of the community life in the Church.

1. *The Blessed Trinity*

Christian joy is the joy of the *presence* of the Three Divine Persons in the regenerated soul of the baptized person. How is it that so many Christians, and even so many consecrated persons, remain so strangely insensitive and unresponsive to this wonderful presence of the "living and true" God? Have they never read the very explicit and formal promises made by Our Lord? Or do they hesitate to take these promises as literally meant? Is it, perhaps, that they regard this pledge given by Christ, as too beautiful to be really possible? One seeks in vain for a reason sufficient to explain this ignoring, in practice, of the magnificent richness possessed by the Christian. For the person who loves—and love is the only condition laid down by Christ—what ecstasy it is to enjoy the presence of the beloved Being, when this Being is God Himself, the Blessed Trinity! The Three Divine Persons are present within the soul of the Christian who loves God! In silent awe at this Presence, he adores and he makes his return of love.

Christian joy is the *gift* of the Three Divine Persons to the soul. Here again, and perhaps to a greater extent, it would seem that there is some fear, some hesitation in accepting the reality of this and in affirming that this is literally what God has willed. Did God intend this divine visit to be reserved to those who, by an exceptional grace, are raised to those states we call mystical? By no means. This is the privilege of every soul which is in the state of grace. Infinite Love gives Itself to the soul; and immediately, in the brilliance of Divine Light and as the effect of the infinite Love of the Three Divine Persons acting together, a created gift rises in the soul. This gift is sanctifying grace, which really transforms the soul, making it all beautiful and all resplendent. It is not the soul which attracts God to itself. It is not in God, but in the soul, that the transformation is produced. Here, as always, but in a very special way, the initiative comes from God, from His infinitely condescending love.

What a joy it is for the Christian, to know that this created gift of grace is the effect of the love of the Three Divine Persons; that the Three Divine Persons come into his soul, in order that together They may impress on the soul a similarity with the Divine Nature, and also a similarity with the Blessed Trinity as One Only God. What a joy for the Christian, to adore the Three Divine Persons, by sanctifying grace and by each increase of that grace.

But that is not all. Sanctifying grace, while being an effect, is in its turn the radical principle *of sublime relations with the Blessed Trinity,* with each of the Three Divine Persons, Who becomes for the soul the object of its knowledge and of its supernatural love, through faith and charity. The soul is thus raised up, by grace and by the theological virtues, to the level of the Divine Family; and it is called to live in community with that Divine Family, to live by Their life of Love, to rejoice in the full happiness with which the Blessed Trinity lives in Itself, and to share in that happiness with joy and with love . . .

With the joy of no longer being without, but within . . .

The joy of no longer being held at a distance, but of being called to enter into the mystery of God, into this current of life, of light and of love, in order to participate in it as sons in the Only Son . . .

The joy of already entering into this life of knowledge and of love, which Christ has said is eternal life, and which will increase more and more within us if we are faithful.

2. *The Whole Christ*

The joy of knowing that Our Head is risen from the dead! He lives in the glory of His Father, as the Conqueror of death and of sin. It is with the Risen Christ that we are in constant relations. It is as risen, that He is our Head and the Source of our supernatural life. This vision, *in faith,* of the triumph of our Head, should fill our souls with joy, if indeed we love Christ for His own sake.

The joy of being certain that He will one day return to complete His work and to judge mankind; that His Kingdom will be definitely established among mankind! *The joy of hope,* which sustains us and lifts up our hearts, at times when the daily cross seems to weigh too heavily upon us!

In Heaven, when the Mystical Body is entirely reconstituted in love, each and all shall enjoy all things from all and from each, and every member shall be happy in the glory which is reflected through the whole Mystical Body by the holiness of each member. We shall rejoice, not only in the happiness of each member, because it will be truly our own happiness, but we shall rejoice also in the happiness of all, in the happiness of unity, where there will no longer be any place for jealousy, for ambition, for divisions and for hatred.

Now, since eternal life is already commenced on earth, and we have already entered into communion with Heaven, we ought to begin here and now this common life in unity—which life is the Church. We should rejoice in the glory which all the Saints of Heaven and of the earth, communicate to the whole Body, to the whole Church. We should seek *the joy of tasting the divine riches*, not in isolation from the other members, but in union with all the Saints of Heaven and earth, and especially with the glorious Virgin Mary, assumed both soul and body into Heaven. Our joy should be a participation in the joy of Christ contemplating His Mother in her triumphs; and a participation in the joy of Mary herself, now associated body and soul with the glorious Mysteries of her Son, just as she was associated on earth with His Mysteries of joy and of sorrow.

And yet, in our exile on earth, our joy is not comparable in intensity with the joy of Heaven. Here we must savor that joy, not in the direct and immediate vision of Glory, but in the light which is also the twilight of faith: "We see now through a glass in a dark manner; but then face to face" (I *Cor.*, XIII, 12).

Then there are all the others, our human brethren, who walk in the night—unenlightened, sad, burdened, and with souls embittered with revolt and despair. There is all the material, moral and spiritual distress of mankind. There is the evil of sin. There is the forgetting and ignoring of God.

The Christian would not be the disciple of His Master, if he sought to stand aside from this suffering and to avoid all this human drama. On the contrary, he must now take on himself, with his brethren in the Faith, the burden of that Cross which his Master has carried alone, two thousand years ago, and which He desires to carry in His Mystical Body, in His members, now that He can no longer suffer in His own Glorified Body.

But Christian joy reaches out even into this sorrow, and has its role to play there; for this joy and this sorrow are perfectly compatible, though they appear to be contradictory one of the other. The unity of these two dispositions is effected in charity—through participation in the charity of the Christ-Head, Who draws His members to Himself for the forming of the Whole Christ. There is the joy of consoling those who weep; of helping those who are striving to bear their cross; of suffering with those who suffer; of meeting, loving and serving Christ in all His members; of cooperating in the Redemption of the world, and thereby giving its most noble and most fruitful meaning to our life.

But, O Lord, it is above all for You and to prove our love for You, to give You joy, that we wish to renew here the oblation of our whole being to Your full redemptive plan. We know very well, of course, that we are powerless to add even in the slightest way to that fullness of joy possessed by Your glorified Humanity in the bosom of the Father. But at least we can offer to the full joy of Your loving Heart, something in which You will deign to take pleasure: our own poor heart itself, in the measure in which we give ourselves to You in Your brethren, and in the measure in which we give joy to You by giving joy to the least of Your brethren, in Your Name.

CONCLUSION

THE WHOLE CHRIST

THE WHOLE CHRIST

*That he would grant you, according to
the riches of his glory . . . that, being
rooted and founded in charity, you may
be able to comprehend, with all the saints,
what is the breadth and length and height
and depth (of the Mystery of the Whole
Christ); to know also the charity of Christ,
which surpasseth all knowledge; that you
may be filled unto the fullness of God.*

(Ephes., III, 16-19)

The Whole Christ is Christ the Man-God, in all the fullness
of His Divinity and of His Humanity: the Whole Christ is the
Christ-Head gathering together in Himself, in the unity of His
Mystical Body, all regenerated mankind. The Whole Christ,
therefore, is Christ the Head in unity with His members. To
understand, with all the Saints, the dimensions of this sublime
Mystery, we must be rooted in charity and must receive from
the Father, through faith, the light which will reveal to us the
incomprehensible love of Christ "which surpasses all understanding."

1. THE MAN-GOD

1. *In the fullness of His Divinity*

a) Christ is *God giving Himself* to men.

Beyond the created gifts of God, and beyond the gift of
God *par excellence* which is the Sacred Humanity of Christ, we
must contemplate this incomparable gift of *Himself*, of God in
Person, which God gives to us. It is the gift of God giving
Himself to men, in Christ; God communicating Himself to man-
kind, in Christ: God penetrating mankind with His Divine Life;
God making Himself ours.

b) Christ is *God revealing Himself* to men.

Beyond the message containing the revealed truths, the plan of our salvation, the moral law, we must contemplate, in Christ, God revealing Himself to us in His intimate Life—the Mystery of His Triune Godhead. Were we to consider this Mystery even as *an exterior* revelation, we would already have an inexhaustible motive for wonder and adoration. But we must enter more intimately into this Mystery. It is in Christ that we reach God and hear His secrets. Christ is the Word, in Whom the Father expresses Himself entirely and speaks to every creature. It is Christ Who reveals God and the life of God to us, by His Spirit Who sounds the Depths of God. The God revealed to us by Christ is not only the God of the philosophers, Who can be known by unaided human reason through the image of His perfections in created things; for Christ also reveals God as the Blessed Trinity. The Son reveals His Father and communicates His Holy Spirit to every person who, living in Christ, humbly allows himself to be introduced by Christ into the mystery of the Triune life of God, and to be assimilated by Christ.

c) Christ is *God reconciling men with Himself.*

The initiative of pardon, of mercy and of salvation, comes from God. This is so, not only as to origin—for, by regarding only this point of departure, however ineffable it may be, we would be in danger of stopping short at the externals of this mystery. We have here an acquittal, a sentence of complete absolution! Christ is God saving sinful men, in His Son. Christ is God drawing us, in order to pardon us, to give us His life; continuing to save each one of us by applying the Redemption to each.

d) Christ is *God uniting Himself* with men, divinizing them, making them participate in the life of the Blessed Trinity, gathering them together as His sons in the Son, in order to make them enjoy eternally in Heaven, and here on earth through faith and charity, the life of His Divine Family, the unity of the Father and of the Son in the Holy Ghost.

2. *In the fullness of His Humanity*

a) In the fullness *of all His virtues and of all His splendors.*
Christ is the ideal of all perfection. He is Holiness itself. He is the glory of mankind: "because in him, it hath well pleased the Father that all fullness should dwell." It would be impossible to imagine a more noble, more generous and more admirable person than the Man-God, Jesus Christ. Anyhow, the imagina-

tion is here completely powerless, since we are dealing with a mystery of faith and of love.

The contemplation of His Sacred Humanity kindles enthusiasm in a soul which is free, adaptable and completely prepared to throw itself wide to Christ and to give itself to Him.

b) In the fulness *of His mysteries.*

All the mysteries of Christ are intimately linked one with another, so as to form but one unified whole in a harmonious synthesis. It is impossible, therefore, to speak about the Whole Christ, if, in our faith or in our spiritual life, we omit one or other of the mysteries of Christ. Were we to do so, the Apostle's words would then again be apposite: "Is Christ divided?" (1 *Cor.,* I, 13).

At the center of all these mysteries, is *the mystery of the Cross.* It illumines and governs all the others. It is by the mystery of the Redemptive Cross that the Whole Christ is formed and developed. The liberating Cross is the Sign of the victory of Christ, and of the salvation of the world. For it is the Cross which ensures the triumphs of the Resurrection.

c) *The fullness of Humanity.*

The Sacred Humanity of Christ is the instrument of our salvation. It is not an inert instrument, devoid of initiative. On the contrary, the Sacred Humanity is endowed with a prodigious Intelligence, with an infinitely loving Heart, and with a magnificent liberty. The personal union of the Word with the Sacred Humanity of Christ, gave an infinite dignity to that Humanity, and made It an absolutely unique instrument of the Divinity, for the salvation of the whole human race.

The Word was made flesh. He did not despise, in any way, our human nature, but assumed it in its entirety.

He did not, of course, assume sin. But sin is not necessary to prove the reality of human nature, which came untainted from the hand of God; nor is it a sign of the grandeur of that nature, since it indicates weakness of will and moral decadence. Moreover, Christ has conquered sin, and He aids men to free themselves from sin.

On the other hand, the consequences of sin—suffering and death—do not imply any moral indignity of human nature. Christ assumed these consequences, in order to show clearly that He was truly man, with a nature like ours, and that He came to restore human nature to its true grandeur, by renewing it "in a yet more wonderful manner."

Christ, of course, has not a human personality in the philosophical sense of the word. The Divine Personality of the Word took possession of Christ's Human Nature from the first instant of its Conception, and thus superseded the human personality that was congenital to it. But for what purpose? Was this in order to deny to the Humanity of Christ, the right and the ability to have thoughts, desires, wishes, actions—in short, all that constitutes the nobleness of man's personality? Certainly not. The purpose of this "replacement" of personality by Personality, was in order that the human thoughts and actions of Christ should not appertain to Him as to a mere *man*, having in his very nature the principle of his autonomy and of his independence; but should be those of a *Divine Person*. It is the Divine Person of the Word Who, through this humanity which He has assumed, thinks, desires and does whatsoever is thought, desired or done by Jesus Christ.

The Personality of Christ is indeed sublime, since it is that of the Son of God. This Personality makes Christ in His Humanity, but by reason of His Divinity, the Mystical Head of the human race, Head of angels and of men, Head of the creation and of the universe.

2. THE DIMENSIONS OF THE WHOLE CHRIST

1. *The DEPTH of the Mystery of the Whole Christ*

a) *Depth in relation to man.* "De profundis clamavi" (*Psalm* 129).

The Incarnate Word came to seek men in the depths of their misery and of their sin. He did not recoil in loathing from this descent into a world flung into disorder by sin, but He entered into it, with all His love, even to the laying down of His life for the salvation of mankind. Through respect for human dignity, He has willed to associate men with the working out of their own salvation, in the Church, and to make them participate in His Redemptive Mission.

This is indeed a profound mystery, which reaches down into the very depths of our being, in order to effect a transformation, by grace, in the very substance of our soul. In His love for us, Christ makes Himself more intimately present to us than we are to ourselves, so as to become the very Source of our supernatural and divinized life.

Again, the depth of this mystery is shown in that it makes us all one in Christ, and establishes an interior union among us, by what is most deep in ourselves, since we are all united together in the same life—the Life of Christ Himself. In Him, as in one single Principle, the life of each member communicates with the life of all the members of the Mystical Body.

b) *Depth in relation to God.* "Etiam profunda Dei" (1 *Cor.*, II, 10).

Whoever lives in the Whole Christ, lives by the Holy Ghost, Who inspires him, directs him, and animates him. Now, the Holy Ghost is He Who "searches the depths of God." The more, therefore, a soul is obedient to the Spirit of Christ, the more also will that soul be urged on to penetrate ever more profoundly into the knowledge and love of Christ and into the Divine Mysteries.

A twofold disposition is then produced in the soul. On the one hand, the soul possesses and enjoys the gift of the Holy Spirit, and tastes peace in the satisfaction of its deepest aspirations; on the other hand, the more it discovers the splendor of what it has received, the more also does it thirst to receive ever more and more abundantly. The more it glimpses the depths of God, the more also does it thirst to penetrate those depths, being convinced that, as long as it is on earth, it can always look for a new discovery of the riches of the Mystery, under the light and inspiration of the Holy Ghost.

c) *Depth in relation to the Church.*

To be in the Whole Christ, is to live by the Church. The whole challenge for a son of the Church, is to become inserted, more and more deeply, in the life of the Church; to nourish his soul ever more abundantly in her Sacrifice; and to immerse himself ever more deeply in the Faith of the Church. What originates merely from ourselves is of no value; for what counts is that we should belong to the Church and should be deeply rooted in the Church. It is in the depths of the life of the Church that the soul finds the Holy Ghost: it is from those depths that the soul draws its life, because the Holy Ghost was given in the first instance to a united community, and not to isolated individuals, on the Day of Pentecost. The life of the Church is a continual Pentecost.

2. *The BREADTH of the Mystery of the Whole Christ*

This Mystery is extended to all men, and no one is excluded. The aim of the Whole Christ is to save all men, in order to reunite all men with God, in Christ. In the Whole Christ, the supernatural unity of mankind is effected by the Redemptive Incarnation, by that continuation of the Incarnation which is the Church, by the Blessed Eucharist and by charity. This supernatural unity is superior to all that divides men and sets them one against another: races, nations, classes, interests, jealousies and hatreds.

We speak of the breadth of this mystery, because it detaches us from our own selfishness, and effects a radical change in us, in our sentiments and in our horizons. It substitutes the communal and universal plan, in place of our individualistic ideas, and makes us think, pray, suffer, live and act as members of one great Body, as sons of the *Catholic* Church.

Again we speak of the breadth of this mystery, because it obliges us to participate in the love which Christ extends to all those who are not yet united with Him, and not to limit our love to those who are actually members of the Mystical Body. We must love these others with the same love that Christ extends to them. "A true love of the Church requires, therefore," writes Pope Pius XII in his Encyclical on the Mystical Body, ". . . that in other human beings not yet united with us in the Body of the Church, we should see brethren of Christ according to the flesh, called with us to the same eternal salvation." We must pray for them, that they may soon be reunited in the Mystical Body of the Redeemer: "For though they may now be related to the Mystical Body of the Redeemer by some unconscious yearning and desire, yet they are deprived of those many great heavenly gifts and aids which can be enjoyed only in the Catholic Church." (*Mystici Corporis Christi*).

Finally, we speak of the breadth of this mystery, because it associates us with the sufferings and the prayers of Christ in His Mystical Body, for those of His brethren who are separated from the Body as long as they remain apart from the true Church.

3. *The LENGTH of the Mystery of the Whole Christ*

Throughout all the centuries, this Mystery remains the same. It is announced in the Old Testament, and is given in the New Testament, but it must unfold its dimensions in the centuries that follow. It will be fully manifested only in the Heavenly Jerusalem.

We must contemplate, with a mind of faith, the centuries up to the coming of Christ. The Old Testament is the preparation for the New, which it announces and frequently prefigures. Always, in accordance with the patient teaching of God, the Old Testament carries out a work of education, by creating in souls an expectation of the Savior. It is completely orientated towards Christ and towards the Whole Christ.

The history of God's alliances with His chosen people, announces and prepares the New Alliance by which God unites regenerated mankind with Himself, in His Son and in the Church.

The very existence of the Jewish people announces and prepares the Church. The people of Israel transmit to the Church the conception of a salvation which is not only individual, but social as well. The Church is the people of God, the people who have a right to the inheritance, the New Israel according to the spirit.

Even while they hold the purifying scourge of anger over those who are faithless to the Alliance, the Old Testament prophets announce the universal religion which will be extended to all nations. The prophecies concerning the Messias were to be accomplished in Christ and in the Church. Jesus would fulfill the promises, by transporting them to a higher level. He would establish the Kingdom. The Church is that Kingdom in the earthly and visible stage of its growth.

But it is not the Jewish People alone who have prepared the world for the coming of Christ, nor all the mighty religious personages of the Old Testament—the patriarchs and the prophets, the kings and the priests of the Levitical priesthood. Apart from the events of the history of the Chosen People, the coming of Christ was prepared by the whole of secular history, with its thinkers, its philosophers, its learned men, its conquerors, right up to the Pax Romana. All these have worked together to prepare the way for the coming of Christ.

Jesus Christ is the center of the whole world.

While the Church fulfills the promises of the Old Testament, she is also fully directed towards the heavenly consummation. All the centuries to come—and the Church is only at the beginning of her career—will have as their role the manifestation of all the riches contained in Christ. The creation itself awaits the manifestation of the Children of God.

Christ guides human history by His Mystical Body, under the action of the Holy Ghost. This is the Christian meaning of history: for the Christian, history is the story of the mighty works of the Holy Ghost, accomplished through the combats between Christ and the world, which will continue as long as the world lasts.

Christians should cooperate earnestly with these works of the Holy Ghost. They should collaborate, in union with all their fellow men, in the plan of the Creation, by labor and by temporal action; and in the plan of the Redemption, in union with the hierarchic Church, by Catholic Action. By work, in order to give man the mastery over nature and the creation, so that they may be made to serve the purposes assigned to them by the plan of God: respect for the human person. By temporal action, in order to build an earthly city more worthy of man, in its laws, its institutions, its structure. By Catholic Action, to make this earthly city more worthy of the sons of God and more open to grace, and to transform it into a first sketch of the Heavenly City, under the powerful radiance of charity. Here we have an admirable unity of the Christian vision of the world, and of the purpose of human history: the building of the Whole Christ.

4. *The HEIGHT of the Mystery of the Whole Christ*

Is there a higher or more sublime vocation, than that of the Christian called to participate in the Mystery of the Whole Christ?

It is a mystery of grandeur and sublimity, because it throws into full relief the *unity* of Christians with Christ and in Christ. We form but *one* with Him and in Him, so that now there is a sense in which it can be said that *Christ alone* exists, we ourselves existing *in* Him. The greatness of a Christian does not lie in his being "another Christ" (the familiar phrase may convey no more than an effort at conformity), but rather, in his being *of* Christ, in his belonging to the Mystical Body. The greatness of Christians lies in their incorporation in Christ, in their mystical identification with Christ. It is not they who make themselves like unto Christ: it is Christ Who makes them like unto Himself by an organic process of assimilation and incorporation into Himself, if they will only permit Him.

Again, it is a mystery of grandeur and height, because it is that of the *life* of Christ in us, by His grace, and His Spirit, by faith and the Sacraments of the Faith, by the indwelling of the Divine Word and of the Blessed Trinity, and by our participation in Christ's Divine Life and in His Mysteries. It is to the very heights of the Divine Life that we are lifted up by Jesus Christ.

When we speak of the life of Christ in us, we think especially, and sometimes exclusively, of all those spiritual and supernatural energies which Jesus brings to us in order that we may live our *human* life; and it is indeed true that He makes Himself our Companion in our journey through life, and that He helps us to carry our cross on earth. This is a wonderful extension of the Incarnation!

But what the Mystery of the Whole Christ especially reveals to us, is that Jesus dwells within us in order that, as members of

His Church, we may participate *together* in His divine life, in His splendors and His Mysteries, and in the dignity of His Sonship. The word "participate" implies total dependence, and preludes any idea of fusion or absorption. Christ introduces us into His relations with His Father, into the intimacy of the Divine Family, and into the ineffable exchanges between the Persons of the Holy Trinity: He introduces us as sons with Him, the Son, and through His Holy Spirit.

Finally, this is a Mystery of height and grandeur, because it is the *action* of Christ which dominates in it. It is He, Christ, Who forms the Whole Christ with His Church, which is His pleroma. It is He, Christ, Who reveals Himself in His fullness, through His Church. It is our greatness to be intimately associated with this work which builds the Mystical Body and which saves the world . . . "until we meet into the unity of faith and

of the knowledge of the Son of God, unto a perfect man, unto the measure of the age of the fullness of Christ" (*Ephes.*, IV, 13) . . . "And afterwards, the end; when he shall have delivered up the kingdom of God and the Father; when he shall have brought to nought all principality and power and virtue. For he must reign... (1 *Cor.*, XV, 24-25).